T0305419

The Reform of Network Industries

The Reform of Network Industries

Evaluating Privatisation, Regulation and
Liberalisation in the EU

Edited by

Massimo Florio

*Professor of Public Economics, Department of Economics,
Management and Quantitative Methods, University of Milan,
Italy and Scientific Coordinator, EUsers Jean Monnet Network*

 Edward **Elgar**
PUBLISHING

Cheltenham, UK • Northampton, MA, USA

Published by
Edward Elgar Publishing Limited
The Lypiatts
15 Lansdown Road
Cheltenham
Glos GL50 2JA
UK

Edward Elgar Publishing, Inc.
William Pratt House
9 Dewey Court
Northampton
Massachusetts 01060
USA

A catalogue record for this book
is available from the British Library

Library of Congress Control Number: 2017947254

This book is available electronically in the **Elgar**online
Economics subject collection
DOI 10.4337/9781786439031

ISBN 978 1 78643 902 4 (cased)
ISBN 978 1 78643 903 1 (eBook)

Typeset by Servis Filmsetting Ltd, Stockport, Cheshire
Printed and bound in Great Britain by TJ International Ltd, Padstow

Contents

PART II   EMPIRICAL EVALUATIONS

Contributors

Philippe Bance is Professor at the University of Rouen (Normandy University). He is President of the International Scientific Council of CIRIEC (International Centre of Research and Information on the Public, Social and Cooperative Economy) and Science Adviser at Hcéres (High Council for the Evaluation of Research and Higher Education). He was Vice-President of the University of Rouen (2007–10). His main recent publications concern multilevel governance and Contingent Valuation Method with A. Chassy (P&P, 2017; rfe, 2016), Public enterprises (APCE, 2015) and two edited books on the strategic state; internalization of the general interest by public organizations (PURH, 2016; 2015).

Roberto Cardinale is a doctoral researcher in Economics of Energy Infrastructure at the Bartlett Faculty of the Built Environment, University College London. He carried out research at the University of Cambridge, Sungkyunkwan University (Seoul) and the Catholic University of Milan. His research, which was awarded the Ermenegildo Zegna Founder's Scholarship, proposes forms of energy governance that reconcile European Union policies with the specificities of the energy sector.

Paolo Castelnovo is a research fellow in Public Economics at the Department of Economics, Management and Quantitative Methods (DEMM), University of Milan, and has been adjunct Professor of Public Finance at Bocconi University since 2015. He has an MSc in Economics and Social Sciences from Bocconi University and a PhD in Economics and Finance of Public Administration from the University of Milano-Bicocca and Catholic University of Milan. His main research interests are within the fields of public economics, applied econometrics and labour economics.

Angélique Chassy holds a PhD in Economics from the University of Rouen, Normandy (laboratory CREAM). Her research concerns the assessment of public policies and more precisely public decisions, willingness to pay through the Contingent Valuation Method and multilevel governance.

Stefano Clò is Assistant Professor at the University of Milan. His research interests include public economics and energy policy. He earned a European Doctorate in Law and Economics at Erasmus University of Rotterdam and at Università degli Studi di Bologna. From 2010 to 2012 he was a research fellow at CEIS Tor Vergata (Rome) and worked as Adjunct Economist at the Italian Ministry of Economics and Finance.

Ajla Cosic holds a PhD in Management from the Scuola Superiore Sant'Anna, Pisa. Her research interests fall under the areas of consumer behaviour. She received her Masters in Business Leadership from Lund University. Ajla holds a BA with honours in Information Systems and Economics from Buckingham University.

Lea Diestelmeier is a PhD researcher at the Groningen Centre of Energy Law, University of Groningen. Lea holds an LL.M. in European Law with a specialisation in Energy and Climate Law from the University of Groningen. She obtained her Bachelor of Science in European Studies at the University of Twente and spent a semester at the faculty of Economics and Administrative Science at the Boğaziçi University in Istanbul.

Julia Doleschel is a graduate student in Economics at the Vienna University of Economics and Business as well as of International Development at the Vienna University. She has gained international experience at Bocconi University, London School of Economics and Universitat Autònoma de Barcelona (UAB). Her research interests include macroeconomics, development economics and growth.

Serena Marianna Drufuca holds a PhD in Economics. Her research interests include media economics, industrial organisation and voting theory. She holds a research scholarship at the Regional Institute for Research, Statistics and Training (Eupolis Lombardia) for the analysis of the competitive position of Lombardy. She is Lecturer in Microeconomics, Industrial Economics and Antitrust and referee for *Journal of Economics* and *European Journal of Law and Economics*. She has collaborated as junior researcher at the Institute of Social Research (IRS) in projects monitoring the labour market and evaluating policies.

Giovanni Esposito is a Doctoral Researcher in public sector organization and reform at the HEC Liège School of Management, University of Liège. His research focuses on organizational change and public governance. He has worked as economic analyst at DG Enterprise and Industry of the European Commission.

Massimo Florio is Professor of Public Economics at the University of Milan. Formerly a Jean Monnet Chair of Economics of European Integration and the Chair 'ad personam' of European Union Industrial Policy, he is currently coordinator of a Jean Monnet network of six

European universities and President of CIRIEC Commission Public Services/Public Enterprises. Recent publications include *Applied Welfare Economics* (2014), *Network Industries and Social Welfare* (2013), and two edited books: *Infrastructure Finance in Europe* (2016) and *The Economics of Infrastructure Provisioning* (2015).

Sonja Grönblom is a PhD researcher and from 2017 Lecturer in Economics at Åbo Akademi University, where she previously worked as research associate, acting lecturer and part-time lecturer. Her research is focused on microeconomic topics such as mixed oligopoly, public services and intrinsic motivation in different types of organisations.

Regina Maria Hirsch is completing a Master's degree in Political Science at the University of Vienna. Her research interests include European integration policies as well as the role of the European Union in the field of individual rights protection. In addition, she studies Arabic and Middle Eastern Studies (BA) at the University of Vienna.

Torben Holvad is Economic Adviser at the European Union Agency for Railways (France), senior research associate at the Transport Studies Unit (University of Oxford) and external Associate Professor at the Department of Transport (Danish Technical University). He obtained Economics degrees from Copenhagen University (MSc) and European University Institute (EUI) (MA and PhD).

Tobias Kaloud is a researcher and lecturer at Vienna University of Economics and Business. He has gained precious international academic experience at the Universities of Maastricht, Milan and Liège. His main research focus lies in the fields of regulatory and infrastructure economics.

Manto Lampropoulou holds a PhD in Political Science and Public Administration from the University of Athens. She is a postdoctoral researcher at Athens University of Economics and Business. Her research interests include state reform, privatisation policies, public policy and public administration.

Alexandru Maxim is a researcher and Associate Lecturer at the Alexandru Ioan Cuza University of Iaşi in Romania. He has a PhD in Marketing focused on the energy sector and previously worked for GE Energy Europe. His current research interests include sustainable development, European Union policies and energy markets.

Annalisa Negrelli holds a PhD in Administrative Law from the University of Milan. She is an administrative lawyer and from July 2015 has a research fellowship in Administrative Law from the University of Milan, concerning the public procurements and organisational models of the Public Administration. She is author of several peer-reviewed scientific publications and a book, edited in 2016, about the influence of the Four Freedoms on the European Union Member States' juridical systems, particularly on the perspective of liberalisation/privatisation of the internal markets.

Tue Anh Nguyen holds a PhD in Energy Policy from the University of Greenwich. She is currently a visiting postdoctoral fellow at Harvard Kennedy School. Her research interests include energy policy, public services, market liberalisation model, World Bank loans, structural reforms and economic growth.

Rogelio Pesqueira Sánchez is a PhD student at the University of La Coruña. His research interests include TAM (Technology Acceptance Model), SEM (Structural Equation Modelling), Millennials, telecommunications policies and public policies. He is author of several books and evaluator of European educational projects. He has been a vocational education and training teacher in La Coruña in Spain since 2004.

Nicolò Rossetto holds a PhD in Economics, Law and Institutions from the Istituto Universitario di Studi Superiori (IUSS) of Pavia. He is a research associate at the Florence School of Regulation. His research interests cover energy economics, energy policy and regulation of the network industries. He has previously worked for the University of Pavia, the Istituto per gli Studi di Politica Internazionale (ISPI) of Milano and the World Bank.

Anastasia Roukouni is a Transportation Engineer with a PhD in the field of Transport Planning and Economics from Aristotle University of Thessaloniki, Greece, funded by a Fellowship of Excellence, awarded by the State Scholarships Foundation of Greece and Siemens. She also holds an MSc in Transport from Imperial College London and University College London, UK (joint program). She is the author or co-author of 30 peer-reviewed scientific publications. She currently works as postdoctoral researcher, at the Policy Analysis Group, Department of Multi-Actor Systems, Faculty of Technology, Policy and Management, TU Delft in the Netherlands. Her research focuses on how games can foster the implementation process of innovation in the field of logistics and transportation.

Steve Thomas is Emeritus Professor of Energy Policy and member of the Public Services International Research Unit (PSIRU) at the University of Greenwich Business School. He is an associate editor of *Energy Policy*. His research interests include economics and policy on nuclear power, liberalisation of energy markets and corporate policies of energy companies.

Jadwiga Urban-Kozłowska is a researcher at the Jagiellonian University in Kraków and a Polish legal adviser. She earned the title of Master of French law at the University of Orléans. Her main areas of expertise include European Union and Polish competition law, German and Polish labour law.

Johan Willner is Emeritus Professor in Economics at Åbo Akademi University. He has been Research Scholar at the London School of Economics, and several times Visiting Fellow or Visiting Professor at the University of Warwick. His research and teaching have mainly dealt with microeconomic theory, in particular public economics and industrial organisation.

Preface

Since the 1990s the role of public services, relabelled Services of General Interest (SGI) in the European Union (EU) legal jargon, has been subject to intense scrutiny and critical evaluation. One driver was the increased political attractiveness of liberalisation policies as part of the 'common market' approach to building a European economic space; another driver was the desire to create a shared social model in the construction of the EU. These two drivers did not necessarily converge in the proposed reforms, despite some consensus about the need to move away from the former approach based on public sector monopoly in service provision.

Today, SGI (some of which, to complicate the wording, are considered Services of General Economic Interest – SGEI) are formally recognised in the EU legislation as a key aspect in fostering European social and territorial cohesion and in ensuring the enjoyment of fundamental rights to the EU citizens.[1] Nevertheless, to many economists and policy makers these are just 'industries', with some characterised by a core segment under natural monopoly, physical or virtual networks.

Although the understanding of what the policy framework for network industries should be is affected by differences in national traditions and practices, the wider notion of SGI is based on a set of overarching values and goals. These include an important concern of legislators and regulators about social affordability, accessibility, sustainability, safety and security of supply. This is because often, even if not always, the network industries provide essential services. Such 'essentiality' notion goes well beyond the universal service obligations as regulatory remedies, which are specific obligations for specific providers, and poses a problem to governments and legislators in the first place: To what extent do the European citizens have the right to enjoy these services, even if they are poor, or live in remote regions or are, in other ways, disadvantaged? This question calls for a critical perspective on the functioning of the industries providing such services to the European citizens. The crucial policy issue is that, in the perspective of the EU project, a network industry providing a service of general interest should contribute, as far as possible, to the European inclusive social model, and this makes the role of competition in this area different from what it would be in other markets, where efficiency and profitability are the sole or main concerns.

This book aims to contribute to such EU policy debate on SGI in several ways. It seeks to expand the existing literature on the empirical evaluation of policy reforms in network industries, focusing particularly on the European policy paradigm and its three main pillars: privatisation, unbundling, (regulated) market entry and liberalisation.[2] Two aspects of the book stand out as possible contributions to the literature. Firstly, reforms are analysed through the lenses of the past and possible future welfare effects on citizens as users, given an evolving panorama, consistently with the notion of SGI. Secondly, the role of State-owned or State-invested players is evaluated in this new perspective.

The chapters included in the book mainly cover six network industries – electricity, gas, railway, local public transport (LPT), telecommunications and postal services. The authors, after taking stock of the notion that such services are in fact essential for EU citizens, discuss to what extent changes in the organisation of these industries promoted by the 'European reform paradigm' are beneficial to consumers. In particular, the authors focus on unbundling of vertically integrated network services, liberalisation and market opening, privatisation of State-owned enterprises. The typical ingredients of reforms, as identified by a well-established literature, are here updated and extended; moreover, countries and sector-specific peculiarities are discussed.

An innovative aspect of this book is the analysis of the role of State-owned or State-invested enterprises (SIEs) that, outside the UK, are still significant players in the market. This is a rather neglected topic in the literature, as if privatisations had wiped away such government-owned players. However, this is not true, and different issues arise about their current role in liberalised markets. Hence, the main research question addressed by this book refers to the impact of these reforms on the welfare of citizens, which sometimes has been unexpected by the initial advocates of reforms.[3] For example unbundling may be necessary in some network industries to promote competition; however, vertical disintegration per se increases transaction costs and when the market tends to oligopolistic equilibrium, even without explicit collusion, the final outcome on consumer prices may be well in excess of marginal costs. Privatisation, in turn, changes the objectives of the former State-owned enterprises and may lead to cost decreases, but also to price increases if regulation is ineffective. Perhaps for these and for other reasons (including substantial revenues accruing to the public budget from profitable public enterprises), the State at central or local level still controls or has important stakes in industries such as energy, transport and telecommunications. What is the role of these players in the liberalised markets? More generally, some network industries are based on critical infrastructures, and the role of government in the provision, management and regulation of infrastructure is still important.[4] Again, what can we say, in an empirical perspective, about the role of governments in this area?

In a methodological perspective, the concept of Policy Framework Reform (PFR) may be helpful. By a PFR we understand here a set of reforms, for example, a 'package' of EU directives and their implementation laws at national level. This is clearly different from the evaluation of the marginal change in a specific provision, for example, a change in the X element in the RPI-X price-cap formula, as for the early regulatory arrangements in some network industries, where RPI is the retail price index and X the estimate by the regulator of productivity change.

The advantages of using the empirics of PFR is that reforms of SGI are too complex to be traced by a myriad of marginal changes, and it is sometimes preferable to look at the general picture, possibly making comparisons over time and across countries. Of course one needs to be particularly careful in dealing with potential errors in what are essentially snapshot pictures of the reform process, given the fuzzy nature of the main variables of interest. Time and effort are needed to understand the historical, political and social circumstances that supported an actual or proposed policy shift in the first place, and its impact.

The material presented in this book draws from the research activities carried out by the Jean Monnet EUsers network,[5] a three-year project linking six universities together (Università degli Studi di Milano, Åbo Akademi University School of Business and Economics, University of Greenwich, Universität Leipzig, Université de Rouen, WU Wirtschaftuniversität Wien).

The book is divided into two parts. Part I begins with a methodological chapter while subsequent chapters deal with the evaluation of cross-cutting issues arising from the reforms of networking industries to provide meaningful examples; these include privatisation, unbundling, performance of State-owned enterprises, determinants of prices, impact of reforms on citizens and so on.

Chapter 1 discusses possible errors and pitfalls of the empirical evaluation of PFR, such as biases related to the research design and to the interpretation of results. More specifically, the chapter deals with issues of measurement of variables representing the PFR; it presents a taxonomy of possible errors along this procedure and turns to the selection of proxies for changes in consumers' welfare, a necessary step for any evaluation of policy reforms.

Chapter 2 focuses on the traditional missions of public services, discussing their performance in an empirical perspective. The authors also critically discuss the privatisation policy and contrast it with a theoretical analysis on how public and private enterprises are likely to perform when it comes to cost efficiency and social welfare (and possible tradeoffs), with and without the potential intrinsic motivation of managers. Moreover, the future of public ownership and the possibility of renationalisation are discussed.

Chapter 3 provides an overview of the unbundled energy businesses – characteristics, ownership, technical and commercial synergies – including a review of the literature that analyses the impact of reforms on market performance, power prices and, more generally, social well-being. The main message is that policies are often contradictory and their outcome less beneficial for citizens than expected.

Railway is another archetypal network industry, where the involvement of governments in service provision is still wide. Over the past 25 years railways in Europe have experienced substantial changes in terms of legislative measures and Chapter 4 provides an overview of the outcomes with particular emphasis on passenger transportation. The author examines the outcomes of these changes in terms of market structure, competition and State involvement explaining how the reforms have impacted the overall performance of the railway sector across EU Member States. The chapter puts forward future perspectives in terms of how the railway industry in Europe may develop in the future.

Evidence of the persistence of public enterprises, even within the industry where privatisation started, is provided in Chapter 5 on the major SIEs operating in the telecommunications industry. This chapter shows that modern SIEs, while not different in size from private companies, have achieved significantly higher profitability. This result is confirmed by an econometric analysis accounting for firm- and country-level characteristics, regulatory constraints in the industry and time fixed-effects. Regression results show that, even when controlling for the full set of covariates, SIEs display higher margins than their private counterparts. An additional determinant of firms' profitability is the probability of being listed on the stock exchange and market regulation, described by the ETCR aggregate indicator (Energy, Transport and Communications Regulation) for the telecom sector.

The issue of public mission is discussed in Chapter 6 with the example of the postal sector, where opening up to competition and the decrease in traditional mail activity resulted in profound changes. The chapter analyses the transformations of operators' ownership and behaviours in a new environment, and the role of the public service obligations assigned to the operators by national authorities. The author shows the great structural diversity of service providers and the variety of national public authorities' visions of the role of this sector, leading to the coexistence of multiple models in Europe.

While Part I largely deals with thematic issues arising from a broad picture of network industries, Part II focuses on the empirical analysis of the PFRs in six industries – electricity, gas, telecommunications, railway and LPT. The aim is to assess changes in PFR from the consumers' point of view and to provide a comparative country analysis. These assessments rely both on a review of the relevant literature and econometric analyses of panel data,[6] financial data from Bureau Van Dijk,[7] quality satisfaction from Eurobarometer,[8] prices data from Eurostat and so on.

The aim of Chapter 7 is to investigate whether reforms in the electricity sector have generated welfare benefits for household consumers across four countries – France, Germany, Italy and the UK. In particular, the chapter investigates the issue of affordability of electricity supply and the reliability of services by considering the proportion of real disposable income spent annually on electricity by households and the severity of service interruptions. In this regard, the authors show that privatisation and liberalisation did not have a consistently positive impact on household consumers.

With respect to the telecommunications industries, Chapter 8 provides a picture of the reform paths at both the EU level and individual Member States' level. The authors show that, despite differences across countries, the privatisation and liberalisation processes have contributed to the development of this sector ensuring more variety in consumer choice, lower prices and higher quality.

Chapter 9 focuses on the transformations of the rail sector over the last two decades. It provides a historical overview of the reform context through outlining the most important regulatory innovations introduced by the EU. The chapter also empirically investigates how regulatory innovations have influenced price, investment and quality of European rail services, using Organisation for Economic Co-operation and Development (OECD) data from 1996 to 2013, showing that prices are very weakly correlated to reform indicators.

The objective of Chapter 10 is to examine the main policy reforms promoted by the EU and adopted by the Member States in the LPT industry. The chapter identifies the existence of different reform patterns across countries and performs an evaluation of the role of enterprises controlled by local governments. The authors also investigate whether European citizens have been served by the evolution of policy reforms in this area and present both positive and negative examples of Member States' policy experiences.

Finally, for the gas industry Chapter 11 discusses the transition from State-owned enterprises to mixed ownership, its rationales and impacts. The author raises general issues about the role of ownership in network industries; in particular, the objective of increasing profitability for mixed ownership enterprises that has prevented States from pursuing some policy objectives such as achieving large-scale plans of economic and technological development or ensuring consumers' price affordability.

There are three main messages arising from this book. Firstly, network services are still 'political industries', meaning that the market-driven approach has been overstated as there are persistent overarching policy concerns in terms of access, affordability, territorial cohesion, continuity of supply, environmental impact. Secondly, the push by the EU institutions for the adoption of a homogeneous paradigm across the Member States conflicts with the variation in national policy goals. Thirdly, the benefits for citizens of the reforms are visible in some cases, not detectable in others, or even reversed by social costs in others, particularly when privatisation has led to price increases for households. Within this complex panorama, in those countries in which public enterprises are still playing a major role, their performance is usually no worse than their private competitors; it also seems that public enterprises are able to complement the efforts of governments in securing social objectives such as fairness of tariffs and long-term sustainability.

Massimo Florio
Milan, April 2017

NOTES

1. See, for instance, https://ec.europa.eu/info/topics/single-market/services-general-interest_en (accessed May 2017).
2. See, for instance, M. Florio (2013), *Network Industries and Social Welfare*, Oxford: Oxford University Press; M. Finger (ed.) (2014), '20 years of liberalization in network industries', *Utilities Policy*, Special issue.
3. See, for instance, D. Newbery (2000), *Privatization, Restructuring and Regulation of Network Utilities*, Cambridge, MA: MIT Press; M. Florio (2004), *The Great Divestiture*, Cambridge, MA: MIT Press.
4. See, for instance, A. Picot, M. Florio, N. Grove and J. Kranz (2016), *The Economics of Infrastructure Provisioning: The Changing Role of the State*, Cambridge, MA: MIT Press.
5. For details see http://users.unimi.it/eusers/ (accessed April 2017).
6. Including policy reforms indicators from the OECD/ETCR, https://stats.oecd.org/Index.aspx?DataSetCode=ETCR (accessed April 2017).
7. https://amadeus.bvdinfo.com/version-201739/home.serv?product=amadeusneo (accessed April 2017).
8. http://ec.europa.eu/public_opinion/index_en.htm (accessed April 2017).

Acknowledgements

The editor and the authors are grateful to the Education, Audiovisual and Culture Executive Agency (EACEA) for funding the EUsers Jean Monnet Network and to the participants at the MEEW (30 June 2016) and the EUsers summer school (27 June–1 July 2016) for their comments.

Thanks are extended to Gelsomina Catalano, research fellow, for her dedicated effort in animating the network and in assisting both the editor and the authors; Valentina Morretta, research fellow, has provided a competent review work on the final manuscript and many helpful suggestions to improve the text. The editor is also grateful to four anonymous reviewers, appointed by the publisher, for their comments provided to the initial editorial project. Several anonymous reviewers have also provided constructive criticisms chapter by chapter and on the entire project.

Abbreviations

AEG:	*Allgemeines Eisenbahngesetz*
CBA:	Cost-Benefit Analysis
CEP:	Courier, Express and Postal
DEA:	Data Envelopment Analysis
EACEA:	Education, Audiovisual and Culture Executive Agency
EBIT:	Earnings before Interest and Taxes
EBITDA:	Earnings before Interest, Taxes, Depreciation and Amortisation
EBRD:	European Bank for Reconstruction and Development
EC:	European Commission
ERA:	European Railway Agency
ETCR:	Energy, Transport and Communications Regulation
EU:	European Union
EU ETS:	European Union Emissions Trading Scheme
GDP:	Gross Domestic Product
GLA:	Greater London Authority
GNI:	Gross National Income
HSR:	High Speed Rail
ICT:	Information and Communications Technology
IM:	Infrastructure Manager
ISDN:	Integrated Services Digital Network
ISP:	Internet Service Provider
ITU:	International Telecommunication Union
LIB:	Liberalisation Index
LPT:	Local Public Transport
LTAs:	Local Transport Authorities
MCF:	Marginal Cost of Public Fund
MEA:	Multi-Directional Efficiency Analysis
MOE:	Mixed-Owned Enterprise
NPM:	New Public Management
NSAs:	National Safety Authorities
OECD:	Organisation for Economic Co-operation and Development
OJEU:	*Official Journal of the European Union*
OLS:	Ordinary Least Squares

OTE: Hellenic Telecommunications Organization
OTT: Over-The-Top
PCA: Principal Component Analysis
PCWs: Price Comparison Websites
PFR: Policy Framework Reform
PO: Public Ownership
PPP: Public-Private Partnership
PSC: Public Service Contract
PSO: Public Services Obligations
PSTN: Public Switched Telephone Network
PTO: Public Telecommunications Operator
QALY: Quality Adjusted Life Years
R&D: Research and Development
RES: Renewable Energy Sources
ROA: Return on Assets
RSG: Ramsey-Samuelson-Guesnerie Tradition
SAIDI: System Average Interruption Duration Index
SAIFI: System Average Interruption Frequency Index
SFA: Stochastic Frontier Analysis
SGEI: Services of General Economic Interest
SGI: Services of General Interest
SIE: State-Invested Enterprise
SISE: Share of Income Spent on Electricity
SOE: State-Owned Enterprise
SWF: Social Welfare Function
TEN: Trans-European Network
TEN-T: Trans-European Network – Transport
TERFN: Trans-European Rail Freight Network
TFEU: Treaty on the Functioning of the European Union
TfL: Transport for London
TMB: Transports Metropolitans de Barcelona
TPA: Third Party Access
TSIs: Technical Specifications for Interoperability
USP: Universal Service Provider
VDI: Volume Development Index
WWII: World War II

PART I

Cross-cutting policy issues

1. The empirical evaluation of regulatory policy reforms in network industries: some methodological issues

Massimo Florio*

1.1 INTRODUCTION

Economists are often confronted with the task of providing assessments of policy reforms. In fact, a very large share of the contemporary economic literature deals with the evaluation of either *ex post* or *ex ante* reforms just proposed or actually implemented by governments. These reforms can be represented by the specific change of the level of a given 'signal'. A signal (Drèze and Stern, 1990) is a microeconomic variable which 'directly' affects the behaviour and welfare of economic agents. Examples are the rate of an indirect tax, the level of a price-cap on tariffs of utilities, the number of years of compulsory primary education or the permitted level of carbon emissions. This is the context of the well-established literature originated by the theory of policy reform, particularly of taxation. For example, Ahmad and Stern (1984, p. 259) summarize their study of indirect taxation reform in India in this way:

> Given a set of value judgements, an initial state, and a model of the economy, one can ask whether some feasible tax change would increase welfare. We do this by defining the marginal cost in terms of welfare of raising an extra rupee from the *i*th good. The inverse optimum problem is the calculation of non-negative welfare weights on households which imply that the initial state is optimum. If no such welfare weights exist, then a Pareto improvement is possible. We illustrate the concepts and results using data from the Indian economy for 1979–1980. Directions of tax reform for a number of specific social welfare functions and for Pareto improvements are presented.

To understand the theory of reform this way has several founding fathers in public economics, starting with Ramsey (1927), the unpublished Samuelson (1951) memorandum to the US Treasury, Diamond and Mirrlees (1971), Guesnerie (1977, 1998), Drèze and Stern (1990), and for a review see Boadway (2012). In spite of its taxation origin, this theoretical stream had the ambition to cover any specific reform in an applied welfare economics perspective (see Drèze and Stern, 1990; Florio, 2014 for marginal reforms in cost-benefit analysis (CBA), and Johansson and Kriström, 2015 for the evaluation of large-scale projects and policy changes). In this context, 'marginal' means that the reform is small, in the technical sense that while it may have general equilibrium effects, it does not change the trajectory of the economy (this is equivalent to the 'small project' assumption in cost-benefit analysis).

However, reforms can often take a rather different shape from the change of a microeconomic signal or macroeconomic instrument. For example, product market reforms are a broad change of public policy arrangements hindering competition in some industries. This 'mesoeconomic' change will only have an indirect impact on agents' utility. For an early discussion of mesoeconomics see Ng (1986). Here I shall refer more loosely to a context where it is the change of an institutional setting that should be evaluated, neither captured by a microeconomic nor macroeconomic variable. Examples are the privatization of public enterprises, unbundling in network industries or the promotion of competition in a formerly monopolistic market. These changes will be embodied in legislation, through several bills or regulatory decisions which are more or less closely linked together by common objectives of a general nature. For policy makers a reform is usually a more comprehensive package than the change of a specific signal (such as a statutory tax rate, a price-cap, the amount of a good provided by a government agency). The reform, in this wider meaning, is in fact a mechanism aimed at promoting a cascade of several punctual changes in a certain desired direction.

In this chapter, I discuss some methodological issues of the latter evaluation, the assessment of changing a 'policy framework', focusing on network industries, drawing from a very selective and purely illustrative review of some literature and from my own experience as an applied economist. My main concern here is to suggest an analytical framework and point out possible methodological errors and pitfalls that may bias the research design and the results when something more comprehensive than the change of a specific signal is at stake. I shall use the concept of 'Policy Framework Reform' (PFR) when the change concerns a set of rules more than the change of a specific signal in the Ramsey-Samuelson-Guesnerie tradition.

The topic is discussed as follows by Parker and Kirkpatrick (2012, p. 7), for example, in their review of the literature:

OECD member countries have been engaged with regulatory reform and improving regulatory processes for a decade or more, in the expectation that there will be significant improvements in economic welfare outcomes. But in the absence of clarity about how and why the changes should lead to improvements, policy failures are likely. The critical public policy challenge is to ensure that the expected economic benefits from regulatory changes are both achieved and outweigh any economic costs imposed. This requires firm evidence on how different policies perform. Evidence on the outcomes of regulatory policies should help policymakers design regulatory measures that work better.

The perspective adopted in this chapter is that of a concise discussion of some frequent pitfalls in the interpretation of results, when the traditional theory of reform is not applicable, or not appropriate, for the empirical analysis of a given context and one needs to rely on reform indicator variables.

The structure of the chapter as follows: Section 1.2 discusses the problem of how to properly define the object of analysis, clarifying the distinction between two different ways to consider policy reforms; Section 1.3 discusses issues in measurement of the change of variables representing the PFR; Section 1.4 presents a taxonomy of possible errors throughout this procedure; Section 1.5 turns to the selection of proxies for welfare changes, which is a necessary step for any evaluation of policy reforms; a generic empirical modelling approach is presented in Section 1.6; Section 1.7 discusses possible misinterpretations of what the empirics of policy reform evaluation can achieve; Section 1.8 concludes.

1.2   DEFINING THE OBJECT OF ANALYSIS

Properly defining the object of analysis in the policy reform context is crucial, and a less trivial step than often understood. In theoretical models, such as those reviewed in Guesnerie (1998) or developed for CBA of projects and policies by Drèze and Stern (1990), things may be mathematically and informationally demanding, but conceptually unambiguous. There is a given constellation of signals, that is, variables that potentially influence the behaviour of agents, households or firms. Signals may include prices, quantity rations, taxes, ownership shares and so on, and one wants to study the welfare effects of marginal changes of such signals. In some models, one may want to study non-marginal effects, which implies different techniques.

In this form, the problem is simple: there are functional relations linking signals, constraints, agents' reactions and government objectives to be maximized, and one studies how changes in signals ultimately have an impact on objectives, possibly through a series of chain effects. Basically, if $W(s)$ is a social welfare function and s is a vector of signals, the theory revolves around the estimation of marginal social values of the form $dW(s)/ds$. This can be done by looking for solutions around the optimum of a program (a second-best way to understand the problem) or starting from the existing set of signals and gradually moving on (see Johansson and Kriström, 2015 for a discussion of the two different applied welfare economics strategies).

To give an example, when the vector s is a set of indirect tax rates, this is how a revenue neutral marginal tax change, in the context of discussing environmental policies, is introduced by Mayeres and Proost (2001, pp. 346–7), where t_m, t_k are indirect taxes, W is the social welfare function, B is exogenous government budget and MCF is the marginal cost of public funds:

> We want to evaluate whether a revenue neutral marginal policy reform is welfare improving or not when starting from an arbitrary tax system and from an arbitrary level of public abatement. In a first instance the analysis concentrates on marginal reforms of the tax system . . . The effect on welfare of a revenue neutral tax change which consists of increasing t_m and reducing t_k is given by:
>
> $$dW = \frac{\partial w}{\partial t_k}dt_k + \frac{\partial w}{\partial t_m}dt_m \text{ with } dB = 1 = \frac{\partial B}{\partial t_m}dt_m = -\frac{\partial B}{\partial t_k}dt_k$$
>
> Defining the marginal cost in terms of social welfare of raising one additional unit of government revenue via the tax on commodity m as:
>
> $$MCF_m = -(\partial W/\partial t_m)/(\partial B/\partial t_m)$$
>
> we find
>
> $$dW \gtreqless 0 \Leftrightarrow MCF_m \gtreqless MCF_k$$
>
> So welfare is increased (reduced) when the tax with the highest MCF is reduced (increased) and when simultaneously the tax with the lowest MCF is raised (reduced).

I shall come back later on this way of looking at the evaluation problem, but here I just claim that in the perspective of applied economists the main limitation in implementing this scheme is that, in the real world, policy reforms are often not easily tracked as a (marginal) change in a signal.

Frequently, economic policy reforms do not take the simple aspect of changing a tax rate or a regulated price, but are embodied in legal acts providing possible mechanisms that may lead to such changes under certain circumstances. Clearly, in the case of adding one year to compulsory education, or lowering by $x\%$ an emission standard, marginal reforms can be analysed without major definitional issues, in the framework of applied welfare economics, such as in the Drèze and Stern (1990) theory discussed in Florio (2014). The general equilibrium frame can be a second-best economy or departures from the existing state of affairs (Johansson and Kriström, 2015), or partial equilibrium (Boadway and Bruce, 1984; Boardman et al., 2016).

Even so, one has to be careful when going from the theory of reform to empirics. For example, suppose a government adds one year to compulsory education, but in fact does not recruit more teachers. This implies that the existing stock of teachers has to work more and if their effort has diminishing returns in terms of students' achievements, the marginal net welfare effect of the reform would be misread without taking into account a quality measure. The quality of the service before-after the reform is assumed to be homogeneous, but it is not. Thus, we would need a 'quality adjusted additional year' as the proper unit of analysis. In some cases, the operative definition of the object of analysis may be problematic in practice – for example, see the notion of Quality Adjusted Life Years (QALY) in health economics as discussed in Johansson and Kriström (2015, p. 208) or the precise definition of an emission standard, but it is not conceptually difficult per se.

However, such policy reforms as the privatization of state-owned enterprises (SOEs), or the unbundling of vertically integrated network services, pose a definition problem: these are generic labels for a range of potential changes in the current circumstances, and in a deep sense such labels are not well defined in the perspective of applied welfare economics. Unbundling gas networks is a set of legislative and regulatory changes, and does not enter explicitly in the utility functions of agents. It can influence their behaviour in many ways. How to evaluate such a reform?

Applied welfare economics is about a quantitative assessment of the social effects of a change of circumstances. If the economic policy reform is described in a form that does not lead to empirical analysis in the specific form of a quantitative evaluation of effects, it may be an interesting object of study for economic historians, or for other social scientists, but not *sensu stricto* for applied economists. I am in favour of interdisciplinary studies in this area. For example, I think that the best approach to the study of privatization in principle should be a comparative political economy, which would blend together the perspectives of history, political sciences and applied economics (a review may be found in Obinger et al., 2016). However, without a definition of privatization or liberalization in the form of measurable variables, the contribution of an applied economist to the possible interdisciplinary policy evaluation would be severely constrained.

Thus, in the rest of this section, I discuss the situation whereby a policy reform cannot be treated in the Ramsey-Samuelson-Guesnerie tradition (RSG from here on) as the (marginal) change of the supply of a good by the public sector or of a signal. It is important to be precise in making the distinction between the RSG 'theory of reform' framework and what is discussed below. A simple example is privatization. In the general theory of CBA one may consider ownership of firms as a signal, taking the possible measurable dimension of a share of equity capital owned by government or households. Thus, a marginal change of such government ownership can be interpreted as a reform, and its welfare effect can be analysed in the same way as one would analyse the change of a price. Drèze and Stern (1990) show how this analysis of privatization may work in a general equilibrium, and there are also some loosely related ideas in Bös (1991) and Jones et al. (1990). This analysis is far from being easy, for example, a marginal reform of selling just one share of a SOE by a government to a private shareholder may or may not be significant according to the fact that such share insures a change of control or not: there are often these discontinuities in the value of signals which make the empirics less straightforward than one would expect (see, for example, Clò et al., 2015).

I turn now, however, to the concept I am more interested in here: a policy reform that is seen as a set of legislative or regulatory packages which are not immediately translated into a change of signal. To simplify, suppose that a government is able to pass a legislation that provides for privatization as a broad framework requiring that in certain industries SOEs' control must be relinquished to investors other than government itself and instructs managers of SOEs to implement such directives. This was the case of British privatization policy (Florio, 2004) – in fact, a set of different acts. When observed at this level, the object of analysis is not the marginal change of ownership of shares in one specific firm, a microeconomic change as in the above discussion, but rather a 'mesoeconomic' change: not as wide as would be described in terms of macroeconomic variables, but not so small to refer to a punctual transaction in the market for corporate control in relation to one firm.

Here the government announces and implements, possibly over some years, an entire set of changes. These can include, for example, the corporatization of SOEs, then listing them in stock markets, then seasoned selling of tranches of equity either by floatation or by deals with some domestic or international investors. Such deals may or may not be pre-determined in the legislation, when the control of a number of firms is actually passed from government to third parties.

A second example, particularly important for network industries, is an act providing for unbundling of some facilities which are the natural monopoly core of the industry. It is very uncommon that such legislation or regulation takes the precise form that is suitable for the RSG theory of reform style of analysis. For instance, the legislation may say that a railway firm should divest tracks from the train operating company; however, such divestiture can take, as a preliminary step, the form of accounting separation, then of functional separation and, finally, of full divestiture of ownership and control (which goes beyond legal separation of ownership). There are many nuances around the implementation of such reforms, as they are not easily described as changes of signals, but are changes of frameworks which are then expected to eventually lead to changes in signals.

The two examples above, selling one share of a SOE by the government, or passing an unbundling legislation, are just illustrations of a more general issue in defining and hence in tracking policy reforms. To distinguish them from changes of signals, I would use the term PFRs. In some interesting cases, such changes are related to an even more comprehensive shift, a change of the policy paradigm, that is, of the theory (sometimes of the ideology) supporting in general the way a government thinks about its policy.

To summarize this discussion, an act passing a quality adjusted increase in compulsory primary education is a (marginal) reform affecting a signal; one or more acts changing the incentives for households to take advantage of primary education is a reform affecting a framework which in turn will change some signals; and a shift away from the view that government is ultimately responsible for the provision of primary education is a change of paradigm in the role of the welfare state.

I will not discuss changes of paradigms below because it is uncommon that an applied welfare economist is able to empirically analyse them in quantitative terms, and because this is the level where the interdisciplinary approach would be most useful. Instead, I claim that the 'mesoeconomic' changes of policy framework lend themselves to empirical analysis, albeit with due caution.

1.3   MEASURING CHANGES OF POLICY FRAMEWORKS

While a change of a signal requires only some ingenuity to appropriately define the unit of measurement of the appropriate variable (a tax rate, a QALY, a price, number of passengers per kilometre provided and so on) the empirics of PFR need the creation of artificial indicator variables, for which usually no natural units of account exist.

An example of this is the Energy, Transport and Communications

Regulation (ETCR) database created and maintained by the Organisation for Economic Co-operation and Development (OECD),[1] which for several industries in the energy, transport and communication sectors, tracks reforms in the European Union Member States, in the form of yearly scores given by experts (Figure 1.1).

I dwell here on this specific example because it has been used by several researchers for the empirical analysis of market reforms (there are, however, other examples of policy indicators released by international organizations – including the European Commission (EC), the European Bank for Reconstruction and Development (EBRD), the World Bank, or built by think-tanks and individual researchers.[2]

At a more elementary level one can think of ETCR as an exercise of assigning normalized scores by experts along certain dimensions of change of a PFR, sometimes based on surveys of policy makers, but also on reviews of legislation and even news in the media.

When scores are given consistently by an expert team over years and across countries, one could track reforms in several ways, including by figures such as Figure 1.2, where different PFR trends are visually displayed for the natural gas industry.

In the ETCR case there may be different layers of analysis of PFR. The progress of reforms in a specific country and industry implies that one may need to aggregate different levels of the scoring system. Table 1.1 shows an example of such layers of analysis from the ETCR.

The methodological issues involved in building such scoring systems are non-trivial. The analyst should, first of all, collapse the legislation or regulatory decisions supporting the reforms along some simplified dimensions, which should be sufficiently recurrent but also variable across countries and time to allow for a consistent measure in different circumstances. Moreover, as the above ETCR example shows, there may be a mixture of qualitative and quantitative variables involved in the attempted measurement of the reforms. However, one should want to normalize the scoring system and this typically leads to transforming continuous variables (for example, market share of the incumbent electricity firm in the generation segment of the industry) into discontinuous scores, defining brackets (such as 0 score meaning that the market share is below $x\%$). For example, in the words of Parker and Kikpatrick (2012, p. 15):

> Multiple regression analysis is central . . . for modelling and measuring the relationship between one dependent variable (e.g. GDP growth) and other, so-called independent or explanatory, variables that can be expected to cause changes in the dependent variable (e.g. labour input, investment and technology). An additional explanatory variable reflecting the nature of regulation or a regulatory change can be added to the independent variables, either as a separate variable

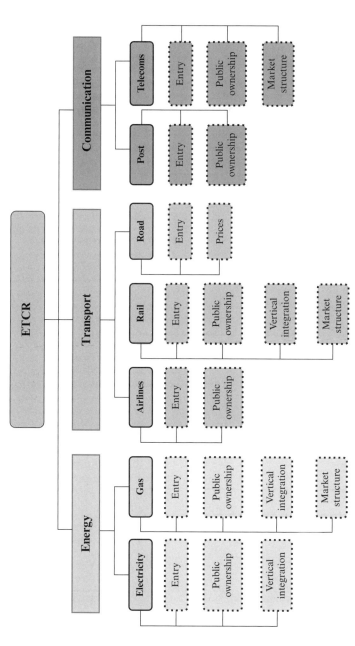

11

Source: OECD Economics Department Working Paper (2006), No. 530, 'Product Market Regulation of Non-manufacturing Sectors in OECD Countries: Measurement and Highlights'.

Figure 1.1   Structure of the ETCR indicators

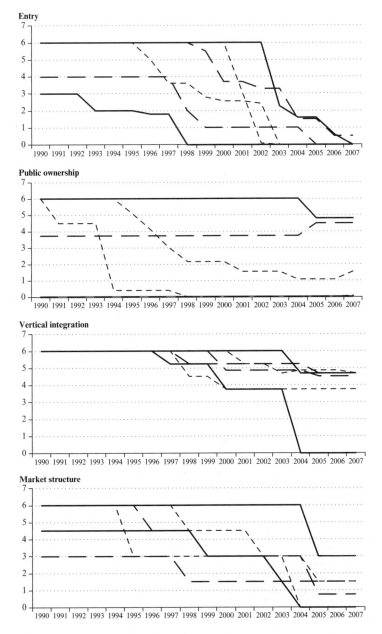

Source: Florio (2013), *Network Industries and Social Welfare*, Oxford University Press.

Figure 1.2   PFR trends for the natural gas industry

Table 1.1   Sectoral indicator of regulatory reform: gas

	Weights by theme (b_j)	Question weights (c_k)	Coding of data		
Entry regulation:	1/4				
			Regulated TPA	Negotiated TPA	No TPA
How are the terms and conditions of third party access (TPA) to the gas transmission grid determined?		1/3	0	3	6
What percentage of the rental market is open to consumer choice?		1/3	(1-% of market open to choice/100)*6		
			No, free entry in all markets	Yes, in some market	Yes, in all markets
Do national, state or provincial laws or other regulations restrict the number of competitors allowed to operate a business in at least some market in the sector: gas production/import?		1/3	0	3	6
Public ownership:	1/4				
			None	Between 0 and 100%	100%
What percentage of shares in the largest firm in the gas production/import sector is owned by the government?		1/3	0	3	6
What percentage of shares in the largest firm in the gas transmission sector is owned by the government?		1/3	0	3	6
What percentage of shares in the largest firm in the gas distribution sector is owned by the government?		1/3	0	3	6

Table 1.1   (continued)

	Weights by theme (b_j)	Question weights (c_k)	Coding of data		
Vertical integration:	1/4				
			Ownership separation	Legal/ Accounting	Integrated
What is the degree of vertical separation between gas production/ import and the other sector of the industry?		1/2	0	3	6
What is the degree of vertical separation between gas supply and the other sector of the industry?		3/10	0	3	6
Is gas distribution vertically separate from gas supply?		1/5	0	3	6
Market structure:	1/4				
			< 50%	Between 50% and 90%	> 90%
What is the market share of the largest company in the gas production/import industry?		1/3	0	3	6
What is the market share of the largest company in the gas transmission industry?		1/3	0	3	6
What is the market share of the largest company in the gas supply industry?		1/3	0	3	6
Country scores (0–6)			$\sum_j b_j \sum_k c_k answer_{jk}$		

Source: Adapted from OECD Economics Department Working Paper No. 530 (2006), 'Product Market Regulation of Non-manufacturing Sectors in OECD Countries: Measurement and Highlights'.

or as an interactive variable (e.g. interacting with the level of investment). This may take the form of a – dummy or – binary form, with a value of 1 when there is good regulation or a regulatory improvement and zero in other cases or there could be a scaling between 0 and 1.

The ETCR scoring has a range 0–6, with 0 indicating the 'completed' reform and 6 the 'no reform'. The binary form is the extreme form of apparently a loss of information, but the advantage is the opportunity to aggregate scores deriving from originally quantitative variables with scores deriving from qualitative variables, where the latter are typically discrete. Such discretization defines an ordering, and it is a delicate issue that is discussed further below.

Finally, the aggregation from the lowest to the highest level of scoring implies using weights and there are no natural ways to define such weights in most cases. For example, there is no theoretical justification for assigning equal 1/4 weights to each of the entry-privatization-unbundling-liberalization scores in ETCR (see Table 1.1). This leads to a discussion of potential errors in this area.

1.4   ERRORS IN MEASURING POLICY FRAMEWORK REFORMS

The above discussion suggests that several types of errors may occur in measuring PFR. We can classify these errors into five types:

1. Conceptual errors in defining the relevant reform dimensions.
2. Errors in discretization of continuous variables.
3. Errors in defining metrics and orderings.
4. Measurement errors deriving from misinterpretation of the information.
5. Scoring aggregation errors.

I briefly elaborate on this classification, with some examples, and how to manage the concerns arising from uncertainty surrounding the PFR data.

'Conceptual errors' are encountered when the team or individual researcher(s) providing the scoring system of the PFR defines a variable, either quantitative or qualitative, that per se does not work in the same way as a signal in the context of marginal reform theory. In the RSG context, there are natural units and natural orderings, such as a given increase in the provision of a public service by the government production plan. In network industries, 'unbundling' can be considered as a categorical variable with an ordering going from full vertical integration to accounting, functional, legal, ownership unbundling. This may be a relatively crude way to define a sequence of steps, but it is not illogical per se if one considers that a new paradigm promotes a PFR in a direction that goes from full vertical integration to full vertical disintegration of an industry. Clearly, each step should be sufficiently well described and unambiguous, but this is a different issue, which I discuss below. However, if one defines as a PFR indicator what in fact is possibly an outcome variable, this may lead to some interpretation problems.

For example, the market share of the largest electricity generator in a country may or may not be legitimate policy reform information: it can be interpreted as PFR when the incumbent has been forced by legislation or regulation to divest generation capacity, thus the observed share is part of the policy, but this is not the case if the observed change is a response to different circumstances, for example, a technological shock decreasing the optimal size of the production for any firm, including obviously the incumbent one. If the latter shock is an omitted variable in the subsequent modelling of the welfare effects of the PFR, there is the risk of misunderstanding some effects as if they were caused by the reform, while they have a different origin. In some cases, some control variables, if available, can cure the problem, but if not available, then the conceptual error of attributing a possibly non-policy related change to a PFR may cause a serious interpretation problem. As a consequence, a prudent applied economist using secondary PFR information, that is, data created by somebody else, should double check if there is the above-mentioned risk in the data he is going to use.

Turning to type-2 errors, any scoring system is intrinsically based on some assumptions about how to build indicators from initial information, and this poses specific problems when the original data are in continuous form. 'Discretization' may or may not have alternatives, but in most cases PFR data are expressed on a multidimensional scale because of the complexity of programs, hence they should be normalized for aggregation, as discussed below. Discretization means that all the variables, whatever the nature of the initial information, are expressed in the form of discontinuous scores, as in the ETCR example. Mistakes in discretization may arise when the distribution of the original data are not such that it is obvious how to define the brackets that will be translated into scores. This problem is not specific to policy reforms and is widely discussed in econometrics. If the original data are not available, concerns arise about discretization; in some cases, it may be better to collapse the scores in a dichotomic variable, or aggregate them in wider brackets: this procedure indeed shrinks statistical variability, but also may reduce the discretization error.

The above-mentioned problem may or may not lead or coincide with 'mistakes in defining orderings and metrics' (errors of type-3). A possible problem arises when there are different reform policy options and it is not entirely clear whether each of them can be considered as 'superior' or 'inferior' to another along an ideal path leading from the less to the most ambitious or advanced. The second problem arises when the empirical analysis uses a categorical variable in such a way that de facto ordinal information is treated as cardinal. While the ordering per se may be right, the metric involved in the implicit cardinalization may be wrong, for example, in linear regressions in which an indicator taking different values is used as the variable of interest. This happens because obviously 'third' is not the same as 'three', but in Ordinary Least Squares (OLS) or other regressions the latter may be taken as the former. Thus, inadvertently, the scoring process may introduce a bias in subsequent analysis. In these cases, again, it may be better sometimes to shrink the information to a dichotomous variable, thus dramatically reducing the error (but unfortunately also variability).

'Measurement errors' (type-4) affect any empirical analysis, but in the context of the study of PFR they are potentially particularly frequent because the source of information may include non-standard sources, for example, reports in the media, parliamentary acts and regulatory documents, in some cases interviews to policy makers or other stakeholders. Occasionally, it is possible to double check the scoring attributed to a PFR in a particular country and sector with alternative sources, and if this is possible a double check on data samples is advisable. As usual, irregular patterns may point to these types of errors and should be removed.

Finally, and most important, the 'aggregation error' (type-5) is pervasive in this context because there is usually no natural way to decide how to 'sum', for example, liberalization scores with unbundling scores. In many cases the existing PFR datasets simply count the items and aggregate them linearly, with equal weights. This error is potentially serious as it makes the aggregate reform score dependent on arbitrary coefficients, which are neither supported by theory nor estimation, but simply plugged into the system for computational ease. In some cases, the problem can be circumvented either by a Principal Component Analysis (PCA) of the individual items or entirely avoiding aggregate indicators and introducing the individual variables in the model, where one of them will be interpreted as the variable of interest and the remaining as additional controls

It is important to acknowledge that in spite of all these problems, in most cases there are limited alternatives to the use of such coded information to perform a quantitative analysis of the effects of reforms. This discussion should be seen more as a set of preliminary tests on the available PFR data, rather than generic arguments not to use them and to revert to a more traditional marginal reform approach, which in turn may beunfeasible or inappropriate.

To sum up, a careful interpretation of the data is always needed in this context, and applied economists working in this area should not take for granted that the information they use is meaningful just because it is provided by authoritative sources, such as international institutions. With this caveat, empirical modelling may be more informative than a simple narrative, or of individual case histories of reforms, even if these may have their place in a comprehensive policy evaluation.

1.5   DEFINING AND MEASURING THE WELFARE EFFECTS

Having defined and measured the policy variable of interest, the other crucial ingredient in the evaluation of reforms is the identification of the dependent variable(s). The choice, which actually specifies the research question, should be firmly based on the analyst's perception of the relevant Social Welfare Function (SWF).

Exactly because the adoption of a SWF is somewhat controversial, one needs to be clear about the perspective of the research question. First, a policy evaluation always takes a normative perspective. A positive analysis of policy reforms is instead often embodied in wide 'political economy' questions such as: 'Are social-democratic governments against privatization?', 'To what extent are regulators independent in less developed economies?', 'Is government debt causing or hindering liberalization policies?' and so on. The core of positive empirical research on policy reforms is the understanding of the historical, political, social, financial and economic drivers of policy adoption, of its success or failure. The core of the normative perspective, however, is the objective analysis of the social welfare effects of such reforms. Examples of research questions are: 'Is privatization beneficial to the poor?', 'Does market opening to foreign investment destabilize the income of small farmers?'

While in the same paper one can try to combine the two perspectives, in this section I focus on the issue that any welfare analysis explicitly or implicitly assumes a SWF (for example, gross domestic product or GDP, which, however, is based on some special assumptions) and aims to explore the impact of a reform on it, at least partially. Any country, or portion of it, is ultimately a society, that is, a set of individuals that can be lumped in convenient aggregates: social classes (shareholders and workers), income groups (the rich and the poor), age groups (the elderly and the youth), regional sub-groups (North and South). Such partitions may overlap, as when welfare effects of a reform on consumers, taxpayers, shareholders, employees are simultaneously considered. In a general equilibrium context, simultaneity of effects is embedded in the structure of the analysis, as a 'local' reform can have 'distant' effects across social groups, regions and so on.

Having in mind a SWF does not imply that all the welfare effects should be tracked, in many cases this could be a daunting task. Nevertheless, even if the study focuses on a specific segment of the society (for example, pensioners and rebalancing of their electricity tariffs), it is often implicit that in the SWF assumed by the researcher a particular group enters in the overall computation of effects with a certain weight. Sometimes such welfare weights are implicit, for example, when in a partial equilibrium frame, changes of consumer surplus and producer surplus are simply summed after a reform that increases the tariff of public service. There is nothing wrong in doing so, but only provided that this is compatible with either a very specific SWF or the welfare level of all the consumers and shareholders should be the same. A Bergson-Samuelson SWF compatible with simply summing consumer and producer surplus must have identical welfare weights (Florio, 2014) or for a larger class of SWF, one may assume that the income or other welfare related variables are more or less similar for the owner of the utility and his client. Both assumptions do not command a wide consensus, however, as just using the textbook sum of surpluses in policy evaluation reveals that the analyst is putting issues of equity under the carpet.

The issue is relatively less important when only a very narrowly defined social group is considered, in a partial equilibrium frame; however, even an analysis of effects on one relatively broad group, such as pensioners, may raise the question of differences in welfare level within the group, and it should be made explicit what welfare weights are assigned by the analyst to high and low income pensioners and so on. One may experiment with different welfare weights in this context, in a sort of sensitivity analysis of the conclusions to the SWF assumptions. Or at least qualitatively discuss the robustness of the normative conclusions to such assumptions.

Having said this, the outcome variable in many empirical analyses of reform is not explicitly the welfare change, but an empirical proxy of it. Thus, in the literature on economic policy reforms it is quite rare that one is able to read the results in the form of a change in a well-defined welfare measure, which necessarily requires at least the estimation of (compensated) demand curves or other appropriate functions, supply curves, quantity constraints, local equilibriums. Such results, if available, would then be expressed typically in a numeraire ('welfare' euro) or in the form of percentage change (before-after or without-with the reform, controlling for confounding factors). More frequently, the results are expressed in empirical variables, which are directly observable by the researcher, such as, for example, consumer or producer prices, profits, household income, quantity consumed and quality of service. This procedure is economical and sensible if there is at least some discussion of the assumptions linking these observables to the unobserved welfare change of the target social group(s).

In many cases, consumer prices are the most important signal relevant for a welfare analysis, as it can be easily demonstrated (Price and Hancock, 1998; Florio, 2004). Though important to use micro data on prices paid, these are rarely available, and one should be aware of the possible aggregation error across types of consumers, as this can be large.

While it may seem a less orthodox approach to welfare analysis, the use of consumers' satisfaction survey data adds an interesting dimension to potential proxies, that is, the perceived welfare change. For example, some Eurobarometer[3] waves allow the individual responses to questions on the subjective appreciation of the fairness of prices, of quality of service, of accessibility to be recorded. Other surveys such as SILC[4] and ECHP[5] (Poggi and Florio, 2010) were particularly useful in the study of utilities poverty, and occasionally regulators commission specific surveys which can feed in research on perception of the welfare impact of PFR.

Interestingly, one can combine micro data originating from a survey with country data, for example, to double check if the average 'objective' information on outcome variables, such as unplanned interruption of electricity services, match with subjective data.

The relationship between subjective and objective information can be framed in terms of behavioural welfare economics, a broader topic that cannot be discussed here, but amounts to making appropriate hypotheses about the observable satisfaction (or happiness) of agents and their unobserved utility. This is a controversial topic as according to some behavioural welfare economists any divergence between happiness and utility can be traced as deviations from rationality, while others would question the notion of rationality itself in this context. This is a subtle controversy with wide epistemological implications for economics, but an applied economist could take a pragmatic approach, and simply focus on convergence or divergence of objective and subjective data, and try to understand the drivers of such divergence. In many cases, there are simple explanations, such as aggregation errors when average objective data on an outcome variable are compared with subjective micro data. Clearly, the question, if such divergence arises, is to rule out these simple explanations, before resorting to the most complex ones, pointing to cognitive issues. Of course, if one has the actual information on prices paid by a sample of individual users of a public service before and after a reform, or with and without a reform, and for exactly the same individuals satisfaction data are available, the usual hypothesis is that price decrease would be correlated to higher satisfaction, after controlling for any confounding factors. If the hypothesis is rejected, there are two possibilities: either there are omitted variables in the controls, or in some sense there are systematic measurement errors either in the subjective or the objective data or in both. Some of these issues are discussed below. However, unfortunately, it is rare that one is able to take advantage of subjective and objective data simultaneously on the same samples of users, and the two sources of information can be seen as heterogeneous but complementary, and combined case by case with due caution.

1.6   MODELLING THE RELATION BETWEEN REFORMS AND OUTCOMES

The basic model for policy reform (of the PFR type) empirical evaluation often takes the generic form:

$$Y = f(R, D, S, Z) \qquad (1.1)$$

where Y is the outcome dependent variable, R is a set of indicator variables which are proxies for the policy reform framework, D are demand-side controls, S are supply-side controls, and Z are additional controls, including, for example, time and fixed effects, and other controls such as individual characteristics (firm level or consumer level).

There is often no fundamental difference at this level with an empirical model where R is replaced by a specific signal, for example, a statutory tax rate, but the discussion below focuses on the PFR context, while in the next section we go back to issues of interpretation of the results.

The justification of the generic form (1.1) is as follows. We want to understand the correlation (if not the impact) between the reform indicators and the outcome variable, which is seen in turn as a proxy of the welfare effects, but we need to control for any possible confounding factors. It is convenient to think of three broad sets of such controls.

First, drivers of *demand* usually have an influence on most outcome variables. Obvious examples are prices of the service, which respond positively, that is, increase with demand and decrease with the price of substitutes. For example, the price of electricity for residential users is correlated to income per capita of households because – at least in the short or medium term – if prices are allowed to vary (that is, there is an upstream electricity market following liberalization) – they will respond to increased consumption of electricity: households will use more electric appliances during the day, or will increase their stock of appliances. Electricity used for cooking or heating, however, has natural gas as a substitute, and a decrease of the price of gas compared to electricity may lower the demand of electricity. Hence, in general at least income per capita and the price of a main substitute will enter into the determinants of price, but other demand-side effects may reflect shifts in preferences (for example, energy saving attitudes may respond to cultural changes, usage of fixed telephony may be sensitive to higher mobility of users, which in turn increases the preference for mobile phones). When micro data are available some individual characteristics may be directly linked to preferences, and considered as drivers of demand (for example, younger people may have a preference for smartphones which goes beyond the price of the service).

On the *supply* side, the core drivers of outcome variables are changes in unit costs, which in turn are related to two sets of data: input prices and technology. Some network services may resort to different inputs, for example, electricity generation to gas, coal, nuclear, hydro, solar, wind, and changes in prices of such inputs have a direct impact on production costs. In relatively long run terms, technological shifts may dramatically change the cost of such services as telecommunications, but less than in relatively stagnant industries, such as water distribution to households. This calls for a good understanding of the essentials of the technological environment of service provision by the analyst.

Finally, there are characteristics which are relatively 'fixed', but are nevertheless important. In the context of international panel data analysis, which is particularly helpful in policy evaluation, country fixed effects may be able to capture demand and supply aspects that are not captured by D and S variables, but also other features that are not easily accommodated in standard economic variables. One example is the average 'optimism' of agents about their perspectives in the country, which may be a complex mixture of memory (for example, of past unemployment or inflation) and expectations (for example, about government effectiveness). Time fixed effects may capture shocks not otherwise identified. Most importantly, according to the type of data available, there are some individual characteristics (of households or firms) which while not being directly correlated to D or S may have an influence on outcomes.

Both objective and subjective outcome data can be fitted with the above-mentioned generic model, with opportune variations. For example, it is obvious that in the perception of price or quality of service, age, gender, ideology may enter as a confounding factor about the evaluation of the reform, and not because they may be directly correlated to D or S, but because social attitudes may vary between the old and the young, male and female, left-wing and right-wing respondents to a survey. However, even with objective micro data available, it would still be helpful in some cases to consider the individual characteristics. Suppose, for example, that we want to understand how profits of firms providing a service respond to regulatory changes. While D and S variables, and year and time fixed effects may be included in the model as controls, there may be firm-level characteristics which are important too: just consider the difference between SOEs and those controlled by private investors, co-operatives, firms listed in the stock exchange and those controlled by private equity funds and unlisted. Ownership often implies different unobservable firm-level objectives, corporate governance mechanisms, managerial responses to shocks. Hence, omitting relatively fixed firm-level characteristics in a price model would imply that coefficients estimates of other covariates would be biased.

To simplify the argument, suppose there are two countries where the reform is unbundling of a network industry in the same year, and we want to understand to what extent this is correlated with a change of price for households after the reform, *ceteris paribus* in terms of cost of inputs, technology, demand drivers. However, in one country the industry after unbundling is split between a private owner of the network and several private competitors, while in the other country the owner of the network is a national government body, and the competitors are firms under the control of local governments. The latter wants to maximize the welfare of citizens under budget constraints (they are not allowed to incur losses), while the former wants to maximize the value to shareholders. In both countries there is a regulator that imposes a price-cap on access to the network, but there is no price regulation for service to the households. There is no reason to expect that if the markets in the two countries are not interconnected, the equilibrium price will be the same because the firms' managers will react to unbundling in different ways, given the difference of their objectives. Omitting the information about ownership of firms may lead to biasing the estimates of other coefficients, including the variable of interest.

Other issues are more technical, and shared with any kind of econometric approaches in similar contexts, for example, whether or not to include a lagged dependent variable among the covariates to account for dynamic effects, to what extent to introduce interaction terms, non-linearity, or how to pick up the appropriate estimation techniques. Some of these aspects are indeed not specific to the empirical analysis of policy reforms, but others take a particular form and are discussed in the next sections.

1.7　INTERPRETATION OF THE EMPIRICAL RESULTS

The main question that arises in our context is how to exactly interpret the estimated coefficients of the variables of interest.

In the more standard theory of reform model, the interpretation is relatively straightforward: for example, one may conclude that the public provision of one additional place in a hospital has an x effect of QALY for the target population, and this result would lend itself to relatively simple cost-benefit tests, including the social cost of increasing distortionary taxes to support public spending in healthcare.

But this simple interpretation does not usually hold when the variable of interest is a PFR indicator. It is important to restate here that in some cases the RSG 'theory of reform' approach is either unfeasible or not appropriate. For example, one would be tempted to represent privatization policy with a decreasing change of a continuous variable such as the first difference of privatization proceeds for the Treasury or the change of the percentage share of firms' assets in one country (or region) from year to year. If data are available, this is perfectly feasible and may be interesting, but not necessarily a really good proxy of the actual scope of reforms. If the intention of the government, through selling public enterprises, is to collect cash proceeds, perhaps to decrease the level of indebtedness of the public sector, it would be entirely appropriate to study the impact of one additional pound of privatization proceeds on the outcome variable, for example, GDP per capita, after controlling for confounding factors. Here the interpretation is simple: perhaps through changes in savers' expectations or those of foreign investors the null hypothesis could be that the privatization proceeds are correlated to GDP because of diminishing debt, hence less burden of interest and repayment for public finance, and ultimately, according to some macroeconomic models, more growth. If one assumes that GDP is the relevant social welfare function (no equity and sustainability concerns) then a 'positive' estimated coefficient of the privatization variable would point to the expected effect. However, if the government objective is to get rid of the control of firms for the sake of assumed greater efficiency of private ownership, it may even be interested in under-pricing SOEs and the continuous variable of cash proceeds would not be the right signal. In such cases, discontinuous thresholds of equity shares held by government may be more appropriate, because what is at stake is a policy framework and not the marginal reform of a specific signal in the traditional meaning. Hence, an indicator variable may be a better description of the change, for example, setting a multinomial ordering such as full ownership at more than 50 per cent of equity, less than 50 per cent but more than 20 per cent, less than 20 per cent but greater than zero.

While this may be seen as reducing the variability of the information, it actually points to a different type of information, which would not be captured by a coefficient expressing the contribution of a small change in ownership to the social welfare proxy variable. Thus, one should read the coefficient as expressing the contribution of a policy reform in a different meaning, as the shift from a regime to another one, each represented by the value taken by the reform indicator.

It is helpful to observe that this issue is not related per se to the well-known problem of causality in empirical analysis: it would arise even if one would loosely interpret the estimated coefficients simply as the expression of correlations. The issue is deeper, and it has to do with the appropriate interpretation of the 'meaning' of the reform and to what extent the empirical proxy captures it. Thus, one should read the coefficient as correlated to the welfare effect of a 'one step further' transition of policy regimes, when the variable of interest is expressed in an appropriate way. Clearly, no statistical test can clarify the issue of such appropriateness, only a careful qualitative interpretation of the 'history' behind the PFRs. Here the economist needs, perhaps more than in other contexts, to be a true social scientist.

1.8   CONCLUDING REMARKS

This introductory chapter contributes to the literature on the empirics of policy evaluation by making the distinction between, on one side, the approach of the theory of reform in the Ramsey-Samuelson-Guesnerie tradition and – on the other side – the approach here described as the evaluation of changes of policy reform frameworks.

Some methodological issues of the two approaches are similar, but the latter departs from the former in certain aspects, the most important being the way the reform is treated as an object of analysis. In the theory of reform approach a precise signal can be identified and its marginal change evaluated, in the PFR context what changes is a broader orientation of the policy makers on some economic governance mechanisms or structures.

This distinction has consequences in the empirical analysis, particularly of the reform of network industries. While some potential errors are common to the two approaches, others are more likely when a PFR is considered. Moreover, the interpretation of estimated coefficients differs because usually it is not meaningful to express it as quantitative changes of the variable of interest, but rather as a transition from a policy regime to another one along an ordering.

In both contexts it is apparent that the dependent variable should be clearly linked, even if indirectly, to a social welfare function assumed as the evaluation criterion. In principle, both objective and subjective outcomes may be considered, with some implications for the interpretation of the results. In the empirics of PFR, apart from being particularly careful in dealing with potential errors given the more fuzzy nature of the variables of interest compared with changes in the RSG theory of reform, an applied economist needs to spend some time and effort in understanding the historical, political and social circumstances that supported an actual or proposed policy shift in the first place. The example of privatization or liberalization shows that indicator variables related to such changes of policy framework can have different meanings in different contexts, and this crucial characterization should be embodied in the empirical proxy of the policy variable of interest.

NOTES

Websites were last accessed April 2017.

*   The author is grateful for helpful comments on a previous version to Andrea Bastianin, Paolo Castelnovo and Valentina Morretta.

1.   Koske et al. (2015) and more recent materials and papers are available at http://www.oecd.org/eco/growth/indicatorsofproductmarketregulationhomepage.htm.

2.   See, for example, the wide range of international data available at the Quality of Government Institute website http://qog.pol.gu.se/data.

3.   http://ec.europa.eu/public_opinion/index_en.htm.

4.   Statistics-on-Income-and-Living-Conditions (SILC) is available at http://ec.europa.eu/eurostat/web/microdata/european-union-statistics-on-income-and-living-conditions.

5.   European-Community-Household-Panel (ECHP) is available at http://ec.europa.eu/eurostat/web/microdata/european-community-household-panel.

REFERENCES

Ahmad, E. and Stern, N. (1984). 'The Theory of Reform and Indian Indirect Taxes', *Journal of Public Economics*, **25**, 5, 259–98.

Boadway, R. (2012). *From Optimal Tax Theory to Tax Policy: Retrospective and Prospective*, Cambridge, MA: MIT Press.

Boadway, R.W. and Bruce, N. (1984). *Welfare Economics*, Oxford: Basil Blackwell.

Boardman, A., Greenberg, D., Vining, A. and Weimer, D. (2016). *Cost-benefit Analysis*, 4th edn, London: Pearson.

Bös, D. (1991). *Privatization: A Theoretical Treatment*, Oxford: Clarendon Press.

Clò, S., Del Bo, C.F., Ferraris Fiorio, C.V., Florio, M. and Vandone, D. (2015). 'Public Enterprises in the Market for Corporate Control: Recent Worldwide Evidence', *Annals of Public and Cooperative Economics*, **86**, 4, 559–83.

Diamond, P.A. and Mirrlees, J.A. (1971). 'Optimal Taxation and Public Production II: Tax Rules', *American Economic Review*, **61**, 3, 261–78.

Drèze, J. and Stern, N. (1990). 'Policy Reform, Shadow Prices, and Market Prices', *Journal of Public Economics*, **42**, 1, 1–45.

Florio, M. (2004). *The Great Divestiture: Evaluating the Welfare Impact of the British Privatizations, 1979–1997*, Cambridge, MA: MIT Press.

Florio, M. (2014). *Applied Welfare Economics. Cost-benefit Analysis of Projects and Policies*, Abingdon and New York, NY: Routledge.

Guesnerie, R. (1977). 'On the Direction of Tax Reform', *Journal of Public Economics*, **7**, 179–202.

Guesnerie, R. (1998). *A Contribution to the Pure Theory of Taxation*, Cambridge: Cambridge University Press.

Johansson, P.O. and Kriström, B. (2015). *Cost-benefit Analysis for Project Appraisal*, Cambridge: Cambridge University Press.

Jones, L.P., Tandon, P. and Vogelsang, I. (1990). *Selling Public Enterprises: A Cost/ Benefit Methodology*, Vol. 1, Cambridge, MA: MIT Press.

Koske, I., Wanner, I., Bitetti, R. and Barbiero, O. (2015). 'The 2013 Update of the OECD's Database on Product Market Regulation', OECD Economics Department Working Papers.

Mayeres, I. and Proost, S. (2001). 'Marginal Tax Reform, Externalities and Income Distribution', *Journal of Public Economics*, **79**, 2, 343–63.

Ng, Y. (1986). *Mesoeconomics: A Micro-Macro Analysis*, London: Harvester Wheatsheaf.

Obinger, H., Schmitt, C. and Traub, S. (2016). *The Political Economy of Privatization in Rich Democracies*, Oxford: Oxford University Press.

Parker, D. and Kirkpatrick, C. (2012). 'Measuring Regulatory Performance. The Economic Impact of Regulatory Policy: A Literature Review of Quantitative Evidence', OECD Expert Paper No. 3.

Poggi, A. and Florio, M. (2010). 'Energy Deprivation Dynamics and Regulatory Reforms in Europe: Evidence from Household Panel Data', *Energy Policy*, **38**, 1, 253–64.

Price, C.W. and Hancock, R. (1998). 'Distributional Effects of Liberalising UK Residential Utility Markets', *Fiscal Studies*, **19**, 3, 295–319.

Ramsey, F.P. (1927). 'A Contribution to the Theory of Taxation', *The Economic Journal*, **37**, 145, 47–61.

Samuelson, P.A. (1951). 'Theory of Optimal Taxation', Unpublished Memorandum, US Treasury.

2. Public and private enterprises, costs and welfare performance: an overview with suggestions for further research

Johan Willner and Sonja Grönblom*

2.1 INTRODUCTION: WHY PUBLIC ENTERPRISES?

In this chapter we identify a number of important research topics related to the costs and benefits of public ownership, privatisation and liberalisation against the background of mixed conclusions in previous literature. The significance of the topic is highlighted by the fact that state-owned enterprises (SOEs) correspond to 6 per cent of world gross national income (GNI) and that the value of their sales is estimated at approximately 19 per cent of the value of cross-border trade in goods and services (Kowalski and Perepechay, 2015).

SOEs in market economies have not usually emerged through nationalisation in well-performing markets, but as a solution where they would have otherwise failed. This explains their presence in particular in public services and network industries with a natural monopoly infrastructure (Florio, 2014), or in the production of public goods.

SOEs have also co-existed with private companies in the so-called *mixed oligopolies*. Public ownership has usually been associated with wider objectives than profit maximisation, for example, in the form of giving some weight to the consumer surplus. Competition between SOEs and private firms is then likely to reduce profit margins in the industry (De Fraja and Delbono, 1990). Public and private producers have co-existed in the car industry in Britain, France and Germany (Sheahan, 1966; Vickers and Yarrow, 1988). The same applies to several industries (for example, paper and pulp, banking, shipyards, the manufacture of trucks, buses, coaches and other road transport and electronic equipment) in Finland (Miettinen, 2000; Willner, 2006), and to the aluminium industry in the USA (Martin, 1959). Some industries in

Argentine may also have worked as mixed oligopolies (see Xu and Birch, 1999).[1]

However, SOEs are not always required to behave differently. Some exist because of a perceived need to rescue ailing companies. Others have been established because of a lack of private venture capital, for example, when it comes to fertilisers and other chemicals, mining, steel, oil products and the manufacture of paper machines in Finland, during the period 1920–70 (Willner, 2006; Willner and Grönblom, 2016). Similar reasons also partly explain public ownership in the generation and transmission of hydroelectric power in the USA (Hausman and Neufeld, 1999). A similar developmental motive as in Finland was present in Argentine as well (Xu and Birch, 1999). Related motives are post-war restructuring, for example, in Austria, Germany and Italy, and countercyclical policies in France, Germany and the UK, among others (Willner, 2003).

Such a growth strategy is not necessarily misguided, as suggested by evidence in favour of a positive relationship between economic growth and size of the public enterprise sector (see Fowler and Richards, 1995).[2] If this is the case, the notion of potential economic surplus (including unemployed resources and incomes that are wasted on luxury and military equipment) in stagnant or less developed countries is in need of a revival (Baran, 1962).

2.2 REASONS FOR PRIVATISATION AND LIBERALISATION

From an economist's point of view, public ownership would hardly be desirable if high production costs overshadow its benefits. Under such conditions, privatisation would seem sensible unless the privatisation process is associated with distortions such as corruption or underpriced assets.

There was scant evidence for lower costs, and economists tended to be sceptical when the second government of Mrs Thatcher in Britain (1983–87) initiated a series of privatisations that were subsequently followed by several countries (see Kay and Thompson, 1986; Vickers and Yarrow, 1988).[3] However, the political rhetoric emphasised cost efficiency (Ikenberry, 1990; Thatcher, 1993), partly inspired by influential think tanks (Pirie, 1988), and the benefits of public ownership were implicitly assumed to be negative. Similar motives were cited in some other countries (but less so than usually believed; see Willner, 2003). The intuitive explanation for expecting lower costs was the belief that private firms, which can go bankrupt or become subject to hostile takeovers, get stronger incentives for monitoring and cost-cutting (World Bank, 1995); see Section 2.4 for a discussion of the literature and Chapters 1–10 for fresh evidence from European network industries.

However, the privatisation wave cannot be explained just by an attempt to cut costs. Mrs Thatcher's thinking included an ideological component as well (see Thatcher, 1993, pp. 676–7). Ideology was present also in other countries such as Portugal and France (Parker, 1998). Other governments may have been less ideological, but it was also believed that small open economies had to follow the bandwagon, like Denmark, Finland and the Netherlands (Hulsink and Schenk, 1998; Willner, 2006).[4]

Recent research reveals, on the other hand, that the motive to raise revenues was stronger than suggested by the rhetoric, as highlighted also by the British government's priority to divest not its weakest but its most successful companies (Parker, 2009). Similar motives occurred in Finland, France and Germany as well, often combined with ambitions to spread popular share ownership, to force firms to emphasise profitability rather than objectives that are seen as distorted, to encourage research and development (R&D) and other investments, and to prevent disloyal competition (Willner, 2003).

Apart from when privatising for ideological reasons, the objectives above can in general be fulfilled through other means than complete privatisation and shall therefore mostly be ignored in what follows. For example, fund-raising and widened share ownership can be achieved without complete divestiture, through partial privatisation in several industries.[5]

Distorted objectives because of political influence (see Section 2.5) can be addressed also by granting autonomy (such as for listed companies, independent central banks and traditional public sector universities). However, as pointed out in Section 2.5, employment and/or output and quality in excess of their profit-maximising levels (see Ferguson, 1988; Boycko et al., 1996) are not necessarily distortions. Moreover, if public sector decision makers have distorted objectives, why would they not cause similar distortions through taxes and subsidies? Are such biased decision makers able to sell assets at adequate prices and to regulate the industry afterwards? Did public ownership really work better under dictatorship than in countries where politicians had to please their voters?

The motive to encourage R&D relates to dynamic efficiency such as low costs (or new products) in the future. However, it is not obvious that full profit maximisation would strengthen the incentive to invest in cost-reducing activities. As for the need to fund other types of investments, state ownership has in some cases meant limited access to the banking sector, but such problems can be addressed through legislation without a change of ownership.

It is also worth noting that there is a tendency to refocus criticism of SOEs from their alleged inefficiency to the aggressive competition caused by their wider objectives (Bernier et al., 2016). This is a more recent privatisation motive that is often seen as associated with European Union (EU) regulations (see Haskel and Szymansky, 1992; Bös, 1993; Berne and Pogorel, 2005; Clifton et al., 2006). However, higher output levels or lower prices than under profit maximisation are anti-competitive only if a firm's purpose is just to maximise profits, but not if they are consistent with a company's Articles of Association (or objective function; see De Fraja, 2009).[6]

Regulation against anti-competitive behaviour also relates to privatisation as a response to globalisation, because competition is often international. Moreover, divestiture often means selling companies to international investors (Florio, 2013), and capital mobility, without federalism, is often perceived as calling for a 'narrow straitjacket' of deregulation, low taxes and privatisation (Rodrik, 2000). While it can be argued that the problem is then not necessarily ownership as such, international competition raises issues about the scope for wider objectives (see Section 2.5).

2.3   COST EFFICIENCY: THEORETICAL RESULTS

Lower costs are a necessary but not sufficient condition for privatisation and liberalisation to increase welfare, but it is obvious that the benefits of wider objectives would dominate if costs are not reduced. Cost reductions are often modelled as depending on managerial efforts. All managers are, in conventional theory, assumed to value incomes and dislike efforts, but owners-managers who are exposed to competition get strong incentives to cut costs.

However, SOEs are usually large organisations that would have to hire a manager also if privatised. Managers usually know more than politicians about the state of nature, but also more than shareholders if the firm is privatised. Owners are unable to monitor the manager and to micromanage the firm. To prevent the manager from shirking, blaming high costs on bad circumstances, she must get an incentive to reveal the true state of nature, without reducing her utility below the outside-option level. To pay such a lazy and greedy manager a constant salary in an SOE would indeed cause efforts to be low. The SOE's performance would then be lower than in a private firm with performance-related pay.[7] However, performance-related pay in combination with wider objectives would in fact make SOEs relatively more cost efficient (De Fraja, 1993; for extensions to a market setting and active and passive ownership, see Willner and Parker, 2007; and to network industries, see Willner and Grönblom, 2013).

The intuition is based on the manager's greed and laziness. An objective function in the form of a weighted sum of profits and the consumer surplus would in fact strengthen the owner's willingness to pay for cost-reducing efforts, whereas a profit maximiser would pay for cost-reducing efforts only to the extent that it promotes profitability. Moreover, entry would reduce the profit margins of private firms, and hence also the ability and willingness to pay for cost reductions (Martin, 1993; Willner and Parker, 2007). This also applies to unbundling (Willner and Grönblom, 2013).[8] While the analysis has to be extended beyond greed and laziness (see Section 2.5), such results provide counterexamples to the conventional views on relative cost performance.

As for overstaffing or excessive wages, privatisation and/or competition can indeed reduce labour rents (Newbery, 2006; Grönblom and Willner, 2008).[9] However, both profits and labour rents are part of the total surplus, so privatisation would increase the total surplus only if pre-privatisation labour rents exceed post-privatisation profits. It follows that the condition for privatisation to increase welfare becomes stronger than if the cost-disadvantage under public ownership is explained by waste (Willner, 1996 [2000]; Grönblom and Willner, 2008).[10] Moreover, while the public sector does not always pay higher wages, this often applies to low-wage workers, which suggests that privatisation can increase inequality (De Castro et al., 2013). It is not self-evident that the private sector should set the norm in such cases.[11] The same applies to the accusation that public ownership leads to excessive quality (Ferguson, 1988; see also Section 2.5).

2.4 COST EFFICIENCY: EMPIRICAL FINDINGS

To substitute private for public provision or the reverse is in practice more than just changing the parameter of an objective function. Privatisation can usually be described as a policy framework reform (see Chapter 1). It is a process that may take several years, including steps such as legislation (for example, in favour of competition), corporatisation, listing on the stock market, and selling equity until the firm becomes controlled by private investors. It is not then obvious that, for example, an observed change in performance is caused by the shift of control. Similar issues arise in the case of unbundling.

The proper procedure to analyse a policy framework reform like privatisation would be to apply some social welfare function; and few such functions would associate an increased emphasis on profits, without cost reductions, with a welfare increase. Dewenter and Malatesta (1997) suggest, based on an international sample of 500 firms, that profitability was often higher after the privatisation process. While this does not rule out other explanations than lost state control, it is also obvious that higher profits may reflect the market failure that was previously addressed through a lower emphasis on profits. It therefore makes more sense to focus on other performance dimensions, in particular cost efficiency or total factor productivity. Results are then mixed, and most improvements seem to have occurred in the run-up to privatisation (Dewenter and Malatesta, 1997, 2001). Costs have tended to change both ways after the British privatisation process as well, and often before rather than after lost state control (Martin and Parker, 1997; Florio, 2004).[12] A study of 39 firms in Italy suggests higher labour productivity but no significant increase in total factor productivity (Fraquelli and Erbetta, 2000). Similar results have been reached in Austria (Dockner et al., 2005) and in a meta-study by Hodge (2000).[13]

Another line of research compares firms under different ownership. Studies or meta-studies such as Millward (1982), Boyd (1986), Molyneux and Thompson (1987) and Iordanoglou (2001) do not support the negative view of public ownership.[14] Moreover, the distinction between services and industrial production in Willner (2001) suggests that higher costs tended to occur somewhat more often among labour-intensive service producers (for example, in the case of 7 out of 13 studies on refuse). Similar findings are reported also when it comes to transport, hospitals, health and social care (although insurance appears as better organised under public ownership). However, such comparisons require reliable quality indicators (see also Chapter 1). Higher quality may cost more, like in many service industries where quality is related to staff size.[15] Costs may also reflect wages and working conditions, and thus also income distribution and social justice.

Such factors are less prominent in the industrial production of relatively homogeneous goods. For example, public ownership is at least no worse, and often even superior, in cement and plastics, electricity and water (Willner, 2001).[16] The tendency to privatise electricity and water, where privatisation would also lead to high profit margins because of low demand elasticity (Willner, 1996 [2000]), is therefore surprising.

Analysing the production function is an alternative if an industry is not mixed or before privatisation has taken place. Such methods suggest that postal services and railways (in 19 and 22 countries, respectively) were fairly efficient in the 1980s (Deprins et al., 1984; Perelman and Pestieau, 1988).

As for the significance of competition, it seems that exposure was no guarantee for higher post-privatisation efficiency at least in Britain and Italy, as also highlighted by the British car industry (Martin and Parker, 1997; Fraquelli and Erbetta, 2000). Moreover, privatisation in an oligopoly can lead to higher prices despite somewhat lower costs.

Privatisation and competition in a network industry requires unbundling, which can cause the upstream monopoly to reduce its spending on the bottleneck infrastructure (Buehler, 2005), as highlighted by staff reductions in rail and gas pipe maintenance (12000–6000 and 1000 persons, respectively) in Britain in the 1990s (Guardian, 2001a, 2001b). Deregulation and unbundling have also been blamed for the Californian electricity crisis in 2001 (Lijesen et al., 2001).

On the other hand, the benefits of vertical integration in the electricity industry might amount to 13 per cent for the median firm and 15–20 per cent for larger firms in a European sample (Gugler et al., 2014). There is evidence of benefits from vertical integration also in European railways (Cantos Sánchez, 2001; Pittman, 2003, 2005). The British upstream monopolist had to become non-profit maximising after safety concerns (Crompton and Jupe, 2003; Newbery, 2006). Moreover, state ownership did not harm the Canadian and US railways (Caves and Christensen, 1980; Caves et al., 1982), and the British restructuring failed to reduce the need for subsidies (Shaoul, 2004; Newbery, 2006). This suggests a need for amending EU policy towards network industries (as described in Martin et al., 2005).

Telecommunications (which are no longer associated with any natural monopoly infrastructure) are usually seen as more suitable (or less unsuitable) for restructuring than railways (Pittman, 2005; Newbery, 2006). Telecommunications became cheaper, but in the USA and Europe at least partly because of technical progress and regulation (Taylor and Taylor, 1993; MacAvoy, 1998; Sung, 1998; Daßler et al., 2002). Moreover, despite initial quality improvements (Boylaud and Nicoletti, 2000), there were also signs of subsequent deterioration (Stephen, 2001; van Dam and Went, 2001). The market is often seen as confusing, and there are concerns about universal access, as highlighted by the need to reduce the digital divide (Guardian, 2000; Clifton et al., 2011; Florio, 2013).

2.5   RECENT AND FUTURE RESEARCH

The assumption that managers and other economic agents are just self-interested may be innocuous in the right context, but cannot sensibly be extended to all our social roles, and it may bias the analysis of organisations with different objectives. An important extension to previous research on organisational performance is to replace greed and laziness by an assumption of (potential) intrinsic motivation, so that efforts (or organisational performance) can yield not only costs to the agent but also benefits (Frey, 1997). To signal a suspicion of low work morale through rewards and punishment (extrinsic work motivation) may then crowd out the intrinsic motivation, and thereby reduce organisation's performance (Frey, 1997).[17]

The existence of potential intrinsic motivation and differences in the pay schedules mean that firms may differ in more ways than by having different owners. Public firms may be more cost efficient under such conditions as well, but they can also become less efficient, for example, because of motivation-reducing reforms in the spirit of the New Public Management (Grönblom and Willner, 2014). This ambiguity stands in contrast to contributions favouring just one form of ownership and suggests the need for more research.

We may also ask whether globalisation really undermines the scope for wider objectives. Do SOEs become unable to break even, or will such objectives crowd out their private competitors, thus creating public monopolies? More precisely, how does international competition affect the permissible range of the weight to the consumer surplus, given that both public and private firms should be able to break even?

Research is also needed on endogenous quality, which is hardly unaffected by privatisation and/or competition (see also Chapter 1).[18] It is well known that a monopoly can over- or underprovide quality (Spence, 1975), and oligopolists might overinvest in quality in order to signal high quality under asymmetric information (Belleflamme and Peitz, 2014). However, some tentative results predict a quality reduction under full information after privatisation and/or entry. This happens if quality and sunk costs (or alternatively marginal costs) are positively related, for example, if a restructuring leads to staff reductions and increased queuing (Willner and Grönblom, 2017).

The public sector can remain a provider if production is outsourced to private firms, but renationalisation might be an attractive option if it turns out that outsourcing leads to an oligopoly with high profits that are transferred to tax havens. Renationalisation may in such cases be expensive, unless there is a way to undermine profitability legally before taking over the activity. It is well known that inelastic demand means low profit margins, and vice versa. Supposing that the public sector is a significant buyer of an output that it provides free of charge; can it then undermine profitability by making its demand more elastic within a given budget, without reducing the quantity demanded at a given price?

Finally, the use of public ownership as a policy instrument requires an institutional setting with benevolent and enlightened decision makers. However, there are large international variations in the quality of governance, for example, when it comes to rule of law, the absence of corruption and the quality of regulation (Kaufmann et al., 2004). It would hardly be surprising to find systematic differences in SOEs' performance between countries, high and low performers in terms of governance. Do top performers (such as Finland and Switzerland; see Kaufmann et al., 2004) also have better SOEs than, for example, high-corruption countries?

2.6   CONCLUDING REMARKS

Views on the inferiority of public ownership have seriously reduced the policy options in markets with unsatisfactory performance, or in economies facing secular stagnation. Favouring a mixed economy has for too long been perceived as old-fashioned, and as doctrinaire in comparison to the standpoint that only private ownership can work. However, neither theory nor evidence suggests that public ownership is always associated with higher costs to such an extent that they overshadow all benefits of public ownership when markets would otherwise fail.

This highlights the need to address some new topics, such as the significance of potential intrinsic motivation for relative performance, the impact of globalisation on the scope for wider objectives, endogenous quality, the possibility of renationalisation under outsourcing, and the significance of governance quality. However, our list is biased by our own research interests, so it is far from exhaustive.

NOTES

*   We are grateful for constructive comments by the editor and two reviewers, and by participants at the XIV Milan European Economy Workshop, June 2016.
1.   Most SOEs (in infrastructure industries but also coal mining, petrol and steel) were oligopolists with wider objectives (such as output maximisation with a maximum permitted deficit, or employment maximisation), with hydroelectric power as the only exception (Xu and Birch, 1999). Thus, some industries must have been mixed oligopolies.
2.   Finland's growth is not inconsistent with this result, given the timing of the development of its state enterprise sector: GDP was higher in 1998 than in 1913 by a factor of 8.7, which is second only to Japan (Maddison, 2001, p. 264).
3.   The earlier privatisations in (West) Germany in the 1950s and 1960s and in Portugal and Chile in the 1970s did not shape the international agenda in the same way.
4.   Certainly, for a small and open economy such as the Netherlands it would be difficult to ignore developments elsewhere in Europe. Thus, the Dutch privatisation programme can be described as a 'curtsy to the times' rather than the result of a positive, grand design to revitalise the economy (Hulsink and Schenk, 1998, p. 255).
5.   Privatisation also reduces dividend incomes, and there are fewer assets to sell when the next budget crisis hits. Moreover, to widen share ownership by selling undervalued assets that are subsequently re-sold to large investors can cause housing bubbles (Vickers and Yarrow, 1988; Bös, 1993; Lashmar, 1994).
6.   For example, the Finnish government defines three groups of firms with (some) state ownership. They may be of a 'shareholder interest', of a 'strategic interest' or they

may be associated with an 'industrial, societal or other political mission' (Willner and Grönblom, 2016).

7. Performance-related pay to top managers did on the other hand not become widespread until the 1990s (Jensen and Murphy, 1990).
8. Such utilities may be regulated, which might on the other hand subordinate managers to principals with conflicting interests (Laffont and Tirole, 1991).
9. Moreover, while public ownership may bias labour intensity upwards, private firms are biased in the opposite direction, with ambiguous consequences for total factor productivity (Pint, 1991).
10. Public sector wages are in general higher in the EU, except in Denmark, Finland, Slovakia, Estonia and Hungary (De Castro et al., 2013), but this does not mean higher wages in SOEs in mixed markets. Note also that the public sector ambition to be a model employer seems to be a thing of the past.
11. Also, the gender gap increased when the Swedish public sector began to adopt private sector practices in the 1980s (Zetterberg, 1994).
12. Martin and Parker (1997, p. 217) conclude that they provide 'little evidence that privatisation has caused a significant improvement in performance. Generally the great expectations for privatisation evident in ministerial speeches have not been borne out. Certainly, privatisation has been associated with improvements in some of the eleven firms studied, especially in terms of profitability and value added per employee, although what performance improvement there was often pre-dated privatisation.'
13. Megginson and Netter (2001) conclude in favour of private ownership, but they focus on third world and transition economies with weak governance traditions (see Section 2.5), while ignoring important contributions cited above.
14. Borcherding et al. (1982) use many non-academic sources, including municipal reports. While they are often cited as favouring private ownership, they avoid premature conclusions and emphasise competition.
15. For example, less costly public or voluntary health care providers in the USA (see Willner, 2001) may have provided cheap services for low-income groups.
16. On the water industry, see also Abbott and Cohen (2009) and *Utility Week* (2011).
17. Frey and Benz (2005) suggest that the public sector can teach private firms to rely on intrinsic motivation, career paths that discourage opportunism and non-pecuniary rewards. See also Guttman and Schnytzer (1989) on why the Israeli *Kibbutz* system outperformed the Soviet *Kolkhoz* system.
18. Competitive tender in cleaning services made the incumbent SOE a loser, until it started following its competitors in leaving more dust in the corridors (Helsingin Sanomat, 1997).

REFERENCES

Abbott, M. and B. Cohen (2009), 'Productivity and Efficiency in the Water Industry', *Utilities Policy* 17(3–4), 233–44.

Baran, P.A. (1962), *The Political Economy of Growth*, New York and London: Monthly Review Press.

Belleflamme, P. and M. Peitz (2014), 'Asymmetric Information and Overinvestment in Quality', *European Economic Review* 66, 127–43.

Berne, M. and G. Pogorel (2005), 'Privatisation Experiences in France', *Journal for Institutional Comparisons* 3(1), 33–40.

Bernier, L., M. Florio and J. Willner (2016), 'Rationales, Performance and Governance of Public Enterprises', Editorial Introduction, *Economia Pubblica/ Italian Journal of Public Economics* 43(3), 5–10.

Borcherding, T.E., W.W. Pommerehne and F. Schneider (1982), 'Comparing the Efficiency of Private and Public Production: The Evidence from Five Countries', *Zeitschrift für Nationalökonomie*, Suppl. 2, 127–56.

Bös, D. (1993), *Privatisation. A Theoretical Treatment*, Oxford: Clarendon Press.

Boycko, M., A. Schleifer and R.W. Vishny (1996), 'A Theory of Privatisation', *Economic Journal* **106**(435), 309–19.

Boyd, C.W. (1986), 'The Comparative Efficiency of State Owned Enterprises', in A.R. Negandhi (ed.), *Multinational Corporations and State-owned Enterprises: A New Challenge in International Business*, Greenwich, CT and London: JAI Press, pp. 179–94.

Boylaud, O. and G. Nicoletti (2000), 'Regulation, Market Structure and Performance in Telecommunications', OECD Economics Department Working Papers No. 237.

Buehler, S. (2005), 'The Promise and Pitfalls of Restructuring Network Industries', *German Economic Review* **6**(2), 205–28.

Cantos Sánchez, P. (2001), 'Vertical Relationships for the European Railway Industry', *Transport Policy* **8**(2), 77–83.

Caves, D.W. and L.R. Christensen (1980), 'The Relative Efficiency of Public and Private Firms in a Competitive Environment: The Case of Canadian Railroads', *Journal of Political Economy* **88**(5), 958–76.

Caves, D.W., L.R. Christensen, J.A. Swanson and M.W. Tretheway (1982), 'Economic Performance of U.S. and Canadian Railroads: The Significance of Ownership and the Regulatory Environment', in T. Stanbury and F. Thompson (eds), *Managing Public Enterprises*, New York: Praeger, pp. 123–51.

Clifton, J., F. Comín and D. Díaz-Fuentes (2006), 'Privatizing Public Enterprises in the European Union 1960–2002: Ideological, Pragmatic, Inevitable?', *Journal of European Public Policy* **13**(5), 736–56.

Clifton, J., D. Díaz-Fuentes, M. Fernández-Gutiérrez and J. Revuelta (2011), 'Is Market-oriented Reform Producing a Two-track Europe? Evidence from Electricity and Telecommunications', *Annals of Public and Cooperative Economics* **82**(4), 495–513.

Crompton, G. and R. Jupe (2003), '"Such a Silly Scheme": The Privatisation of Britain's Railways 1992–2002', *Critical Perspectives on Accounting* **14**(6), 617–45.

Daßler, T., D. Parker and D. Saal (2002), 'Economic Performance in European Telecommunications, 1978–98: A Comparative Study', *European Business Review* **14**(36), 194–209.

De Castro, F., M. Salto and H. Steiner (2013), 'The Gap Between Public and Private Wages: New Evidence for the EU', European Economy, Economic Papers No. 508, October.

De Fraja, G. (1993), 'Productive Efficiency in Public and Private Firms', *Journal of Public Economics* **50**(1), 15–30.

De Fraja, G. (2009), 'Mixed Oligopoly: Old and New', University of Leicester, Department of Economics, Working Paper No. 09/20, September.

De Fraja, G. and F. Delbono (1990), 'Game Theoretic Models of Mixed Oligopoly', *Journal of Economic Surveys* **4**(1), 1–18.

Deprins, D., L. Simar and H. Tulkens (1984), 'Measuring Labour-efficiency in Post Offices', in M. Marchand, P. Pestieau and H. Tulkens (eds), *The Performance of Public Enterprises. Concepts and Measurement*, Amsterdam: North-Holland, pp. 243–68.

Dewenter, K. and P.H. Malatesta (1997), 'Public Offerings of State-owned and

Privately-owned Enterprises: An International Comparison', *Journal of Finance* **52**(4), 1659–79.

Dewenter, K. and P.H. Malatesta (2001), 'State-owned and Privately Owned Firms: An Empirical Analysis of Profitability, Leverage, and Labour Intensity', *American Economic Review* **91**(1), 320–34.

Dockner, E.J., G. Mosburger and M.M. Schaffhauser-Linzatti (2005), 'The Financial and Operating Performance of Privatized Firms in Austria', Mimeo, University of Vienna.

Ferguson, P. (1988), *Industrial Economics: Issues and Perspectives*, Houndmills, Basingstoke: Palgrave Macmillan.

Florio, M. (2004), *The Great Divestiture. Evaluating the Welfare Impact of the British Privatizations 1979–1997*, Cambridge, MA: MIT Press.

Florio, M. (2013), *Network Industries and Social Welfare. The Experiment that Reshuffled European Utilities*, Oxford: Oxford University Press.

Florio, M. (2014), 'The Return of Public Enterprise', University of Milan, Centre of Industrial Studies, Working Paper No. 01/2014.

Fowler, P.C. and D.F. Richards (1995), 'Test Evidence for the OECD-countries, 1965–85: The Relationship Between the Size of the Public Enterprise Sector and Economic Growth', *International Journal of Social Economics* **22**(3), 11–23.

Fraquelli, G. and F. Erbetta (2000), 'Privatisation in Italy: An Analysis of Factor Productivity and Technical Efficiency', in D. Parker (ed.), *Privatisation and Corporate Performance*, Cheltenham and Northampton, MA: Edward Elgar Publishing, pp. 537–57.

Frey, B.S. (1997), 'On the Relationship Between Intrinsic and Extrinsic Work Motivation', *International Journal of Industrial Organization* **15**(4), 427–40.

Frey, B.S. and M. Benz (2005), 'Can Private Learn from Public Governance', *Economic Journal* **115**(507), F377–F396.

Grönblom, S. and J. Willner (2008), 'Privatisation and Liberalization: Costs and Benefits in the Presence of Wage Bargaining', *Annals of Public and Cooperative Economics* **78**(1), 133–60.

Grönblom, S. and J. Willner (2014), 'Organisational Form and Individual Motivation: Public Ownership, Privatisation and Fat Cats', *Journal of Economic Policy Reform* **17**(3), 267–84.

Guardian (2000), 'Ringing up the Right Numbers', Jobs and Money section, *Guardian*, 14 October, p. 2.

Guardian (2001a), 'Shockwave for Transco', *Guardian*, 18 June, p. 10.

Guardian (2001b), 'The Breaking Point', *Guardian*, 3 April, pp. 4–5.

Gugler, K., M. Liebensteiner and S. Schmitt (2014), 'Vertical Disintegration in the European Electricity Sector: Empirical Evidence on Lost Synergies', Wirtschaftsuniversität, Department of Economics, Working Paper No. 190, Vienna.

Guttman, J.M. and A. Schnytzer (1989), 'Strategic Work Interaction and the *Kibbuz-Kolkhoz* paradox', *Economic Journal* **99**(397), 689–99.

Haskel, J. and S. Szymanski (1992), 'A Bargaining Theory of Privatisation', *Annals of Public and Cooperative Economics* **63**(2), 207–28.

Hausman, W.J. and J.L. Neufeld (1999), 'Falling Water: The Origins of Direct Federal Participation in the U.S. Electric Utility Industry 1902–1933', *Annals of Public and Cooperative Economics* **76**(1), 49–74.

Helsingin Sanomat (1997), 'Palkka putosi ja työt lisääntyivät', *Helsingin Sanomat*, Talous & Työ, 30 November, p. E2.

Hodge, G.A. (2000), *Privatization. An International Review of Performance*, Boulder, CO: Westview Press.

Hulsink, W. and H. Schenk (1998), 'Privatisation and Deregulation in the Netherlands', in D. Parker (ed.), *Privatisation in the European Union: Theory and Policy Perspectives*, London and New York: Routledge, pp. 242–57.

Ikenberry, G.J. (1990), 'The International Spread of Privatisation Policies: Inducements, Learning and Policy Bandwagoning', in E.N. Suleiman and J. Waterbury (eds), *The Political Economy of Public Sector Reform and Privatisation*, Boulder, CO: Westview Press, pp. 88–110.

Iordanoglou, C.H. (2001), *Public Enterprises Revisited. A Closer Look at the 1974–79 UK Labour Productivity Record*, Cheltenham and Northampton, MA: Edward Elgar Publishing.

Jensen, M.C. and K.J. Murphy (1990), 'Performance Pay and Top-management Incentives', *Journal of Political Economy* **98**(2), 225–64.

Kaufmann, D., A. Kraay and M. Mastruzzi (2004), 'Governance Matters III: Governance Indicators for 1996, 1998, 2000, and 2002', *World Bank Economic Review* **18**(2), 253–87.

Kay, J.A. and D.J. Thompson (1986), 'Privatisation: A Policy in Search of a Rationale', *Economic Journal* **96**(1), 18–32.

Kowalski, P. and K. Perepechay (2015), 'International Trade and Investment by State Enterprises', OECD Trade Policy Papers, No. 184, Paris.

Laffont, J.-J. and J. Tirole (1991), 'Privatisation and Incentives', *Journal of Law, Economics and Organization* **7**, 84–105.

Lashmar, P. (1994), 'Going for Brokers?', *New Statesman*, 1 January, pp. 24–5.

Lijesen, M., H. Mannaerts and M. Mulder (2001), 'Will California Come to Europe?', Mimeo, CPB, Netherlands Bureau for Economic Policy Research.

MacAvoy, P.W. (1998), 'Testing for Competitiveness of Markets for Long Distance Telephone Services: Competition Finally?', *Review of Industrial Organization* **13**(3), 295–319.

Maddison, A. (2001), *The World Economy. A Millennial Perspective*, Paris: OECD.

Martin, R., M. Roma and I. Vansteenkiste (2005), 'Regulatory Reforms in Selected EU Network Industries', European Central Bank, Occasional Paper Series, No. 28.

Martin, S. (1993), 'Endogenous Firm Efficiency in a Cournot Principal-agent Model', *Journal of Economic Theory* **59**(2), 445–50.

Martin, S. and D. Parker (1997), *The Impact of Privatisation. Ownership and Corporate Performance in the UK*, London and New York: Routledge.

Martin, W.H. (1959), 'Public Policy and Increased Competition in the Synthetic Ammonia Industry', *Quarterly Journal of Economics* **LXXIII**(4), 373–92.

Megginson, W.L. and J.M. Netter (2001), 'From State to Market: A Survey of Empirical Studies on Privatisation', *Journal of Economic Literature* **XXXIX**(2), 321–89.

Miettinen, T. (2000), 'Poikkeavatko valtionyhtiöt yksityisistä?', The Research Institute of the Finnish Economy, Discussion Papers No. 730.

Millward, R. (1982), 'The Comparative Performance of Public and Private Ownership', in Lord E. Roll (ed.), *The Mixed Economy*, London: Macmillan, pp. 58–93.

Molyneux, R. and D. Thompson (1987), 'Nationalised Industry Performance: Still Third-rate?', *Fiscal Studies* **8**(1), 48–82.

Newbery, D.M. (2006), 'Privatising Network Industries', in M. Köthenbürger,

H.-W. Sinn and J. Whalley (eds), *Privatisation Experiences in the European Union*, Cambridge, MA: MIT Press, pp. 3–49.

Parker, D. (1998), 'Privatisation in the European Union: An Overview', in D. Parker (ed.), *Privatisation in the European Union: Theory and Policy Perspectives*, London and New York: Routledge, pp. 10–48.

Parker, D. (2009), *The Official History of Privatisation. Volume I: The Formative Years*, London and New York: Routledge.

Perelman, S. and P. Pestieau (1988), 'Technical Performance in Public Enterprises. A Comparative Study of Railways and Postal Services', *European Economic Review* **32**(2–3), 432–41.

Pint, E.M. (1991), 'Nationalization vs. Regulation of Monopolies: The Effects of Ownership on Efficiency', *Journal of Public Economics* **44**(2), 131–64.

Pirie, M. (1988), *Privatisation. Theory, Practice and Choice*, Aldershot: Wildwood House.

Pittman, R. (2003), 'Vertical Restructuring (or Not) of the Infrastructure Sectors of Transition Economies', *Journal of Industry, Competition and Trade* **3**(1), 5–26.

Pittman, R. (2005), 'Structural Separation to Create Competition? The Case of Freight Railways', *Review of Network Economics* **4**, 181–96.

Rodrik, D. (2000), 'How Far Will International Economic Integration Go?', *Journal of Economic Perspectives* **14**(2), 177–86.

Shaoul, J. (2004), 'Railpolitik: The Financial Realities of Operating Britain's National Railways', *Public Money & Management* **24**, 26–36.

Sheahan, J. (1966), 'Government Competition and the Performance of the French Automobile Industry', *Journal of Industrial Economics* **VIII**, June, 197–215.

Spence, A.M. (1975), 'Monopoly, Quality, and Regulation', *Bell Journal of Economics* **6**(2), 417–29.

Stephen, A. (2001), 'Coast to Coast Chaos with the Baby Bells', *New Statesman*, 27 August, p. 20.

Sung, N. (1998), 'The Embodiment Hypothesis Revisited: Evidence From the U.S. Local Exchange Carriers', *Information Economics and Policy* **10**(2), 219–36.

Taylor, W.E. and L.D. Taylor (1993), 'Postdivestiture Long-distance Competition in the United States', *American Economic Review* **83**, May, 185–90.

Thatcher, M. (1993), *The Downing Street Years*, Glasgow: HarperCollins.

Utility Week (2011), 'Vertical Separation of Water Firms' Inefficient and Expensive', *Utility Week*, 5 July, accessed on 3 November 2016 at http://utilityweek.co.uk/news/vertical-separation-of-water-firms-inefficient-and-expensive/770212#.WBtX9zFA6ZY.

van Dam, J. and R. Went (2001), 'Liberalizing Network Utilities: What's in it for the Citizen?', Mimeo, The Netherlands Court of Audit.

Vickers, J. and G. Yarrow (1988), *Privatization: An Economic Analysis*, Cambridge, MA: MIT Press.

Willner, J. (1996), 'Privatisation of Natural Monopolies: A Comment', *Review of Industrial Organization* **1**(6), 869–82, reprinted in D. Parker (ed.) (2000), *Privatisation and Corporate Performance*, The International Library of Critical Writings in Economics, Cheltenham and Northampton, MA: Edward Elgar Publishing, pp. 14–27.

Willner, J. (2001), 'Ownership, Efficiency, and Political Interference', *European Journal of Political Economy* **17**(4), 723–48.

Willner, J. (2003), 'Privatization: A Sceptical Analysis', in D. Parker and D. Saal (eds), *International Handbook on Privatisation*, Cheltenham and Northampton, MA: Edward Elgar Publishing, pp. 60–81.

Willner, J. (2006), 'Privatisation and Public Ownership in Finland', in M. Köthenbürger, H.-W. Sinn and J. Whalley (eds), *Privatisation Experiences in the European Union*, Cambridge, MA: MIT Press, pp. 141–62.

Willner, J. and S. Grönblom (2013), 'Reforming a Network Industry: Consequences for Cost Efficiency and Welfare', *International Review of Applied Economics* **27**(2), 265–84.

Willner, J. and S. Grönblom (2016), 'The Organisation of Services of General Interest in Finland', *Economia Pubblica/Italian Journal of Public Economics* **43**(3), 89–116.

Willner, J. and S. Grönblom (2017), 'Quality Provision Under Conditions of Oligopoly', Mimeo, Åbo Akademi University.

Willner, J. and D. Parker (2007), 'The Performance of Public and Private Enterprise under Conditions of Active and Passive Ownership and Competition and Monopoly', *Journal of Economics* **90**(3), 221–53.

World Bank (1995), *Bureaucrats in Business. The Economics and Politics of Government Ownership*, Oxford: Oxford University Press.

Xu, Z. and M.H. Birch (1999), 'The Economic Performance of State-owned Enterprises in Argentina: An Empirical Assessment', *Review of Industrial Organization* **14**(4), 355–75.

Zetterberg, J. (1994), 'Effects of Changed Wage Setting Conditions on Male-Female Wage Differentials in the Swedish Public Sector', *Public Administration Quarterly*, **18**(3), 342–58.

3. Market reforms, governance and performance: lessons learned from the experience in the EU energy industries

Steve Thomas and Stefano Clò

3.1 INTRODUCTION

The electricity industry has always been an amalgamation of four distinct businesses: power generation; the high voltage transmission network, generally national, but sometimes regional, taking power from power stations to centres of demand; the low voltage distribution network, taking power from the transmission system to final consumers; and retail including buying wholesale power and selling to final consumers including metering and billing. However, while it was a monopoly, usually lightly regulated, the special characteristics of these separate businesses were little recognised and the electricity industry was in the hands of integrated companies, often publicly owned. In some cases, an integrated company carried out all four functions; in others, a distributor carried out distribution and retail while a generator carried out generation and transmission. In the latter case, the distributor was effectively captive to the generator.

The economic and social rationale at the base of this organisational model has been evident since the middle of the nineteenth century. The establishment of legal monopolies in services characterised by network industries led to significant economies of scale being achieved, allowing the recovery of costs, while controlling increases in consumer tariffs (Mill, 1848).

After the Second World War, state-owned enterprises (SOEs) played a key role in providing services of general interest such as the provision of energy (Willner, 2001), to create new markets and support emerging industries where private enterprises were reluctant to invest due to significant start-up costs, high uncertainty, long-term and sometimes non-economic positive returns (Kaldor, 1980). Government intervention through SOEs has not only been justified on economic grounds, it has gone well beyond the correction of market failures. SOEs have deliberately deviated from profit maximisation behaviour to achieve social goals: territorial development and cohesion, employment support, income redistribution and inflation control through pricing mechanisms (Atkinson and Stiglitz, 1980; Bös, 1994).

Massive public investments in network industries were aimed at achieving universal service access, generally interpreted as an obligation for the operator to provide, on an ongoing basis, a good quality service to all consumers at an affordable price, regardless of their income and locational conditions (Cremer et al.,1998).

The limits of this model started to become evident from the end of the 1970s. Increasing public debt, assumed inefficiency of the incumbent stemming from public ownership and the lack of competition progressively brought a change to the dominant paradigm. Privatisation was increasingly advocated as a required process to lower public debt and improve management and SOEs' efficiency (Peltzman et al., 1989). The attempt to transform the electricity industry into a competitive one, largely followed the 1990 UK reforms and the European Union (EU) Electricity Directive of 1996 revised in 2004 and 2009.[1] These Directives first concerned the pillars of liberalisation, unbundling and regulation, and then market integration, while no official position was taken concerning privatisation.

The main objective was to make generation and retail competitive activities. Transmission and distribution would remain monopolies but more rigorously regulated by autonomous national regulators. To ensure fair competition, the networks had to be 'unbundled' from the competitive activities so companies owning the networks could not give their generation or retail businesses an unfair advantage through preferential access to the networks. In turn, these reforms were deemed to be essential to make sure that the desired improvements in productive efficiency would result in lower prices and improvements of social welfare, rather than in higher private profits. The transformation has been slow and competition is far from perfect in any of the EU Member States. However, the distinctive character of the different sectors is increasingly being reflected in their ownership. In this chapter, we discuss how the governance of the electricity system has evolved after the major market reforms. In detail, we examine: the structure of the industry prior to and after its reform; the nature of the four businesses including synergies between them; the progress in creating a competitive generation market; the progress in creating a competitive retail market; how the incumbent companies have responded to market reforms. We also offer an overview of the literature that has analysed the impact of these reforms on market performance, power prices and, more generally, on social well-being.

3.2   THE PRE AND POST-REFORM STRUCTURE

Prior to the reforms to European energy industries initiated in the 1990s, there was a variety of structures and ownership patterns. At one end of the spectrum, a number of countries had nationally publicly owned monopoly companies, for example, France, Greece, Ireland, Italy and Portugal. In others, there was a publicly owned integrated national company and a large number of local companies, some publicly owned companies mainly involved in distribution and retail, for example, Sweden, Finland and much of Eastern Europe. Countries like Austria, Denmark and the Netherlands were dominated by a large number of integrated, locally owned companies. Some involved a mixture of local, publicly owned distributors and large privately owned generators, such as Germany. Private ownership was relatively unusual with the UK (privatised in 1990), Spain (part privatised in the 1980s) and Belgium as the clearest examples.

The UK reforms were usually seen by the British public as privatisation rather than an introduction of competition. However, the EU has no jurisdiction over ownership so privatisation could not be a requirement of the Electricity Directives.[2] Unbundling of the four activities can have varying degrees of separation. As a minimum, accounting unbundling requires that an integrated company does no more than keep separate accounts for the different activities. Legal unbundling requires that the activities are carried out by legally separate companies although they could be owned by a common parent company. The fullest form of unbundling is ownership unbundling under which the two companies cannot have a common parent company.

By 2016, France, Greece and Ireland were still dominated by a nationally owned company with a few new entrant privately owned companies. Austria remained in local public ownership while Germany was still a mixture of local, publicly owned distributors and large privately owned generators. The Netherlands had joined the UK, Spain and Belgium as privately owned. The largest category was countries with one nationally owned, sometimes part-privatised company and locally owned mostly distribution companies, and some private ownership – for example, Sweden, Finland, Italy, Denmark, Portugal and Eastern Europe.

In 1998, the Organisation for Economic Co-operation and Development (OECD) developed several indicators to monitor the evolution of market reforms in network industries. The OECD ETCR database, where ETCR

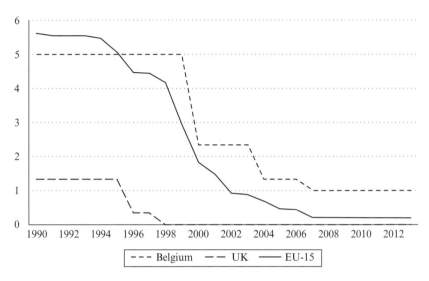

Source: Authors' elaboration on OECD ETCR database.

*Figure 3.1   Opening of the electricity market – OECD Entry Regulation
            Index*

stands for Energy, Transport and Communications Regulation, is composed of cross-country time series data on an annual basis, starting in
the mid 1970s of four key indicators: (1) public ownership; (2) entry
regulation; (3) vertical integration; and (4) market structure. Each reform
is valued annually on a 0 to 6 scale, where a lower value reflects a higher
degree of reform. A score of 6 is assigned when no reform is adopted,
while 0 is assigned to indicate the maximum degree of reform.[3] The OECD
database was updated in 2003, 2008 and 2013 (Koske et al., 2015).

Here, we focus on the EU-15, as data on new Member States are not
always complete. All these countries have largely liberalised their energy
markets, reduced entry barriers, opened wholesale and retail markets to
competition and promoted non-discriminatory access to the grid. These
reforms, summarised by the OECD 'Entry Regulation Index', strongly
progressed over time and reached a value close to zero in 2013 (Figure
3.1). This indicates a pronounced process of market opening, and a wide
convergence towards the creation of a liberalised wholesale market with
non-discriminatory Third Party Access (TPA) to the grid and customers'
freedom to choose their own supplier. Some divergence between countries
can be found in the timing of market liberalisation, with the UK having
started before the others.

3.3 THE NEW BUSINESSES

3.3.1 Transmission

In terms of security of supply, the transmission network is the key part of the industry and a failure in the transmission system can black out an entire country. A shift in the generation mix might require significant investment in transmission to take power from new generation to demand centres. This has been a particular issue in Germany due to the rapid increase in the use of renewables. However, transmission represents a relatively small part of the bill for small consumers, perhaps 10 per cent. This combination of strategic importance and relatively low added value has persuaded some governments to retain or even take the transmission network into national public ownership. This is particularly the case in the Nordic countries and the Netherlands. In other cases, transmission is owned by privately owned companies, some with activities outside their home market. The EU Directive requires transmission networks to be ownership unbundled and this has taken place in most Member States.

In technical terms, there would appear to be some synergies with distribution and perhaps natural gas transmission and distribution, but not generation or retail. Various papers have found evidence of economies of scale stemming from vertical integration with generation and distribution (Kwoka, 2002; Gugler et al., 2013). Arocena (2008) estimates that the integration of generation, transmission and distribution brings quality gains, in terms of lower number and shorter duration of supply interruptions, and cost savings up to 5 per cent.

In commercial terms, provided the sector regulator is competent enough to ensure preferential access to the transmission network is not given, there should be no commercial synergies with generation or distribution. Transmission is generally seen as a low risk business because electricity demand is stable and predictable. However, the more important decentralised generation is, which generally feeds directly into the distribution network and is used locally, the less the transmission network will be used. It will retain its vital role in ensuring security of supply but as income is determined by units of power transmitted, income from the network could fall. For example, in Australia, much of the transmission network is now claimed to be a 'stranded asset' because of the increased use of solar panels.

3.3.2 Distribution

Distribution might comprise about 30 per cent of a typical small consumer bill. Distribution is not as strategically important as transmission and governments have not chosen to intervene to retain control of the network. Nevertheless, a failure of the distribution network can have serious consequences. The EU Directive requires distribution networks to be legally unbundled although this has yet to be completed in some Member States. Like transmission, distribution is seen as a relatively low risk activity although greater use of decentralised generation could increase the strategic importance of distribution with new generators requiring significant investment in distribution to get their power onto the network.

As with transmission, in technical terms, distribution would appear to have some synergies with transmission and perhaps natural gas transmission and distribution, but not generation or retail. In commercial terms, provided the sector regulator is competent enough to ensure preferential access to the distribution network is not given, there should be no commercial synergies with generation or retail.

Ownership of the sector is beginning to change, though the impact of ownership change on efficiency is not univocal and significantly depends on the quality of institutions and on regulation. Borghi et al. (2014) analyse the impact of ownership on total factor productivity of more than 300 electricity distribution firms during the period 2002–09. They do not find that privatisation uniquely improves firms' productivity. Quite the contrary, this depends on the quality of governing institutions: when the governance institutional quality is poor, public ownership is associated with lower productivity levels; however, public ownership is associated with higher productivity in countries characterised by higher quality of the institutional environment.

The UK is probably most advanced in these changes. Prior to privatisation, there were 14 nationally publicly owned regional companies carrying out distribution and retail. In 2002, the UK regulator required the networks to be legally unbundled and by 2016 these 14 networks were owned by six companies: a US utility; a UK utility and a Spanish utility with UK generation and retail businesses; a company owned by a Hong Kong billionaire, Li Ka Shing; a company owned by a US billionaire, Warren Buffet; and infrastructure funds such as the Australian MacQuarie venture capital business.

3.3.3 Generation

Generation represents the largest component of a typical bill accounting for about 60 per cent. Ensuring sufficient power station capacity is key to security of supply but all systems are designed so that a breakdown of a single power station is highly unlikely to cause a blackout. The Directive requires that generators are unbundled from transmission and distribution, but it is silent on integration with retail even though this form of integration is likely to be far more destructive of competition.

There are no technical synergies with the other sectors but a strong commercial synergy with retail. An integrated generator/retailer will be able to sell its generation directly to its retail business at terms known only to the company and at a predictable and profitable price. This dramatically reduces the risk of investment in new generation because it avoids being dependent on volume and prices of generation sold on an unpredictable wholesale market. As a result, where integration of generation and retail is allowed by national authorities, generators try to sell most of their output to their own retail division. In the UK, the six large integrated generator/retailers dominate generation and retail.

3.3.4 Retail

Retail represents a relatively small part, 10–20 per cent, of the typical bill. As noted above, integration with the networks is not allowed but there is no limit on integration with generation. It is an unusual business and a pure retailer has few physical assets other than what is necessary to buy power from the wholesale market and send and collect bills. Its prime assets, and what makes retail so attractive to generators, is the loyalty of its customers and its brand name, which is known and largely trusted by its consumers. In all Member States, most consumers have switched retailer once or not at all and are unlikely to switch in the future. This inertia and lack of price sensitivity means that demand from an integrated generator/retailer's power plants is stable and predictable, making investment in new generation much less risky than if the output was sold to a competitive market. As an illustration of this, when the UK's retail businesses were sold to generators around the year 2000, the price was typically based on a valuation of £200 per customer so a retailer with 1 million consumers was valued at about £200 million (Thomas, 2014).

The OECD 'Vertical Integration Index' shows that in the EU-15 Member States, the electricity industry still presents a high level of vertical integration. The OECD index, however, does not allow segments of the electricity industry that are still integrated to be disentangled from ones that have been progressively unbundled. Indeed, most Member States have ownership unbundled the transmission and generation segments and, in various cases, the distribution networks are also ownership unbundled from transmission and retail segments. Conversely, in many countries the generation and retail segments are not legally separated (like Germany, France, UK) or, at most, accounting separated (such as Spain, Sweden, Ireland, Belgium). This should not come as a surprise. Indeed,

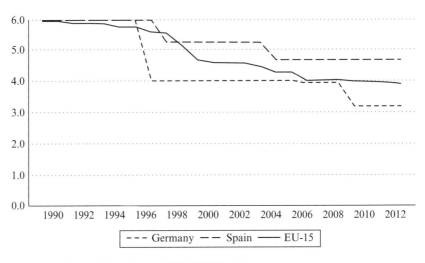

Source: Author's elaboration on OECD ETCR database.

*Figure 3.2   Unbundling in the electricity industry – OECD vertical
              integration indicator*

the European Directives aim at unbundling the segments with features of
natural monopoly (transmission and distribution networks) from generation and retail, while no provisions are specified concerning integration
between generation and final retail. These features are not wholly captured
by the OECD Vertical Integration Index, as it does not distinguish the
generation-retail unbundling from the transmission-generation or distri-
bution-retail unbundling types (Figure 3.2).

3.4   WHOLESALE MARKETS

While there is much discussion about the detail of electricity reforms, such
as unbundling and retail competition, by far the main justification for the
reforms is the claim that generation could be transformed to a competitive
market that would reduce prices. The market design would generally be
based on the commodities market model. Generation is the largest element
of the bill, while transmission and distribution would remain regulated
monopolies, so the promise of lower prices was based on competition producing lower prices than a regulated monopoly.

Experience with wholesale electricity markets since 1990 raises two significant questions: first, is an efficient commodities-style market feasible

for electricity; and second, even if an efficient commodities market is feasible does the priority to combat climate change mean that governments will have to introduce measures that override markets in order to ensure sufficient 'low-carbon' generation is built?

3.4.1   Is an Efficient Wholesale Market Feasible?

Electricity has important differences to other commodities that are bought and sold in a commodities market. These include the following:

- Electricity cannot easily be stored. For other commodities, the effect of periods of low and high prices can be mitigated by building or drawing down stocks.
- Supply and demand must exactly match at every instant or the system will collapse calamitously and stocks cannot be used to deal with short-term market failures.
- There are no ready substitutes for most uses of electricity.
- A constant, reliable and affordable supply of electricity is essential to life in a modern developed country.

If the wholesale market is to be efficient and produce low prices, it must achieve three things:

- It must set the price for bulk power purchase either directly through buyers and sellers relying on the market for their transactions or indirectly through indexation of prices for transactions outside the market.
- It should give investment signals for new generation so that decisions on entry to (or exit from) the market are based on price signals.
- It should offer low entry barriers to new generators and retailers so that if the existing companies charge higher than justified prices, new entrants can easily come into the market offering lower prices and forcing the existing companies to reduce their prices.

In Europe, some of the regional markets, notably the Nordic market, appear to meet the first objective, but it would be hard to argue that any of the regional markets achieve the other two objectives. In 2012, the European Commission stated: 'Properly functioning long-term & short-term wholesale markets, which reflect the economic value of power at each point in time in each area can steer investments to where they are most efficient.'[4]

Various authors have stressed that under market uncertainty, the generators are unable to reach the optimum level of reserve margin required to face all the exceptional situations (Joskow, 2007). The peak shaving effect, induced by strong renewable energy sources (RES) penetration in the energy mix (Ketterer, 2014) and by a number of market and regulatory imperfections, created a problem of accurate long-term price signalling, as short-term prices lead to the 'missing money' issue and to lower investment compared to the socially desirable level (Finon and Roques, 2013).

If market signals do not drive investment, this puts security of supply in doubt because investment will not be forthcoming when needed. This can be overcome by reintroducing system planning processes, for example, calls for tenders for new required capacity, but these seriously compromise the market. From a practical point of view, the timescales from start of planning to first power for a new plant, which can range from less than three years for small-scale renewables to more than 15 years for nuclear, mean that signals must be visible at an implausibly early stage if the investment stimulated is to arrive in time to meet need.

If there are not low entry barriers, existing companies will be able to charge higher than what is necessary. They will not need to collude to do this, they will recognise that reducing their prices would simply lead to other suppliers following suit, so their market share would not be increased and their profits reduced.

If the market is competitive, the volumes sold and the prices achieved would be unpredictable. Commodities markets typically show 'hog cycles' under which, when prices are high, investment is triggered leading to overcapacity and prices collapse, which in turn leads to companies exiting the market and prices rising rapidly. Power generation is a very capital-intensive sector with a typical large power station costing in the order of a few billion Euros, much more for nuclear power. Fixed costs, which must be recovered whether or not the plant is operated, are therefore high. This combination makes investment in new generation very risky. In the long run, investment in generation might yield a net profit but periods of low prices might bankrupt the company even though, in the long term, these losses might have been balanced by profitable periods.

Market reforms have brought undesired and unexpected long-term effects in terms of reliability and security of supply. The UK, the first country that launched massive privatisation programmes and deep liberalisation reforms, is nowadays claimed to be facing a serious problem of energy security linked to underinvestment. Whether the risk is real or whether it is simply the generators seeking measures, such as capacity payments, to reduce the market risk is hard to know. A decade ago, Helm (2005) and Maugis and Nuttall (2008) stressed the need for a new UK energy policy – including nuclear policy and primary energy supply security. More recently, Helm (2014) has argued that the first countries that adopted market reforms in the energy industry are experiencing serious problems that call for a re-intervention of the government and regulation aimed at correcting market failures.

3.4.2 Meeting Climate Change Targets

Markets can only work if competing companies are free to choose any of the generation options. Whether this was the case in the 1990s is arguable, but following the signing of the Kyoto Protocol in 1997, there is a general recognition that action must be taken to prevent the consequences of man-made climate change being catastrophic. This means that investment in new fossil fuel generation sources, almost always the cheapest generation option, must be discouraged in favour of investment in, generally more expensive, renewable sources or energy efficiency. The market will not deliver low-carbon options and governments have had to impose measures that override the market. These include 'feed-in tariffs' under which low-carbon generation is paid a guaranteed fixed price unrelated to the market price and capacity auctions under which companies bid to supply a given amount of power with long-term power purchase contracts being given at non-market prices. An extreme example of this overriding of the market is the decision in 2013 by the UK government to give a 35-year contract to the 3.2 GW Hinkley Point C nuclear power plant at a fixed real price of £92.5/MWh (2012 prices), more than double the prevailing wholesale market price.

Until and unless prices for low-carbon sources fall to a level at which companies will choose them without these non-market incentives, the amount of power that can be traded in the open market will diminish, making an efficient free wholesale market implausible. Even when that point arrives, the transition to a competitive market, if it is possible, will be slow as existing contracts of 20 years or more unwind.

To get around this issue, with the Directive 2003/87 EC the EU has introduced a 'carbon' market, the European Union Emissions Trading Scheme (EU ETS) under which companies generating power using fossil fuel must buy a permit to do so (European Commission, 2003). The EU ETS is a so-called 'cap and trade system' under which permits are traded in an open market and the number of permits is limited and diminishes over time. In theory, the price of permits should tend to the level that the cost of generating using fossil fuels and buying a permit is as high as generating using low-carbon sources so that generators will have no financial incentive not to choose low-carbon options.

In 2012, the European Commission stated: 'A sufficiently high carbon price also promotes investment in clean, low-carbon technologies.'[5] This system was introduced in 2005 but has failed to produce prices that are anywhere near high enough to bridge the gap between low-carbon sources and fossil fuel generation and few commentators expect the market to operate efficiently. This was due to the over-allocation of allowances, the unexpected reduction of the demand of allowances induced by the economic crisis, and to the overlapping with national instruments that support renewable sources. Even if, in the short term, carbon prices are sufficiently high to support investments in low-carbon technologies, the market will have all the risk issues of any market, of volatile and unpredictable prices, which are likely to mean that few companies will be willing to invest on the basis of their forecasts of the future carbon price. The cost of renewables is highly location specific so the carbon price necessary to stimulate investment in renewables in one country could be much lower than in other countries.

From a practical point of view, the increased level of renewables will tend to require a redesign of the wholesale market. In a commodities market that is not under-supplied, the price will tend to be set by the marginal cost of the most expensive producer. It will be in the interests of such a producer to bid down to their marginal cost because while this will not cover their total costs, it will generate more income than not bidding at all. While fossil fuel, often in old amortised power plants, is the marginal source, this does not cause major problems because the dominant cost of such a generator is the cost of fuel so their marginal cost is only a little lower than their total cost. However, for most renewables, the marginal cost is close to zero and already in a number of European power markets, the wholesale price is collapsing and is negative in some periods (Fanone et al., 2013).

3.4.3   Compromises to the Wholesale Market

In addition to schemes to stimulate low-carbon technologies, a number of other compromises are being introduced in response to the failure of efficient wholesale markets to emerge. While these may have useful effects, they will inevitably further compromise the market. These include:

1. Carbon price floors. To overcome the ineffectiveness of EU ETS carbon price in stimulating investment, countries such as the UK and France are introducing carbon price floors, under which the price of carbon is guaranteed, so that those investing in low-carbon sources will be able to predict the price (Clò et al., 2013). Any shortfall between the market price and the floor price is made up by a consumer subsidy.
2. Capacity payments. Generation shortages can occur because of insufficient new generation, but also because generating plant that is needed to maintain secure supplies is unprofitable and their owners choose to

retire it (Gottstein and Schwartz, 2010). Capacity payments should, in theory, be set at a sufficient level that the plant owner is sure not to make a loss even if the plant is not required to generate any power.

3. Liquidity measures. In the UK, to counteract the chronic lack of liquidity in the wholesale market, the regulator has introduced measures to force integrated generators to offer a minimum proportion of their power to the open market.

Ironically, the UK, often seen as the example of a free market that other Member States should copy, has been a pioneer for all these market compromises.

3.5 RETAIL COMPETITION

With the approval of the Directive 2009/72/EC included in the third energy package, all final consumers should in principle be free to choose their own supplier. According to various analysts, the full introduction of competition should have fostered consumers' choice, promoting switching to more competitive suppliers. However, market trends reveal that the expected results did not always materialise (Defeuilley, 2009). Retail competition has been of little significance in reducing prices. Electricity is a standard product delivered in a monopoly network so it is not feasible to get 'better quality' electricity. The service consumers require is simply that the retailer reads their meter and sends out the bill efficiently, a function that electricity retailers have been carrying out for more than a century. This leaves price as the only criterion for consumers to choose by. This begs two important questions: are the costs of competition (for example, marketing and switching) less than the benefits of competition; and are consumers able to use competition to their advantage?

The European Commission seems to sidestep these questions by claiming that the EU Treaty requires that any product that can be supplied by a competitive market is delivered in this way. The 2009 Electricity Directive states: 'The freedoms which the Treaty guarantees the citizens of the Union are achievable only in a fully open market, which enables all consumers freely to choose their suppliers.'[6]

If the wholesale market is working efficiently, retailers will buy their power at the same market or market-related prices as their competitors. The price retailers must pay for use of the transmission and distribution system will be a standard one, the same as their competitors. This leaves only the retailers' own costs, typically only 10 per cent of the electricity bill, to compete over, leaving too little a margin to get a competitive advantage. Price differences between retailers will only be possible if the wholesale market is not efficient and retailers buy their wholesale power at significantly different prices.

The annual rate of switching, the percentage of consumers that switch each year, is often used as an indicator of how competitive the electricity retail sector is. This is intuitively reasonable if a low switching rate reflects, for example, difficulty of switching or the lack of a large enough price differential. However, if the market is operating efficiently, any supplier offering significantly higher prices than its competitors would risk a large loss of market share and would be forced to reduce their prices to a level similar to that of their competitors. Consumers would not need to switch because they would know their existing supplier would match the lowest price in the market. In this situation, a low switching rate would be indicative of a very healthy market.

A particular problem for consumers is that when they switch, they only know the price their supplier charged yesterday, whereas what they need to know to make an informed choice is the future price. So a consumer could switch to the cheapest supplier only to find that supplier increases its prices soon after. Companies do offer fixed price deals. However, fixed price deals are only likely to appear to offer savings if the energy company believes wholesale costs will fall. So consumers switching to fixed price deals may initially make savings, but in the long term may pay more.

In practice, in most EU markets, the switching rate is low and there is no suggestion that this is because the market is so efficient. The country with consistently the highest switching rate is the UK with a rate of up to 25 per cent per annum. It is therefore worth examining the UK experience to see if it does show a well-functioning market.

3.5.1   UK Experience

From 2002, the UK retail market for residential consumers has been dominated by a group of integrated generator/retailers widely known as the 'Big Six'. From 2003 to 2015, the real price of electricity to residential consumers increased by more than 80 per cent,[7] a higher rate of increase than any other EU Member State and by 2015, pre-tax electricity prices for residential consumers in Britain were higher than in any other Member State.[8]

In 2012, these companies accounted for 99 per cent of the residential retail market and the annual switching rate was 12 per cent. Continued price rises and suspicions that the Big Six were operating as an oligopoly made the Big Six very unpopular.[9] By 2015–16, the annual switching rate was still only 13 per cent and by the end of 2015, the Big Six share had fallen but was still 86 per cent.[10]

In terms of the two questions raised above – are the costs of competition less than the benefits and can consumers identify the best deal? – the evidence is that competition in electricity supply is not a benefit to consumers. The costs of competition are difficult to quantify. The cost of switching – moving the registration of the consumer from the old to the new supplier – spread over all consumers has not been estimated recently but a small proportion of switches do go badly wrong, resulting in lengthy delays and high costs to the energy companies as they try to sort out the problems. These costs are passed on to consumers but there is no authoritative estimate of what the cost is. The cost of marketing is only known by the companies, who regard such data as commercially confidential and will not release it. The best-known cost is the commission paid to the price comparison websites (PCWs), which are the vehicle for most switches and was estimated at between £15 and £35 per fuel.[11] So the total cost per switch is likely to be in excess of £100 and the higher the switching rate, the higher the cost all consumers will have to bear. There will also be the loss of scale economies from having just one supplier to many.

There is now a significant volume of research that shows that the majority of consumers cannot identify the cheapest deal for them using a PCW and a significant proportion would end up with a worse deal than they had before (Wilson and Waddams-Price, 2010; Hills, 2012).

3.6 OWNERSHIP AND CORPORATE ASPECTS

3.6.1 Ownership

While the EU has no jurisdiction over ownership and cannot require Member States to privatise publicly owned companies, the Electricity Directives significantly diminished the attractions of public ownership, especially national public ownership. Nevertheless, there has been a significant degree of privatisation, in part following the example of the UK. In addition, the introduction of competition removed much of the scope for governments to use their ownership of electricity companies as tools of policy, for example, through influencing tariffs or choice of generating technology. The remaining argument is that publicly owned companies will be less likely to profiteer and more likely to treat consumers fairly. As a result, Portugal fully privatised its electricity company (EDP), Italy (ENEL), Finland (Fortum), Greece (PPC), Denmark (DONG) and France (EDF) have sold between 15 per cent and 70 per cent of the central government stake in the national company. Only Ireland (ESB) and Sweden (Vattenfall) have retained full public ownership of the main company.

Local public ownership has also declined, particularly in the Netherlands and, to a lesser extent, Italy. However, in Germany, there is evidence that distrust of the large private companies is leading to local authorities taking their companies back into public ownership.

The OECD 'Ownership Index' measures the degree of privatisation in the power market. It ranges from 0 to 6: it equals 0 when national, state or provincial governments do not hold any equity stakes in the largest power company, while it equals 6 when the largest firm in the sector is entirely owned by a public institution.

In 1990, the biggest power company was controlled by the government in almost all countries, with the notable exceptions of Austria, Belgium and Germany, where the government owned the majority, but not the full control over the major power company. The OECD Ownership Index shows that the process of privatisation brought a progressive dilution of public ownership in the power sector. Nevertheless, public ownership still represents a relevant feature of the European electricity industry, though with remarkable divergences among countries both in the timing and intensity of the privatisation pattern (Figure 3.3).

Various papers which focused on OECD countries used the ETCR indicators to disentangle the impact of ownership and other market reforms

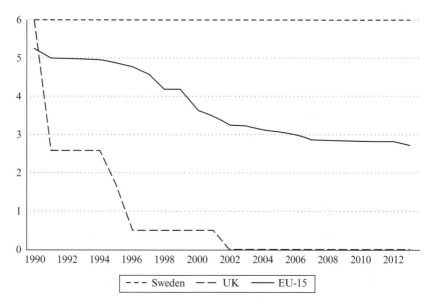

Source: Authors' elaboration on OECD ETCR database.

Figure 3.3   Ownership in the electricity industry – OECD ownership indicator

on a variety of factors, such as prices, efficiency gains and social welfare. In an attempt to estimate the impact of early reforms in 19 OECD countries over the period 1986–96, Steiner (2000) argues that reforms including vertical separation of the industry, liberalisation of the wholesale market and privatisation had a favourable impact on efficiency, which was partly transferred to consumers. Conversely, Hattori and Tsutsui (2004) find that unbundling and privatisation did not have any significant impact in terms of price reduction, while they may possibly have resulted in a higher price.

More recently, Fiorio and Florio (2013) analyse the impact of change in corporate ownership on the power price in the former 15 EU Member States over a longer period, 1978–2007. They find that private ownership and privatisation are associated with higher residential net-of-tax electricity prices in Western Europe.

Bacchiocchi et al. (2015) analyse the impact of electricity regulatory reforms, distinguishing between former EU-15 Member States and new Member States. They find that uniform EU-driven liberalisation reforms had different impact on these two blocs of countries, lowering prices in the EU-15 countries, while having the opposite effect in the new Member States. This points out the importance of ensuring high quality of institutions, including government quality, regulatory quality and government effectiveness. Hyland (2016) focuses on the former 27 EU Member States plus Norway over the decade 2001–11 and finds that, once accounting for the endogeneity of the reforms, the restructuring process of the electricity market did not have any significant impact on electricity prices for industrial consumers.

Empirical analysis on the impact of the reforms in the electricity market has not focused only on prices, but on a variety of factors: such as: consumer welfare and satisfaction (Fiorio and Florio, 2013); research and development (Jamasb and Pollitt, 2008); investments (Gugler et al., 2013); market efficiency, labour and total factor productivity (Pompei, 2013).

Other studies have analysed the impact of market reforms on market efficiency, labour and total factor productivity. Polemis (2016) analyses 30 OECD countries during the period 1975–2011 and finds that the introduction of competition and independent regulation has a positive impact on the electricity sector performance (net generation per capita, installed capacity and labour productivity): conversely, privatisation is negatively associated with its performance activity and with labour productivity.

3.6.2 Corporate Aspects

While there has been considerable policy effort to make wholesale and retail markets work efficiently, there has been little concern about market

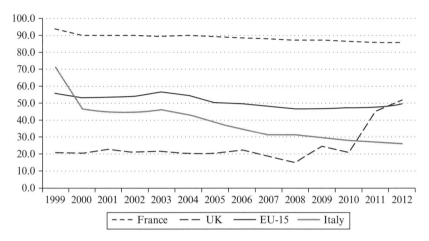

Source: Authors' elaboration on Eurostat.

Figure 3.4   Market share of the largest generator in the electricity market

concentration. In most countries, the electricity market remains, at worst, effectively a monopoly (France and Belgium), or at best an oligopoly. Even in the UK, which has an apparently relatively healthy field of six major companies, the high barriers to entry have led to strong suspicions the market operates effectively as an uncompetitive oligopoly.

Eurostat reports for the period 2003–14 the number of main companies that have a market share of at least 5 per cent of the total national net electricity generation. National markets show a high level of concentration, where the UK and Belgium present, respectively, the highest and lowest number of relevant power companies, which in 2014 was 7 and 2 (Figure 3.4).

Eurostat reports also the market share of the largest generator in the electricity market (as percentage of the total net electricity production) for the period 1999–2013. On average, in the EU-15 the largest power generation companies own about 50 per cent of the market share, with important heterogeneity among countries. While in France the incumbent still owns more than 80 per cent of the market share, the Italian incumbent lowered its market share from 70 per cent in 1999 to 27 per cent in 2012. Interestingly, the UK experienced an opposite trend, as in the last years the largest power generator increased its market share from slightly less than 20 per cent to slightly more than 50 per cent.

Where there has been change of ownership, it has frequently involved companies being acquired by the handful of large European companies with international activities. The group of seven biggest companies (the Seven Brothers EDF, RWE, EON, ENEL, Electrabel, Vattenfall and Endesa) had, through a process of takeovers and mergers, shrunk to five (EDF, RWE, EON, ENEL and ENGIE).

Despite this lack of a competitive field in many countries and the evidence of an emergence of a handful of dominant internationally based companies, there is little evidence of any concern in the European Commission, which believes it knows how to deal with oligopolies.

However, while on the face of it the remaining Five Brothers have strengthened their grip on the market since 2003, there are signs of serious weakness amongst them. The challenge to their dominance comes not so much from competition but from the growth in decentralised power generation. One of the strengths of these large companies was that their size and expertise allowed them to handle large, complex, capital-intensive technologies that new entrant companies could not. By 2010, these companies were relying heavily on the emergence of new complex technologies that would be seen as low carbon. These included a re-launched nuclear power sector, carbon capture and storage systems that would make coal-fired generation low carbon and Desertec, a plan to build thermal solar plant on a large scale in North Africa, exporting the output to Europe.

The prospects for these technologies now look poor and new generating capacity in Europe is dominated by small-scale renewables. These require a much lower level of user skills and therefore allow small, new entrant companies into the market. Such companies may well be better suited to exploiting small-scale options All of the Five Brothers have high levels of debt that is adversely affecting their credit rating. Both EON and RWE have restructured their businesses, EDF is struggling to finance its investments and is seeking to sell some of its foreign acquisitions.

3.7 CONCLUSIONS

The reforms required by the EU Electricity Directives have led to a massive restructuring of the European electricity industry. Governments have progressively chosen to remove themselves from the direct provision of this public service and from the full control and direct management of power companies. Over the past 20 years, there have been remarkable differences in the timing and intensity of market reforms between Member States. Nevertheless, they have now converged on a common market model, characterised by the establishment of a wholesale market, network unbundling, reduction of entry barriers and competition in the final retail segment of the industry. Moreover, electricity companies have now been largely corporatised, they have budgetary autonomy and they must comply with European state aid rules, which limit the possibility of direct transfer from the public budget to the company. In many cases, they are publicly traded companies competing against private operators in an open market.

While the need for a monopolistic market and the direct public management and provision of this service has been questioned and progressively superseded by a new organisational model, the intrinsic strategic nature of electricity as well as the very basic principle of service universality and accessibility at reasonable prices must remain broadly unchanged. On top of that, new political paradigms – environmental protection and energy security – have emerged in parallel with the process of liberalisation and privatisation. This has exacerbated the friction between public priorities and private choices. Private companies competing in a liberalised market are free to choose which technology to adopt, where, when and how much to invest. These choices are driven by a profit maximisation goal and may conflict with public preferences towards some technological solutions – such as nuclear and renewable sources – which, on the one hand, might be socially desirable in terms of reduction of energy dependency, internal energy security and greenhouse gas reduction, while, on the other hand, will not be chosen by the market due to their high fixed unit costs.

As a result, European and national institutions continue to define objectives and policies that constrain and shape the future development of energy systems. Moreover, 20 years after the launching of this market reform, it has become clear that the rationale behind the reforms, that creating an efficient competitive wholesale electricity market would be beneficial to consumers, has not been achieved so far. Some general lessons can be learned from the EU energy industry market reform experience. Various researches agree on the fact that similar EU-driven liberalisation reforms had differentiated impacts on different countries, mainly depending on the quality of internal institutions. This points to the importance of ensuring high institutional quality and suggests caution with the idea of designing uniform policy recipes, as reform prescription for a specific country cannot easily and successfully be transferred to another one.

It is now increasingly recognised that market reforms have brought undesired and unexpected long-term effects in terms of reliability and security of supply. The UK, the first country to launch massive privatisation programmes and deep liberalisation reforms, is now facing a serious problem of energy security linked to underinvestment. Even early supporters of privatisation and liberalisation recognise that the security of energy supplies has re-emerged as a central issue in the energy policy arena in the UK and elsewhere against a backdrop of increased liberalisation of the energy markets. As a consequence, countries that adopted market reforms in the energy industry are now experiencing serious problems that have required a re-intervention of the government and regulation aimed at correcting market failures. The handful of dominant companies are now in serious difficulties partly because the technology trend towards small scale does not suit them and partly because they over-stretched themselves financially expanding into international markets. It may be that a new wave of restructuring will now happen as these big companies divest assets that they regard as no longer core to reduce their debts. Who would buy these assets is difficult to see. Renationalisation or remunicipalisation on a large scale seems unlikely given the heavy pressure on public finance most countries are still under. The most likely 'private' sector buyer appears to be Chinese companies or Middle East wealth funds if and when the world oil price recovers.

Another widely agreed conclusion is that effective competition and regulation are considerably more important in improving performance than privatisation. Conversely, unbundling and privatisation did not bring any significant impact in terms of performance and price reduction, and they may possibly have resulted in a higher price. Privatisation has been associated with higher residential net-of-tax electricity prices, while vertical separation of generation, transmission and distribution is associated with negative quality implications, in terms of cost increase, higher number and longer duration of supply interruptions. Finally, retail competition has not proved of benefit to small consumers with consumers apparently unwilling to risk switching to an untested alternative even when it appears savings could be made.

How far this has been because of the underlying difficulty of creating a wholesale market, fundamentally because of the special characteristics of electricity and how far it is due to the policy dominance of replacing fossil fuel generation with low-carbon sources and energy efficiency is a moot point. However, unless and until low-carbon options can compete on equal terms with fossil fuel, this question will be unanswerable.

NOTES

1. Directive 96/92/EC of the European Parliament and of the Council of 19 December 1996 concerning common rules for the internal market in electricity, http://eur-lex. europa.eu/LexUriServ/LexUriServ.do?uri=CELEX:31996L0092:EN:HTML (accessed 11 October 2016). It was revised in 2003, http://faolex.fao.org/docs/pdf/eur72803.pdf (accessed 14 October 2016) and 2009, http://eur-lex.europa.eu/LexUriServ/LexUriServ. do?uri=OJ:L:2009:211:0055:0093:EN:PDF (accessed 14 October 2016).
2. Article 345 of the Treaty on the Functioning of the European Union states: 'The Treaties shall in no way prejudice the rules in Member States governing the system of property ownership', http://eur-lex.europa.eu/legal-content/EN/TXT/HTML/?uri=CE LEX:12008E345&from=EN (accessed 14 October 2016).

3. The OECD indicators are built by computing information on regulatory structures and policies collected through a questionnaire sent to governments in OECD and non-OECD countries. The related responses are integrated by publicly available data to create cross-country time series data of annual frequency starting in the mid 1970s. Collected information can be quantitative or qualitative and are standardised by assigning a numerical value to each response over a 0 to 6 scale.
4. European Commission (2012), 'Making the internal energy market work', Communication from the Commission to the European Parliament, the Council, the European Economic and Social Committee and the Committee of the Regions' SWD(2012) 367 final, http://eur-lex.europa.eu/LexUriServ/LexUriServ.do?uri=CELEX:52012DC0663:EN:NOT (accessed 14 October 2016).
5. Ibid.
6. http://eur-lex.europa.eu/LexUriServ/LexUriServ.do?uri=OJ:L:2009:211:0055:0093:EN:PDF (accessed 14 October 2016).
7. https://www.gov.uk/government/statistical-data-sets/monthly-domestic-energy-price-statics (accessed 13 October 2016).
8. http://ec.europa.eu/eurostat/statistics-explained/index.php/File:Electricity_-_share_of_taxes_and_levies_paid_by_household_consumers,_2015s2_(%25)_V2.png (accessed 13 October 2016).
9. Arguably, the UK is not a single oligopoly but 14 duopolies. In each region the market is dominated by the incumbent electricity retailer and British Gas selling electricity and gas as a 'dual fuel' offer.
10. https://www.ofgem.gov.uk/chart/electricity-supply-market-shares-company-domestic-gb (accessed 13 December 2016) and https://www.ofgem.gov.uk/data-portal/retail-market-indicators (accessed 13 December 2016).
11. https://assets.publishing.service.gov.uk/media/54ef378a40f0b61427000005/Price_comparison_websites.pdf (accessed 13 December 2016).

REFERENCES

Arocena, P. (2008), 'Cost and quality gains from diversification and vertical integration in the electricity industry: a DEA approach', *Energy Economics*, **30**, 39–58.

Atkinson, A.B. and Stiglitz, J. (1980), *Lectures in Public Economics*, London: McGraw-Hill.

Bacchiocchi, E., Florio, M. and Taveggia, G. (2015), 'Asymmetric effects of electricity regulatory reforms in the EU15 and in the new Member States: empirical evidence from residential prices 1990–2011', *Utilities Policy*, **35**, 72–90.

Borghi, E., Del Bo, C.F. and Florio, M. (2014), 'Institutions and firms' productivity: evidence from electricity distribution in the EU', *Oxford Bulletin of Economics and Statistics*, Wiley Online Library.

Bös, D. (1994), *Pricing and Price Regulation*, Amsterdam: North-Holland.

Clò, S., Battles, S. and Zoppoli, P. (2013), 'Policy options to improve the EU ETS: a multi-criteria analysis', *Energy Policy*, **57**, 477–90.

Cremer, H., Gasmi, F., Grimaud, A. and Laffont, J. (1998), 'The economics of universal service: theory', Economic Development Institute of the World Bank Working Paper.

Defeuilley, C. (2009), 'Retail competition in electricity markets', *Energy Policy*, **37**(2), 377–86.

European Commission (2003), 'Directive 2003/87/EC of the European Parliament and the Council of 13 October 2003 Establishing a Scheme for Greenhouse Gas Emission Allowance Trading within the Community and Amending Council Directive 96/61/EC', European Commission, Brussels.

European Commission (2009), 'Directive 2009/72/EC, Concerning Common Rules for the Internal Market in Electricity and Repealing Directive 2003/54/EC', European Commission, Brussels.

Eurostat, 'Market share of the largest generator in the electricity market - annual data (nrg_ind_331a)', available at: http://ec.europa.eu/eurostat/web/energy/data/database.

Eurostat, 'Statistics explained – Electricity market indicators', available at: http://ec.europa.eu/eurostat/statistics-explained/index.php/Electricity_market_indicators.

Fanone, E., Gamba, A. and Prokopczuk, M. (2013), 'The case of negative day-ahead electricity prices', *Energy Economics*, **35**, 22–34.

Finon, D. and Roques, F. (2013), 'European electricity market reforms: the "visible hand" of public coordination', *Economics of Energy & Environmental Policy – International Association for Energy Economics*, **2**(2), 1–19.

Fiorio, C.V. and Florio, M. (2013), 'Electricity prices and public ownership: evidence from the EU15 over thirty years', *Energy Economics*, **39**(C), 209–18.

Gottstein, M. and Schwartz, L. (2010), 'The role of forward capacity markets in increasing demand-side and other low-carbon resources: experience and prospects', May, RAP project Roadmap 2050.

Gugler, K., Rammerstorfer, M. and Schmitt, S. (2013), 'Ownership unbundling and investment in electricity markets: a cross country study', *Energy Economics*, **40**, 702–13.

Hattori, T. and Tsutsui, M. (2004), 'Economic impact of regulatory reforms in the electricity supply industry: a panel data analysis for OECD countries', *Energy Policy*, **32**(6), 823–32.

Helm, D. (2005), 'The case for regulatory reform', http://www.dieterhelm.co.uk/assets/secure/documents/TheCaseForRegulatoryReform.pdf (accessed April 2017).

Helm, D. (2014), 'The return of the CEGB? – Britain's central buyer model', http://www.dieterhelm.co.uk/energy/energy/the-return-of-the-cegb/ (accessed April 2017).

Hills, J. (2012), *Getting the Measure of Fuel Poverty. Final Report of the Fuel Poverty Review*, CASE report 72, Centre for Analysis of Social Exclusion, London School of Economics, p. 27.

Hyland, M. (2016), 'Restructuring European electricity markets: a panel data analysis', *Utilities Policy*, **38**, 33–42.

Jamasb, T. and Pollitt, M. (2008), 'Liberalisation and R&D in network industries: the case of the electricity industry', *Research Policy*, **37**(6–7), 995–1008.

Joskow, P. (2007), 'Competitive electricity markets and investment in new generation capacity', in D. Helm (ed.), *The New Energy Paradigm*, Oxford: Oxford University Press, pp. 76–122.

Kaldor, N. (1980), 'Public or private enterprise – the issue to be considered', in W.J. Baumol (ed.), *Public and Private Enterprises in a Mixed Economy*, New York: St Martin's Press, pp. 1–12.

Ketterer, J. (2014), 'The impact of wind power generation on the electricity price in Germany', *Energy Economics*, **44**, 270–80.

Koske, I., Wanner, I., Bitetti, R. and Barbiero, O. (2015), 'The 2013 update of the OECD's database on product market regulation: policy insights for OECD and non-OECD countries', OECD Economics Department Working Papers, No. 1200, OECD Publishing, Paris.

Kwoka, J. (2002), 'Vertical economies in electric power: evidence on integration and its alternatives', *International Journal of Industrial Organization*, **20**(5), 653–72.

Maugis, V. and Nuttall, W.J. (2008), 'Metapolicy options for energy in England', EPRG 081.

Mill, J. (1848), *Principles of Political Economy*, New York: A.M. Kelley.

Peltzman, S., Levine, M.E. and Noll, R.G. (1989), 'The economic theory of regulation after a decade of deregulation', Brookings Papers on Economic Activity: Microeconomics.

Polemis, M. (2016), 'New evidence on the impact of structural reforms on electricity sector performance', *Energy Policy*, **92**, 420–31.

Pompei, F. (2013), 'Heterogeneous effects of regulation on the efficiency of the electricity industry across European Union countries', *Energy Economics*, **40**, 569–85.

Steiner, F. (2000), 'Regulation, industry structure and performance in the electricity supply industry', OECD Economics Department Working Papers, No. 238, OECD Publishing, Paris.

Thomas, S. (2014), 'Progress with energy markets in Europe', *Economics and Policy of Energy and the Environment*, **1**, 5–26.

Willner, J. (2001), 'Ownership, efficiency, and political interference', *European Journal of Political Economy*, **17**(4), 723–48.

Wilson, C. and Waddams-Price, C. (2010), 'Do consumers switch to the best supplier?', *Oxford Economic Papers*, **62**(4), 647–68.

4. Market structure and state involvement: passenger railways in Europe

Torben Holvad*

4.1 INTRODUCTION AND BACKGROUND TO RAILWAY REFORM INITIATIVES

Over the past 25 years substantial legislative initiatives at the European level (starting in 1991) have been put forward. This has been notably realised through a series of European Union (EU) directives and regulations, in particular Directive 91/440 and the four so-called Railway Packages (from 2001, 2004, 2007 and 2016) as well as various follow-up measures. Key aspects addressed in these legislative measures included: (1) commercialisation and managerial independence of railway companies; (2) unbundling (particularly provisions for some degree of separation between railway operations and infrastructure); (3) market opening (including independent regulation) with a particular focus on freight and limited focus on passenger transport until 2016; and (4) technical harmonisation.

Some EU Member States have already gone much further in terms of market opening for passenger rail transport (e.g. Sweden, UK, Germany, Italy) but from a European perspective only international passenger services have so far been opened for the possibility of competitive entry (although this is changing with the adoption of the Fourth Railway Package by the end of December 2016).

These reforms, involving a greater role for market forces, aim to improve cost performance and enhance customer focus (European Commission, 1996), thereby providing the basis for improvement in rail services; for instance, the competitiveness of rail vis-à-vis other modes is enhanced contributing to sustainable transport as set out in the 2001 European Commission Transport White Paper (European Commission, 2001).

In particular, the impetus for this type of railway reform in Europe in the 1990s was linked to significantly reduced modal share for rail in both the passenger and freight markets over the last decades. For example, for

Table 4.1   Railway debts in 1994 for selected countries

	1994 railway debts (million ECU)	1994 rail debt in % GDP
Austria	2892	1.7
Belgium	3539	1.8
Denmark	2782	2.3
Finland	166	0.2
France	28731	2.6
Germany*	5795	0.3
Greece	937	1.1
Ireland	323	0.7
Italy	42067	4.9
Luxembourg	168	1.4
Netherlands	2807	1.0
Portugal	1529	2.1
Spain	8140	2.0
Sweden	1958	1.2
UK	10709	1.2
Total	112543	
Approximate 2005 prices	€150 billion	

Note: * After recapitalisation; debt in 1993 was 33788 million ECU.

Source: Mercer Management Consulting reported in ECMT (1998).

the EU15 countries as a whole the modal share for rail passenger transport was 10 per cent in 1970 and had reduced to 6 per cent in 2000; in the case of freight the decline (in the EU15 countries) is even more significant with rail having a 20 per cent modal share in 1970 but less than 8 per cent by 2000. These trends have created significant economic, social and environmental problems (Di Pietrantonio and Pelkmans, 2004). The reduced market shares for rail have resulted in financial difficulties for the public monopolies that throughout Europe had been mainly responsible for railways since the end of the Second World War (see Table 4.1 for an indication of the level of debt relating to the railway sector by country in 1994). These monopolies were in general organised as vertical integrated companies with responsibility for infrastructure management and operations, as well as in many cases other non-rail transport services such as long distance coach services and ferry services.

At the same time there has been increased recognition of the need for more sustainable transport with the rail mode being seen as critical in order to achieve this. The importance of rail in supporting sustainability was confirmed in the European Commission's mid-term review of the 2001 White Paper (European Commission, 2006) emphasising the need to complete the market opening process, take forward the rail priority projects, remove technical barriers and improve infrastructure charging approaches. The role of rail was reiterated in the 2011 Transport White Paper where goals included (European Commission, 2011, p. 9):

1. By 2030, 30 per cent of road freight over 300 kilometres (km) should shift to other modes such as rail or waterborne transport, and more than 50 per cent should be facilitated by efficient and green freight corridors by 2050.
2. By 2050, complete a European high-speed rail network. Triple the length of the existing high-speed rail network by 2030 and maintain a dense railway network in all Member States. By 2050 the majority of medium-distance passenger transport should go by rail.

This chapter focuses on the EU railway reforms with respect to the passenger market. The chapter is structured as follows. Section 4.2 provides an overview of the legislative reform elements. Section 4.3 considers the extent to which the different EU legislative measures have been implemented at the national level. In Section 4.4 the possible outcomes of the railway reforms are discussed. Section 4.5 concludes with final remarks.

4.2   OVERVIEW OF REFORM ELEMENTS

In this section, the main elements in the legislative measures are set out. Table 4.2 provides an overview of the different EU directives and regulations which are then discussed in terms of overarching features. More detailed information on the core legislative measures is provided in Chapter 9.

Below, the following features of the bundle of legislative initiatives are considered further: (1) commercialisation and managerial independence of railway companies; (2) unbundling; (3) market opening (with independent regulation); (4) technical harmonisation.

4.2.1   Commercialisation and Managerial Independence of Railway Companies

Directive 91/440/EEC provided for the first European legal steps towards increased commercialisation and managerial independence of railway companies. In particular, Article (4) stated that 'Member States shall take

Table 4.2   Overview of EU rail legislation since 1991

Date	Directive/ Regulation	Subject
Initial reform attempts		
29/07/1991	91/440/EEC	Development of the Community's railways including limited rights of network access
19/06/1995	95/18/EC	Licensing of railway undertakings
19/06/1995	95/19/EC	Allocation of railway infrastructure capacity and the charging of infrastructure fees
23/07/1996	96/48/EC	Interoperability for the trans-European high-speed rail
The 'First Railway Package'		
26/02/2001	2001/12/EC	Amending Directive 91/440 – providing for the opening up to competition of the Trans-European Rail Freight Network from 2008
26/02/2001	2001/13/EC	Amending Directive 95/18 – extending the licensing principle to all railway undertakings
26/02/2001	2001/14/EC	Repealing Directive 95/19 – allocation of railway infrastructure capacity, the levying of charges for the use of railway infrastructure and safety certification
19/06/2001	2001/16/EC*	Interoperability for the trans-European conventional rail
The 'Second Railway Package'		
29/04/2004	881/2004/EC	Establishment of the European Railway Agency
29/04/2004	2004/49/EC	Railway Safety Directive
29/04/2004	2004/50/EC	Amending Directives 96/48 and 2001/16 – interoperability of the conventional and high-speed trans-European railway network
29/04/2004	2004/51/EC	Amending Directive 91/440 – complete opening of rail freight network in the EU from 1 January 2007
The 'Third Railway Package'		
23/10/2007	2007/58/EC	Amending 91/440 and 2001/14 – opening up the market in international passenger rail services by 1 January 2010
23/10/2007	2007/59/EC	Certification of train crews operating locomotives and trains on the Community's rail network
23/10/2007	1371/2007/EC	Rights and obligations of international rail passengers
Intermediate steps		
23/10/2007	1370/2007/EC	Public passenger transport services by rail and by road – repealing Regulations 1191/69 and 1107/70

Table 4.2   (continued)

Date	Directive/ Regulation	Subject
17/06/2008	2008/57/EC	Recast of the Interoperability Directive
16/12/2008	2008/110/EC	Amended Railway Safety Directive
16/12/2008	1335/2008/EC	Amending Regulation (EC) 881/2004 establishing a European Railway Agency
21/11/2012	2012/34/EU	Recast of the First Railway Package Directives
The 'Fourth Railway Package'		
11/05/2016	2016/796/EU	Technical Pillar: Regulation on the European Union Agency for Railways and repealing Regulation (EC) No. 881/2004
11/05/2016	2016/797/EU	Technical Pillar: recast of the Interoperability Directive
11/05/2016	2016/798/EU	Technical Pillar: recast of the Safety Directive
14/12/2016	2016/2338/EU	Market Pillar: amending Regulation 1370/2007/ EC concerning the opening of the market for domestic passenger transport services by rail
14/12/2016	2016/2370/EU	Market Pillar: amending the Single European Railway Area Directive (Directive 2012/34/EU) as regards the opening of the market for domestic passenger transport services by rail and the governance of the railway infrastructure
14/12/2016	2016/2337/EU	Market Pillar: Regulation repealing the Regulation on common rules for the normalisation of the accounts of railway undertakings (Regulation 1192/69/EEC)

Note: * Formally, Directive 2001/16/EC is not part of the First Railway Package.

Source: Author's elaboration of information from EUR-Lex, updated from Holvad (2009).

the measures necessary to ensure that as regards management, administration and internal control over administrative, economic and accounting matters railway undertakings have independent status in accordance with which they will hold, in particular, assets, budgets and accounts which are separate from those of the State.' This provision is intended to place railway companies on a more independent footing from government/ political control. Moreover, the following Article (5) establishes that railway companies shall adjust their activities to the market and manage those activities in order to provide efficient and appropriate services at the lowest possible costs and at the quality required. This latter provision introduces a clear commercial orientation of railway companies.

The successive four Railway Packages (2001, 2004, 2007 and 2016) are gradually commercialising the sector, for example, in terms of providing for clearly specified contracts between state and the railway service provider, defined track access agreements between infrastructure manager and railway operator, and increased market orientation. However, these legislative measures also contain certain restraints on railway companies of particular relevance to the incumbents (Olsen et al., 2015). These restraints include elements such as: (1) reduced possibilities for cross-subsidisation; (2) access charges to be paid by the railway operators to use the infrastructure and related services; (3) gradual opening up of the rail service market to competition (see below); (4) certifications and passenger rights.

4.2.2   Unbundling

Directive 91/440 provided the starting point for the introduction of vertical separation between infrastructure management and rail service operations, in order to support transparency of cross-financing within integrated railway companies and to ultimately facilitate non-discriminatory access for non-incumbent operators and new entrants to the rail network. It should be noticed that only accounts separation[1] was in fact required to be implemented rather than organisational[2] or institutional separation[3] (both were optional). The next step towards vertical separation between infrastructure management and rail service operations was taken in the First Railway Package (Directive 2001/12/EC). In particular, this required that independent organisational entities must be specified for transport operations and infrastructure management. In this case, vertical separation should involve at least organisational separation (holding company model) and could optionally be extended to institutional separation. Furthermore, essential functions such as rail capacity allocation, infrastructure charging and licensing should be separated from transport operations to enable new rail operators fair access to the rail market. The latter requirement implies that if infrastructure management is being organised within a holding company, these essential functions would need to be entrusted to separate bodies. In addition to the provisions regarding separation between infrastructure and operations, Directive 2001/12/EC contained requirements regarding accounting separation for railway operators. In particular, railway operators were required to set up separate accounts for passenger and freight operations as well as separate accounting for public service and other passenger operations. In the latter case, it was specified that funds received under public service contracts may not be transferred to activities relating to the provision of other transport services. The First Railway Package, through Directive 2001/14/EC, also initiated unbundling in the domain of regulation by providing for national regulatory bodies to oversee the railway market. These regulatory bodies should be independent from any infrastructure manager, charging body, allocation body or railway operator, thereby moving away from the traditional model of self-regulation by the integrated incumbent national railway company.

A major next step in the area of unbundling and securing the independence of the infrastructure manager was introduced in the so-called recast of the First Railway Package, through Directive 2012/34/EU, which permitted simplification of the legal text such that all provisions were in one directive rather than three. The recast also addressed a number of key issues, including: (1) enhanced transparency of the rail market access conditions (e.g. in the case of rail-related services); (2) strengthening the independence and competences of national regulatory bodies; (3) clarification of the rules for the funding and management of infrastructure (e.g. requiring multi-annual contractual agreements between the state and the infrastructure manager and more precise access charging principles).

Further steps regarding unbundling are introduced in the so-called Market Pillar of the Fourth Railway Package, especially aimed at ensuring the independence of the functions of path allocation and infrastructure charging as well as strengthening the provisions for transparency in relation to any transfer of funding between infrastructure manager and railway operator in order to avoid cross-subsidisation within railway holding companies. However, the Fourth Railway Package will still permit the so-called holding company model such that railway operations and infrastructure management can be organised within one (holding) company albeit as distinct organisational entities.

4.2.3 Market Opening (with Independent Regulation)

The EU legislative initiatives have provided for market opening by extending access rights to the railway infrastructure for non-incumbent entities as well as to essential service facilities (e.g. terminals and maintenance depots). These started in 1991 (Directive 91/440) with defining access rights to rail infrastructure in one Member State in the cases of operators[4] in other Member States wishing to provide international combined (freight) services and associations of railway operators and offering international (passenger) services between the countries in which they are established. The next major steps towards market opening only occurred in 2001 focusing exclusively on rail freight in the context of the First Railway Package, whereby access rights would be gradually extended such that by 2003 any railway operator licensed within the European Community would have the right to obtain access on an equal and non-discriminatory basis to the national sections of the so-called Trans-European Rail Freight Network (TERFN) while from 2008 the entire European rail network would be opened up to competition for international freight services (though no provision for cabotage[5]). Following the Second Railway Package adopted in 2004 the entire European rail network would be open from January 2007 including cabotage. This is not the case for the passenger rail market where extensions to the 1991 access right provisions (Directive 91/440/EEC) were introduced only in the Third Railway Package from 2007, where Directive 2007/58/EC provided for opening of the market in international passenger rail services by 1 January 2010 including cabotage. However, a number of exemptions were introduced in the directive; in particular, it is possible to limit access rights if routes concerned are covered by public service contracts. The Fourth Railway Package is addressing the domestic passenger rail market for which no European legislative initiative regarding access rights for non-incumbent operators had been provided for until that point. In particular, from December 2023, public service rail contracts should be provided mainly through competitive tenders open to all EU railway operators, except in specific cases where direct award is permitted. Moreover, enhanced possibility for open access operation across Europe is also put forward from December 2020. However, restrictions on open access may be allowed to ensure the continuation of subsidised services provided these are determined according to objective assessment by regulators.

4.2.4   Technical Harmonisation

As part of the rail reform initiatives, enhancing interoperability of the railway system has been given priority since the mid 1990s in order to contribute towards its competitiveness (European Commission, 1996). An initial measure towards ensuring interoperability of the European rail networks was taken by the Council of the European Union in 1996 when it adopted Council Directive 96/48/EC from July 1996 on the interoperability of the trans-European high-speed rail system. The aim of this directive was to achieve the interoperability of the European high-speed rail network at the various stages of its design, construction, gradual introduction into service and operation.

Similar arrangements were put in place for the conventional trans-European rail network, initially through Directive 2001/16/EC and now according to Directive 2016/798/EU (part of the Technical Pillar of the Fourth Railway Package). Furthermore, this directive requires that the scope is progressively extended to the entire railway system in Europe.

Particular objectives for the Interoperability Directive(s) include: (1) facilitate, improve and develop international rail transport services within the EU and with third countries; (2) contribute to the progressive creation of the internal market in equipment and services for the construction, renewal, upgrading and operation of the rail system within the Community; (3) contribute to the interoperability of the rail system within the Community.

The core instrument used for achieving interoperability within the European legislative framework is preparation and adoption of so-called Technical Specifications for Interoperability (TSIs). The TSIs provide the minimum set of rules to achieve interoperability. In parallel, legislation has been introduced (2004) in order to promote harmonisation in the railway safety regulatory framework among EU Member States (see the Railway Safety Directive). The European Railway Agency (ERA) was established in the Second Railway Package (see the Agency Regulation) to lead and manage the technical development of the interoperability and safety work set out in the Safety and Interoperability Directives. It has the mission of contributing to the creation of an integrated and competitive European railway sector.

Following the adoption of the Technical Pillar of the Fourth Railway Package in 2016 the ERA was replaced and succeeded by the European Union Agency for Railways. Of particular importance is that the new Agency Regulation (Regulation 2016/796/EU) introduces a stronger role for the Agency regarding applications for vehicle authorisation and safety certification. These applications have so far been assessed and granted by National Safety Authorities (NSAs) but from 2019 these tasks will be shared between ERA and the relevant NSA. If an application concerns an area of use/operation in more than one Member State, ERA will exclusively be involved, whereas for applications linked to an area of use/operation in one Member State only the applicant has the choice to address the file to either the NSA or ERA. Of particular importance is that the provisions will introduce a single safety certificate and vehicle authorisation valid across Europe.

Following the Fourth Railway Package it is expected that new legal initiatives for railways will be relatively limited in scope such that the regulatory framework would be stable over the medium term.

4.3 IMPLEMENTATION OF REFORM MEASURES

The implementation of the EU rail legislation by Member States concerns two aspects. Firstly, the Member States need to transpose the directives into national law. Secondly, correct arrangements (in accordance with the EU legislation) are required. Common problems regarding the EU railway legislation have delayed the introduction of required national legislation of the various directives or not even started the national implementation process of EU directives, thereby creating obstacles towards achieving the objectives behind the EU railway reform initiatives as well as increasing the possibility for diverging arrangements in place between EU Member States. In this section different aspects of the implementation of the railway reform measures are examined, including: (1) extent of railway legislation transposition and implementation; (2) national governance structure for main infrastructure manager; (3) composite assessment of the law in the books and law in action (Rail Liberalisation Index (LIB Index)); and (4) degree of market opening for domestic passenger services.

4.3.1   Extent of Railway Legislation Transposition and Implementation

An overall indication of the extent to which EU railway legislation is transposed is provided by the transposition deficit measure used as part of the Commission's Single Market Scoreboard[6] by DG MARKT.[7] It measures the percentage of (rail-related) EU directives not transposed by a Member State that should have been transposed by a given cut-off date (either 10 November or 10 April each year according to the biannual calculation of the Scoreboard indicators). In Figure 4.1 the rail-specific transposition deficit indicator is shown together with the transposition deficit indicator

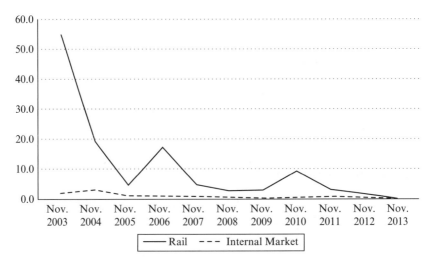

Source: European Commission (2014).

Figure 4.1   Extent of railway legislation transposition, 2003–13

for all internal market-related directives for the period from 2003 to 2013. The comparison of the two indicators shows clearly that transposition concerning the rail directives is slower than for the entire set of internal market-related directives. The figure suggests also that the extent of transposition for rail directives is converging such that the percentage of EU rail directives not transposed on time by a Member State was at the same level as for the internal market directives towards the considered period (2013). However, it should also be remarked that the gap in transposition deficit is expected to increase again with new directives being adopted (notably the Fourth Railway Package as well as the recast Directive 2012/34) drawing on the experience from the previous Railway Packages (Figure 4.1 shows that peaks in the transposition deficit difference seem to be at the highest level shortly after rail directives are due to be transposed).

If EU legislation has not been transposed timely and correctly by a Member State, the Commission can start formal infringement proceedings, which have been used in relation to the various railway legislative measures. A particular case was the First Railway Package for which the Commission in 2008 sent letters of formal notice (first step in infringement proceedings) to 24 EU Member States regarding their failure to implement the First Railway Package. The only EU country that did not receive a letter was the Netherlands (excluding Romania and Bulgaria that became EU members only in 2007). This occurred five years after the directives should have been introduced in national law. More recently, for the recast Directive (2012/34) transposition was due in 2015, though by December 2016 not all Member States had transposed the new provisions in national legislation (European Commission, 2016).

4.3.2   National Governance Structure for Main Infrastructure Manager

One of the core elements in the European legislative programme of railway reform has been to introduce a degree of separation between infrastructure management and rail service operations in order to ensure non-discriminatory access conditions for new entrants and non-incumbents to the rail infrastructure. In particular, the organisation of the so-called essential functions (capacity allocation and charging) was given attention such that these would have to be provided by separate bodies if the infrastructure manager (IM) belonged to a (holding) company also providing rail transport services. Figure 4.2 provides an overview of how the EU Member States have established the institutional setting for their main IM. Two dimensions are considered (thereby indicating the different combinations in a matrix format): (1) overall organisational set-up and (2) scope of the functions of the IM. The overall organisational set-up

	Integrated	Integrated, separate body for essential functions	A holding structure with limited independence guarantees	A holding structure with strong independence guarantees	Separated
IM in charge of all functions (including capacity allocation and charging)	IE		AT FR DE IT PL	BE LV PL SI	BE BG CZ HR DK EE UK (GB part) FI EL NL PT RO SK ES SE
IM in charge of functions except the essential functions		SI HU IE LT LU			
IM in charge of the essential functions, some parts delegated to the railway undertaking			FR		

Source: European Commission (2016).

Figure 4.2   Institutional setting in the Member States (end 2015)

distinguishes between: (a) integrated company (including railway operations and infrastructure management); (b) integrated, separate body for essential functions; (c) a holding structure with limited independence guarantees; (d) a holding structure with strong independence guarantees; and (e) separated. Scope of IM functions is distinguished as follows: (a) IM in charge of all functions (including capacity allocation and charging);

(b) IM in charge of functions except the essential functions (capacity allocation and charging) which are under the responsibility of a separate body; (c) IM in charge of the essential functions with some parts delegated to a railway operator.

The figure highlights several aspects regarding how the EU Member States have implemented the relevant provisions. Firstly, a number of combinations are in use among countries, although less than half of the possible combinations are in fact in use. It appears that a majority of EU Member States (15) have chosen the institutional setting of a separated IM that is also in charge of all functions (including capacity allocation and charging) given that the IM is separated from the rail transport service provision. Other combinations are less used with between one and five countries choosing these. Moreover, there seems to be a move towards combinations that provide a higher level of independence and separation of the infrastructure management function (e.g. the recent cases of Belgium,[8] Poland and Slovenia) albeit complete institutional separation is still far from being achieved in all EU Member States.

4.3.3 Composite Assessment of the Law in the Books and Law in Action

An overview of the extent to which law in books[9] and law in action[10] in the different EU Member States are in line with the goal of market opening is provided by the so-called LIB Index (IBM, 2011). The analysis has been undertaken in 2002, 2004, 2007 and 2011 and covers all EU countries as well as Norway and Switzerland. This index is comprised of two sub-indices: the LEX index and the ACCESS index. In particular, the sub-index LEX considers the extent to which law in the books provides a legal basis for rail liberalisation, market entry and the extent of the powers of the national regulatory authority. Law in action is covered by the ACCESS index that measures information, administrative and operational barriers as well as the share of the domestic market accessible and the level of accessibility to sales service for external railway operators.[11] In Figure 4.3 the latest values for the LIB Index (2011) are shown for rail passenger transport only. It should be remarked that the LIB-based assessment of the legal framework takes into account both the EU legislation as well as any national provisions that could go beyond the European requirements. As noted above, the latter provisions are of particular importance with respect to market opening for domestic passenger services (where EU requirements have only been introduced in the Fourth Railway Package adopted at the end of December 2016).

The figure highlights substantial differences in the legal basis and its application among the Member States concerning rail passenger market

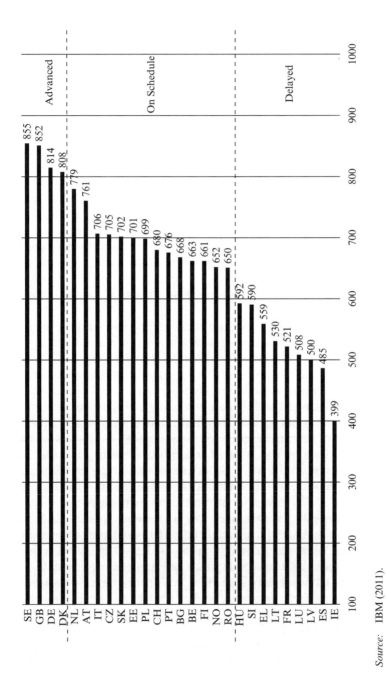

Source: IBM (2011).

Figure 4.3   Rail Liberalisation Index for passenger transport (2011)

opening. Three country groups are defined: advanced (LIB Index over 800), on schedule (LIB Index between 600 and 799) and delayed (LIB Index below 600). The four countries in the 'advanced' group, which have reached the furthest regarding passenger market opening, are Sweden, Great Britain, Germany and Denmark, while the legal frameworks in place and applied conditions in Hungary, Slovenia, Greece, Lithuania, France, Luxembourg, Latvia, Spain and Ireland provide the lowest support for access from external passenger railway undertakings. However, it should be noted that progress regarding the legal framework conditions for market opening has improved since the earlier LIB Index studies from 2002, 2004 and 2007. This is illustrated by comparing the index values given in Figure 4.3 (2011 values) with those shown in Figure 4.4 (2007 values).[12] Overall, a country-by-country comparison suggests that the 2011 values are in general higher than the ones recorded for 2007. In particular, it can be seen that in 2011 only nine countries have index values lower than 600 whereas in 2007 twelve countries had index values less than 600. Indeed, the lowest value (Ireland) was 206 in 2007 compared to 399 (also Ireland) in 2011. Moreover, four countries had values larger than 800 in 2011 compared to only one in 2007.

4.3.4 Degree of Market Opening for Domestic Passenger Services

As noted earlier, there are no requirements in EU legislation (until the Fourth Railway Package) concerning access rights in the case of the domestic rail passenger services (in contrast to international passenger services which have been opened since January 2010 and freight since January 2007). Obviously, market entry would still be supported by other elements of the European reform programme such as unbundling of infrastructure management and technical harmonisation. As a result, the degree of market opening for domestic passenger services is the result of any national requirements for market opening in the form of access rights and/or use of tendering for awarding public service contracts. Figure 4.5 provides an overview of the domestic rail passenger market structure as the situation was in 2012 (European Commission, 2014). The available information indicates that this would still be a reasonably correct reflection of the situation in 2016. Overall, the figure reveals significant country differences with only the UK and Sweden[13] having opened their passenger markets fully (commercial and Public Services Obligations (PSO) services), and nine countries not having introduced any opening of the domestic passenger market (Belgium, Greece, Spain, Finland, France, Hungary, Ireland, Luxembourg and Slovenia). It should be mentioned that in the case of Estonia, Latvia, Lithuania and Slovakia where complete open

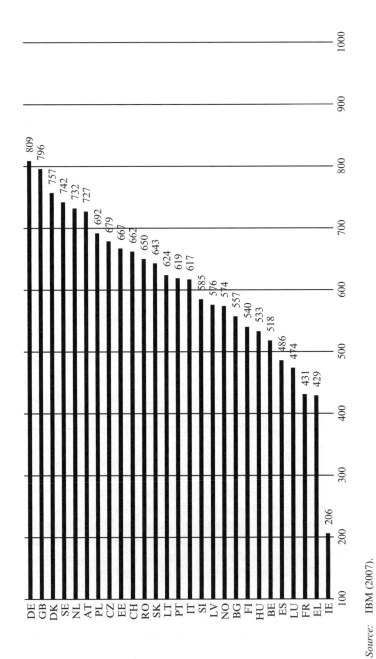

Source: IBM (2007).

Figure 4.4 Rail Liberalisation Index for passenger transport (2007)

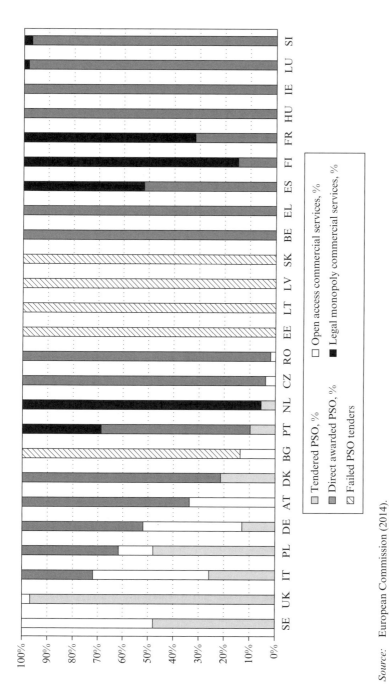

Source: European Commission (2014).

Figure 4.5   Rail market structure (2012)

access provisions exist, PSO services should be tendered according to the national law. However, in the end only the incumbent operator participated in the tender (European Commission, 2014). Overall, available information (not deduced from the figure) suggests that about 40 per cent of the domestic rail market is open for new entrants measured in terms of passenger-kilometres (European Commission, 2014).

4.4   OUTCOMES OF REFORMS

The previous sections have set out the European legislative initiatives for reforming the railways as well as how these measures have been implemented in the EU Member States with particular focus on passenger transport. In this section the focus is on considering what the implications have been of the adopted reforms. As such, it should be remarked that an assessment of reform outcomes is complex at this point for several reasons including: (1) the legal framework is still evolving (notably the recently adopted Fourth Railway Package); (2) implementation of the legal framework is not complete at Member State level; (3) separation of the influence on outcomes linked to the legislative initiatives from other possible factors. The section covers the following aspects: (1) structure of passenger rail companies; (2) passenger rail market competition; (3) cost and efficiency implications; (4) modal share. The first two outcome measures can be considered necessary factors for possible influences on cost, efficiency and modal share.

4.4.1   Structure of Passenger Rail Companies

Prior to the onset of the reform process in the early 1990s the railway sector in Europe was predominantly organised in monolithic public-owned integrated companies (such as NS, ÖBB, SNCB and FS) responsible for almost all passenger transport in the country along with freight transport services and other ancillary services as well as management, development and maintenance of the railway infrastructure. Third Party Access (TPA) possibilities were largely not available in practice. Often the national railway company was subject to substantial political influence and independent regulation was non-existent, instead the railway system was mainly managed through self-regulation.

Following more than 25 years of railway reform at European and national levels this structure is no longer typical for the incumbent passenger railway company (see, e.g., Olsen et al., 2015). Although these companies are almost in all cases still in public ownership (Great Britain being the main exception with privatised operators), other changes have taken place that have changed their characteristics. Firstly, the incumbent (passenger) railway companies have a more independent status from the state where PSO are specified in public service contracts setting the level of transport services to be provided, quality requirements and payments between government and transport provider. Secondly, a minimum level of (organisational) separation between infrastructure management and rail transport operations (with the majority of countries having established full separation) has been introduced. Thirdly, the incumbent passenger companies in a number of countries are facing the possibility of competing operators in the market (or for the market). However, in most countries the incumbent passenger company is still responsible for most of the provided transport services (see further details below). Fourthly, in a number of cases separate companies for passenger and freight have been created from the old integrated company (such as in Sweden where separate incumbent passenger and freight operators exist, SJ and Green Cargo, respectively). Finally, new authorities and organisations have been introduced to the railway system, including: (1) independent (national) regulatory bodies regarding access to the rail network; (2) NSAs with responsibilities for safety certification, authorisation for placing vehicles in service; (3) National Investigation Bodies concerning accident investigations; (4) Notified Bodies (companies notified by Member States with responsibility for checking conformity of railway-related equipment in terms of interoperability).

4.4.2   Passenger Rail Market Competition

Two main forms of competition can be identified in the case of passenger railway transport: (1) competition in the market (or on-track competition), where several railway operators are in competition by providing services on the same network during the same time period – this form of competition is based on open access arrangements for third-party railway operators; (2) competition for the market (or access competition) whereby two or more railway operators are competing (through a bidding process) to get access to the market and the winner of the bidding process can operate services for a time-limited period (usually under exclusive rights). An overview of the market share of competitors in the passenger market for 2014 is provided in Figure 4.6.

In general, the market shares for competitors (non-incumbents) remain relatively low for most EU countries with only the UK, Poland and Italy having shares over 15 per cent. Sweden should also be added, taking into account earlier 2012 figures of +40 per cent reported in European Commission (2014) – unfortunately the 2014 figures are confidential

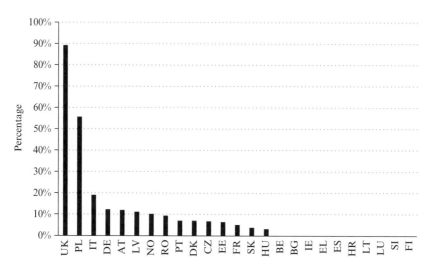

Note: The 2014 data are provided through the Rail Market Monitoring Scheme
(RMMS), except for Ireland (2013 data used for 2014), the Netherlands and Sweden
(confidential), Luxembourg (estimates) and Italy (data from IRG Rail, 2016). This implies
that the figure includes data for 24 out of the 26 EU Member States with railways as well as
Norway.

Source: European Commission (2016).

*Figure 4.6   Market share of competitors in the passenger market (2014,
              per cent of passenger-kilometres)*

according to European Commission (2016). According to Figure 4.6 in 12
countries (including Norway) non-incumbent railway undertakings hold
market shares below 15 per cent. To this group the Netherlands should be
added taking into account earlier 2012 figures of about 8 per cent reported
in European Commission (2014). However, for a number of countries (10)
the market share for non-incumbent railway undertakings remains at 0
per cent; in these countries the incumbent passenger operator provides all
passenger services. The average market share for competitors in the passenger market was reported to be around 20 per cent in 2012 according to
European Commission (2014). A similar figure would be expected to be
the case in 2014.

Overall, the type of competition emerging seems to be linked to the
market segment involved. For regional and suburban passenger rail
services these are typically organised through public service contracts
between authorities and the rail operator where the use of competitive

tendering as the mechanism for contract award has been introduced in a number of countries. On the other hand, long distance and high-speed rail services would tend to be more frequently operated under open access providing the possibility for competition in the market. As for the newcomers appearing as competitors to the incumbents, Bergantino (2015) notes that these are very heterogeneous mainly covering the following: (1) subsidiaries of existing national champions (that enter the market in other countries, including international services); (2) companies partially owned by other incumbents; (3) companies established by other (private) operators active in the rail sector or other type of transportation (coach transport, airline travel and so on). On the other hand, it is seldom that new entrants are completely external to the transport industry.

Below, a brief overview of the progress to date regarding competitive tendering and open access competition is provided. As for competitive tendering, only Great Britain has introduced competitive tendering (franchising) for all passenger services (since 1996–97), whereas Sweden has introduced competitive tendering for regional passenger transport (since 1989–90) and non-profitable interregional passenger transport (since 1992). Germany has provided the possibility for competitive tendering for regional and local transport (since 1996), indeed over 50 per cent of PSO train-kilometres have been tendered (European Commission, 2014). Other countries are using competitive tendering although on a much smaller scale compared to Great Britain, Sweden and Germany: these are Poland, Italy, Denmark, Portugal, the Netherlands, the Czech Republic and Slovakia (e.g. in Denmark there have been two tenders of regional/suburban passenger services[14] representing some 20 per cent of the passenger services, as expressed in terms of passenger-kilometres, though presently less than 10 per cent are provided under contract by external railway operators). In addition, there are countries where the possibility for using competitive tendering is available but this has not been used to date (e.g. in Austria). Other countries continue to award public service transport contracts without a competitive tendering procedure to the national (monopolistic) rail operator on the basis of reimbursement for PSO (e.g. the situation in Finland, France, Greece, Hungary, Ireland, Slovenia and Spain).

Available evidence suggests an increased use of competitive tendering in recent years as illustrated by Figure 4.7. The figure shows the number of (rail) Public Service Contract (PSC) notices published in the *Official Journal of the European Union* (OJEU).[15] Contract notices can be taken as a call for submitting bids and not only used in order to ensure transparency for contract awards. In 2006 the number of PSC notices was 18 and by 2012 the number had increased to 41. Following the adoption of the Fourth Railway Package it is expected that further use of competitive

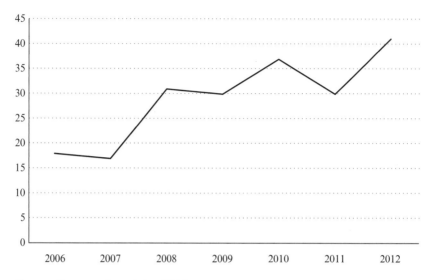

Source: European Commission (2014).

Figure 4.7   Public Service Contract notices in OJEU

tendering across the EU Member States will take place. Below, considerations regarding the possible effects of competitive tendering are given with
a particular focus on cost aspects.

Until recently, limited open access competition had emerged in Europe
with the exception of a few operations in the UK (Hull Trains and Grand
Central), Germany (Interconnex) and Italy (Arenaways). However, during
the last five years more instances of competitive entry have occurred across
a number of European countries (mostly within the long distance passenger market). Table 4.3 provides an overview.

For example, in the Czech Republic there are now two external passenger operators (RegioJet and Leo Express) in direct competition with
the incumbent operator, České dráhy (commonly shortened to ČD), on
the same corridor (between Prague and Ostrava). Similarly, in Austria
WESTbahn[16] is operating long distance services between Vienna and
Salzburg in competition with the incumbent ÖBB. The first example
of open access competition in the high-speed market segment occurred
in Italy with the entry of NTV[17] (Nuovo Trasporto Viaggiatori) providing services on routes connecting major Italian cities (e.g. Turin-
Salerno and Venice-Salerno both serving Bologna, Florence, Rome and
Naples).

Table 4.3   Market entry by domestic open access operators

Country	Open access operator	Service	Begun	Ended
AT	Westbahn	Long distance	December 2011	
CZ	RegioJet	Long distance	September 2011	
	Leo Express	Long distance	December 2012	
DE	HKX	Long distance	July 2012	
	InterConnex	Long distance	December 2001	December 2014
IT	NTV	High speed	April 2012	
	Arenaways	Long distance	November 2010	February 2012
SE	BlåTåget	Long distance	November 2011	
	Öresundståg (Veolia)	Long distance	December 2011	
	MTR express	Long distance	March 2015	
SK	RegioJet	Long distance	December 2014	
UK	Grand Central	Long distance	December 2007	
	First Hull Trains	Long distance	September 2000	
	Wrexham Shropshire & Marylebone	Long distance	January 2008	January 2011

Note: Excluding cabotage by high-speed international services and airport-only operators.

Source: European Commission (2016), originally included in Steer Davies Gleave (2016).

4.4.3   Cost and Efficiency Implications

The possible effects on costs and efficiency of the passenger railway reforms in Europe to date are examined in this subsection. In particular, consideration is given to the effects linked to examples of competitive tendering and open access competition as well as more aggregated analysis of the reform implications.

Available evidence from countries that have already introduced competitive tendering for awarding public service contracts of passenger services suggests typically (though not uniformly) the possibility for cost savings. A number of studies have been undertaken at country level regarding the possible (cost) effects and these are briefly reviewed below focusing on the following countries: Sweden, Denmark, Germany and Great Britain.

Overall, the experience in Sweden suggests significant scope for cost savings of some 20 per cent due to the use of competitive tendering rather than direct award (Alexandersson, 2009). These savings were achieved in the first round of tendering in the early 1990s without the contract going to a non-incumbent operator. Once non-incumbent operators started winning contracts further savings were achieved.

Denmark has more limited experience with competitive tendering compared to Sweden. Two tenders have taken place to date. In the case of the first tender in Mid and West Jutland, won by Arriva, cost savings of some 15 per cent compared to continuing with DSB (the incumbent as the provider) have been achieved (Thelle, 2013). Moreover, the contract prolongation in 2009 is reported to have resulted in additional savings for the Danish government of 10 per cent. Available information also indicates that customer satisfaction is high and increasing as well as being higher than before the tender. As for the second tender (concerning services between Elsinore and Malmö in Sweden) the experiences are less positive. The contract was won by DSB First (a company affiliated to the incumbent, DSB), but DSB First ceased to exist and the services are now operated by DSB. However, despite the latter outcome, it is still estimated that further tendering could result in additional cost savings and service quality improvements.

Similar to Sweden the experience with competitive tendering in Germany is extensive although the scope is limited to public service contracts for suburban and regional services. Link (2016) reports indications that for first round tendering significant cost savings have been achieved (measured in terms of unit costs) in the order of magnitude of 26 per cent. Moreover, as for public subsidies, these have also decreased as measured by operation subsidies per output unit over the period 1996–2010. Apart from reduced costs and subsidies it is also noted that the use of tendering in Germany has in general resulted in better targeted services.

Great Britain adopted the most drastic approach to competitive tendering by including essentially all passenger services as part of the restructuring and privatisation of British Rail in the mid 1990s. In contrast to the experience elsewhere in Europe (see above), cost savings have to date not materialised, instead there have been cost increases: unit costs increased by 14 per cent between 1997 and 2006 (Smith, 2016). As for the possible reasons for this unusual result, several aspects can be put forward, including problems of incentives for the company being awarded the franchise linked to the relative short duration of the contract as well as the size of the franchise (significantly bigger than the ones elsewhere in Europe), which increases complexity as well as not facilitating significant organisational changes in the existing company responsible for the operations. Smith (2016) also highlights that besides the negative effects on costs, there have been successful aspects linked to demand, fares and quality.

So far, there are only limited studies into the effects of open access competition given that most of the examples have occurred in the last five years (see, e.g., Bergantino, 2015 for a recent overview of the experiences to date in the Czech Republic, Slovakia, Austria, Germany and Italy). Another recent analysis of the possible effects is included in Steer Davies Gleave (2016) with reference to five open access competition examples: Hull Trains (UK), Grand Central (UK), NTV (IT), RegioJet (CZ) and Leo Express (CZ).

The analysis suggests a mixed picture of the possible effects for this relatively small sample. For example, as to whether the incumbent adds services in response to entry, in Italy and the two Czech examples, the incumbent did add services, whereas this did not happen for the two UK examples. As for fares, the examples indicate that the entrant lowers fares compared to the incumbent. There is uncertainty concerning the response from the incumbent: in the case of the Czech Republic, the entry resulted in a price war with some fares down 75 per cent. Information about the incumbent's response regarding fares was not available for Italy and the UK.

A recent econometric study examined the extent to which open access competition is influencing efficiency measured in terms of operating expenses per train-kilometre (Casullo, 2016). The preliminary results suggest that at this point it was not possible to detect an improvement in efficiency. On the contrary, there seem to be incurred additional costs linked possibly to problems of coordination as well as duplication of investment costs. In part, these findings may be linked to a time horizon that is too short since the open access competition started and it is possible that a longer time period will allow the dynamic effects of competition to be captured. Therefore, a recommendation put forward in the paper is to revisit the analysis when longer time series are available as well as considering improvements in the econometric modelling and data availability.

Further analysis of on-track competition in the rail passenger market is being undertaken within an ongoing research project REGUTRAIN (see Finger et al., 2016). The particular focus is on the experiences in several European countries, including Austria, the Czech Republic, Sweden, Italy and the UK. So far, conclusions highlight that instances of on-track competition in these countries are limited to a few routes and a small number of competing railway operators. Moreover, the research suggests that whereas there are positive impacts for passengers (lower fares) it remains an open question whether the overall effects are beneficial. This points to the importance of appropriate regulatory frameworks in order to ensure net benefits of on-track competition in the passenger rail market.

A comprehensive framework for assessing the implications for efficiency is represented by the so-called efficiency measurement techniques where a best practice frontier is determined using methods such as Data Envelopment Analysis (DEA) and Stochastic Frontier Analysis (SFA) (see, e.g., Fried, et al., 2008 for an overview of these techniques). Although a number of such studies have been undertaken for the European railway sector there are to date only few that explicitly examine the links between regulatory reform and efficiency. Below, we briefly consider the findings in two of these studies: Friebel et al. (2010) and Asmild et al. (2009). Friebel et al. (2010) assess the changes in (technical) efficiency as a result of railway reform measures with a particular focus on passenger transport within a stochastic production frontier approach. The study covers the period from 1980 to 2003 and includes 12 of the EU Member States though the UK had to be excluded as the data required were not complete for that country. The best practice frontier was determined on the basis of the following inputs and outputs: (1) inputs: staff and route-kilometres; (2) outputs: passenger-kilometres and tonne-kilometres (though the estimation is structured such that tonne-kilometres is only included in order to take into account its effect on passenger traffic efficiency). Moreover, the regulatory reform elements focused on three aspects included as dummy variables in the econometric modelling: (1) separation of infrastructure and operations; (2) TPA; (3) independent regulatory entity. Overall, the analysis provides two main results: (1) reforms appeared to have a positive impact on passenger rail traffic efficiency; (2) however, the positive effect seems to be dependent on the sequencing of reforms. In fact, if the reform elements are introduced at the same time (packaging) rather than gradually over time the positive effect on efficiency disappears.

Asmild et al. (2009) examine the railway operations in 23 European countries during 1995 to 2001 (covering both passenger and freight) in order to determine whether the reform initiatives underway improved the efficiency of the railway systems. In particular, a non-parametric frontier method was used for the analysis, the so-called Multi-Directional Efficiency Analysis (MEA), which is similar to the more widely used DEA. MEA allows the identification of efficiency improvement potential per production factor rather than an aggregated indication of efficiency gains. The following inputs and outputs were used: (1) discretionary inputs: staff costs and material purchases/external charges (both in million euros); (2) non-discretionary inputs: network length (measured in line kilometres); (3) outputs: passenger train-kilometres and freight train-kilometres (in thousands).

The following reform aspects were considered in the analysis: (1) accounting separation: indicating whether or not infrastructure and services are separated on an accounting basis; (2) complete separation: indicating whether or not infrastructure and services are institutionally separated; (3) independent management: indicating whether or not legislation is transposed that assures independent management by railway companies without government involvement; (4) competitive tendering for passenger services: indicating whether or not competitive tendering is used to procure (some or all) passenger railway services; (5) market opening for freight transport: indicating whether or not legislation is transposed that allows entry of competitors.

The main findings are that these reform initiatives generally improve technical efficiency but potentially not the same for different cost drivers. Specifically, the study suggests that accounting separation is important for improving efficiency in the use of both material and staff costs, whereas other reforms only influenced one of these factors. Moreover, in the case of competitive tendering of passenger services the results show that there is a significant positive impact on efficiency with respect to material costs (whereas for labour costs the efficiency improvement effect recorded is not significant). Given that this study is based on data from 1995 to 2001 an updated analysis with more recent data would be of interest to examine the effect of the reforms undertaken and implemented in subsequent years.

4.4.4 Modal Share of Passenger Rail Transport

Overall, it is difficult to demonstrate a direct linkage between rail regulatory reform initiatives and the rail modal share in the passenger transport market. As such, the competitiveness of rail vis-à-vis other modes as reflected in its modal share would be determined by a range of influencing factors, some of which are within the domain of public policy, while others are linked to railway industry practices as well as preferences and constraints faced by individuals. This also implies that there would be limits to how much can be expected to be delivered from railway regulatory reform measures only, as other connected measures would need to be in place as well. Moreover, the influence of regulatory reform on the modal share for passenger rail would be rather indirect through changes in cost performance (e.g. leading to lower fares) and customer orientation (e.g. resulting in higher quality of service), which in turn may encourage higher rail passenger patronage. These changes may either come as a result of competitive entry with new transport providers or as a reaction by the incumbent to the threat of market entry. A further challenge to identify any linkages is that European-level initiatives towards market opening in the passenger market were rather limited until the Fourth Railway Package was adopted in December 2016 (although some Member States have gone further than EU legislation requirements as discussed above). Figure 4.8 shows the trend in passenger rail modal share for the EU Member States (EU28) as a whole covering the period 1995 to 2011. The passenger rail modal share has stayed in the range between 6 and 7 per cent throughout the period. However, the

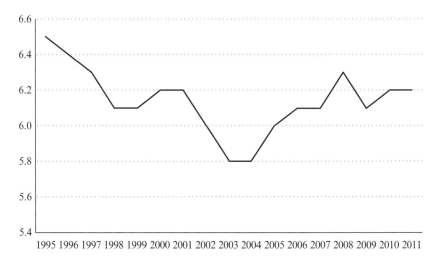

Source: European Commission (2014).

Figure 4.8   Passenger rail modal share 1995–2011 (per cent of passenger-kilometres of all modes)

trend suggests that in the first part of the period (from 1995 to 2003) there was a small reduction in modal share which was reversed in the second part of the period (from 2004 to 2011). Moreover, recent data for (2012 to 2014) indicate that the improvement in rail passenger modal share has continued in those years. A pragmatic interpretation of the linkage could be that the regulatory reforms of passenger rail in Europe have contributed to stabilise the modal share and possibly even stimulated modest improvements. On the other hand, a more appropriate approach for determining the linkage between regulatory reform and passenger rail competitiveness may be to use a case study approach and examine the impact on passenger demand with specific examples of tendering and/or open access competition. Particular insight about how a competitive railway can be provided may be gained by examining successful (country) examples within and beyond Europe as put forward by Nash (2015) (e.g. Sweden as an efficient low-density, mixed-traffic railway and Switzerland as a densely used mixed-traffic railway).

4.5   CONCLUSIONS AND FUTURE PERSPECTIVES

This chapter has offered an overview of how the passenger railway sector has been changing across Europe following the legislative reform initiatives introduced gradually over the past two to three decades. It outlines the narrative behind the railway reforms by setting out the background to the reform initiatives and then follows the successive steps in the reform process: (1) European legislative measures; (2) implementation of legislative measures in the EU Member States; (3) outcomes of passenger railway reform. As such it is apparent that substantial changes are already occurring in this sector and that these can be linked to legislative measures. Indeed, a comparison of the European passenger railway sector from 1980 with that of 2016 would demonstrate the magnitude of the changes that have taken place. However, the review also suggests that there are country differences regarding how the organisation of the railway sector is being shaped during this period. At the very least, differences regarding the timing and speed of implementing the European reforms would create variation between countries. In contrast to rail freight, where European-driven market opening was achieved by 2007, for rail passenger transport progress has been significantly slower in particular with respect to the domestic passenger market. This difference in focus between freight and passenger market liberalisation is probably linked to the political sensitivity regarding the provision of (national) passenger services with a specific focus on the justification of services in general interest that may not be financially profitable but socially desirable (Di Pietrantonio and Pelkmans, 2004). Indeed, only the recently (December 2016) adopted Fourth Railway Package provided for market opening of this market segment. The implication of this is that most progress regarding market opening for passenger rail was mainly linked to national initiatives going further than the European requirements. In general, the incumbent still retains a dominant position as provider of passenger services in most cases, although there are country exceptions. As for the outcomes linked to the regulatory reforms (covering both European and national measures), the available evidence suggests the possibility for positive effects on costs and efficiency, although this result is not necessarily guaranteed. In particular, there appears to be scope for competitive tendering to generate significant cost savings without leading to negative effects on quality and customer satisfaction provided safeguards regarding contract specification, operator incentives and allocation of risks are properly addressed. Limited empirical evidence is available concerning open access competition in order to draw robust conclusions. However, this form of competition may be of importance in the long distance/high-speed market segment where profitable corridors may encourage entry in certain cases.

Over the coming years it is likely that there will be increased competition in the European passenger rail market linked particularly to the Fourth Railway Package provisions. This would cover both competition for the market (competitive tendering) and competition in the market (entry as open access operations). Moreover, it is likely that external railway operators will capture a higher market share compared to the present situation. By 2025 it may be pertinent to undertake an in-depth review of the experiences with extensive rail passenger liberalisation in order to determine the extent to which these reforms were in fact welfare generating.

NOTES

* The views expressed in this paper are those of the author and do not necessarily reflect the European Union Agency for Railways' or the European Commission's view on the subject.
1. Accounts separation requires that if rail service operations and infrastructure management are organised within the same entity (as was typically the situation for the incumbent railway companies across Europe), there should be distinct accounts for the rail service operations and infrastructure management.
2. Organisational separation requires that rail service operations and infrastructure management should be placed in distinct/separate organisations within a (holding) company with independent decision-making procedures in addition to separate accounts.
3. Institutional separation requires that rail service operations and infrastructure management should be organised in distinct companies. If institutional separation is required then for the typical incumbent railway company the infrastructure management part would have to be transferred to a distinct company (though both entities could still have the same owner, normally the state).
4. In this chapter we refer to railway operators as the entities responsible for producing rail services (passenger and freight), which is more frequently used in practice, rather than railway undertakings, which is used in EU legislation.
5. Cabotage is the transport of goods or passengers between two points in the same country. Cabotage is commonly used as part of the term 'cabotage rights', the right of a company from one country to trade in another country.
6. Information about the Single Market Scoreboard is available at http://ec.europa.eu/internal_market/scoreboard/.
7. DG MARKT is the EU Commission Directorate-General for internal market and services (since 2015 part of DG GROWTH).
8. In Belgium since January 2014 the IM (Infrabel) is no longer part of the SNCB holding company but a separate autonomous public company.
9. Legal rules found in texts.
10. The application of legal rules in practice.
11. Railway operator which has entered the rail market in the course of liberalisation and offers rail transport services (usually in addition to the incumbent).
12. Comparisons between LIB Index studies should be undertaken with care given that the method for calculating the indices may be subject to limited adjustment.
13. In three other countries more than 50 per cent of the domestic passenger market is open: Italy, Poland and Germany.
14. The two tenders concerned: (1) contract for services on regional rail network in Mid and West Jutland; (2) contract for services on the line between Elsinore (Denmark) and Malmö (Sweden).
15. Government procurement contracts over a certain amount (100000 euros) have to be published in OJEU.
16. SNCF has a 26 per cent ownership stake in WESTbahn.
17. SNCF has a 20 per cent ownership stake in NTV.

REFERENCES

Alexandersson, G. (2009), 'Rail privatization and competitive tendering in Europe', *Built Environment*, **35** (1), 43–58.

Asmild, M., T. Holvad, J.L. Hougaard and D. Kronborg (2009), 'Railway reforms: do they influence operating efficiency?', *Transportation*, **36** (5), 617–38.

Bergantino, A. (2015), 'Incumbents and new entrants', in M. Finger and P. Messulam (eds), *Rail Economics, Policy and Regulation*, Cheltenham and Northampton, MA: Edward Elgar Publishing, pp. 171–209.

Casullo, L. (2016), 'The efficiency impact of open access competition in rail markets: the case of domestic passenger services in Europe', ITF Discussion Paper 2016-07, International Transport Forum, OECD, Paris.

Di Pietrantonio, L. and J. Pelkmans (2004), 'The economics of EU railway reform', Bruges European Economic Policy Briefings No. 8, Bruges.

ECMT (1998), *Rail Restructuring in Europe*, Paris: OECD Publishing.

European Commission (1996), 'A Strategy for Revitalising the Community's Railways', EC White Paper, COM(96) 421 final, Brussels.

European Commission (2001), 'European Transport Policy for 2010: Time to Decide', EC White Paper, COM(2001) 370, Brussels.

European Commission (2006), 'Keep Europe Moving: Sustainable Mobility for Our Continent', Mid-term review of the 2001 Transport White Paper, COM(2006) 314 final, Brussels.

European Commission (2011), 'Roadmap to a Single European Transport Area – Towards a Competitive and Resource Efficient Transport System', EC Transport White Paper, COM(2011) 144 final, Brussels.

European Commission (2014), 'Fourth Report to the Council and the European Parliament on Monitoring Development of the Rail Market', COM(2014) 0353 final, Brussels.

European Commission (2016), 'Fifth Report to the Council and the European Parliament on Monitoring Developments of the Rail Market', COM(2016) 780 final, Brussels.

Finger, M., D. Kupfer and J.J. Montero (2016), *Competition in the Railway Passenger Market*, Florence School of Regulation Research Report, Florence, November.

Friebel, G., M. Ivaldi and C. Vibes (2010), 'Railway (de)regulation: a European efficiency comparison', *Economica*, **77**(305), 77–91.

Fried, H.O., C.A.K. Lovell and S.S. Schmidt (eds) (2008), *The Measurement of Productive Efficiency and Productivity Change*, New York: Oxford University Press.

Holvad, T. (2009), 'Review of railway reforms in Europe', *Built Environment*, **35** (1), 24–42.

IBM (2007), 'Rail Liberalisation Index 2007: market opening – rail markets of the Member States of the European Union, Switzerland and Norway in comparison', IBM Global Business Services.

IBM (2011), 'Rail Liberalisation Index 2011: market opening: comparison of the rail markets of the Member States of the European Union, Switzerland and Norway', Study commissioned by Deutsche Bahn AG, Munich.

IRG Rail (2016), *Fourth Annual Market Monitoring Report*, Independent Regulators' Group – Rail, March.

Link, H. (2016), 'Liberalisation of passenger rail services: case study Germany', Centre on Regulation in Europe (CERRE), December.

Nash, C. (2015), 'What does a best practice railway look like?', in M. Finger and P. Messulam (eds), *Rail Economics, Policy and Regulation*, Cheltenham and Northampton, MA: Edward Elgar Publishing, pp. 232–47.

Olsen, S., N. Fearnley and J.R. Krogstad (2015), 'Commercialisation and managerial independence', in M. Finger and P. Messulam, (eds), *Rail Economics, Policy and Regulation*, Cheltenham and Northampton, MA: Edward Elgar Publishing, pp. 89–111.

Smith, A. (2016), 'Liberalisation of passenger rail services: case study Britain', Centre on Regulation in Europe (CERRE), December.

Steer Davies Gleave (2016), *Study on the Prices and Quality of Rail Passenger Services*, Final report prepared for DG MOVE.

Thelle, M.H. (2013), *Productivity Gains in Danish Network Industries*, Background report prepared for the Danish Productivity Commission by Copenhagen Economics, Copenhagen.

5. Ownership and firm performance: empirical evidence from the European telecommunications industry (2006–14)

Paolo Castelnovo

5.1 INTRODUCTION[1]

The telecommunications sector was the first network industry affected by market reforms in Europe (Florio, 2013), which were applied starting from the 1980s with the aim of establishing competition. Such reforms included the liberalization of the sector by opening the fixed and mobile segments to competition, the privatization of the fixed-line incumbents and the creation of independent regulatory agencies (Gasmi et al., 2013). At the same time, a process of technological change deeply reshaped the industry (Galperin, 2007; Florio, 2013): the analogue to digital technology transition, requiring costly investments by the governments, contributed to the privatization shift.

The pioneer of privatization reforms in Europe was Great Britain with the sale of 51 per cent of British Telecom shares in 1984, followed by Italy (1991), Denmark (1992), the Netherlands (1994), Belgium, Greece and Portugal (1995), Germany (1996), France (1997), Switzerland (1998), Austria, Norway and Sweden (1999) (see Alonso et al., 2013). However, three decades after the beginning of the privatization process, public ownership is still widespread in the European telecommunications industry: large segments of the industry remain dominated by incumbent Public Telecommunications Operators (PTOs), where the State often maintains controlling shares (Boylaud and Nicoletti, 2001). The result of the implementation of the liberalization and privatization reforms is often a mixed oligopoly, where private and State-invested enterprises (SIEs) coexist.

Nevertheless, there is some heterogeneity in public involvement among countries, the speed and the rate of privatizations being indeed very different across Europe. Spain and Denmark completed the privatization process in a few years, the UK, Italy and Netherlands took about a decade, while until the present governments in Germany, France, Sweden, Finland, Belgium, Austria, Norway and Switzerland have important stakes in the former incumbents (Castelnovo, 2016).

After around three decades of policy reforms, the benefits from market liberalization and privatization seem controversial for consumers. Bacchiocchi et al. (2011) studied the impact of privatization and liberalization on prices and consumers' satisfaction in the telecommunications sector in the EU15 countries. They found that market regulation is important for price reduction while ownership change, from public to private, plays no role (or a very limited one) to explain the prices of international, national and local calls and connection charges. The analysis conducted using Eurobarometer data on consumers' satisfaction about the quality of the telecommunications service confirmed the importance of market regulation and the small effect of privatization per se. Therefore, the authors conclude that there is only mixed and somewhat contradictory evidence that all the reforms have worked in a similar way across the European Union (EU) and that, up to now, have provided substantial benefits for the consumers. While there is evidence that the market share of new entrants contributed to welfare improvements, the impact of competition does not seem to be affected by public ownership.

Looking at company performance, given the prominent role still played by State-controlled enterprises in the telecommunications industry, it is also important to investigate whether there are significant differences between State-invested[2] and private enterprises.

The relationship between ownership type and firm performance has been broadly investigated. However, the evidence is still unclear. Earlier literature often suggested that private ownership is associated with higher productivity than government ownership (see, for example, Boardman and Vining, 1989) because it guarantees stronger incentives to productive efficiency: profit maximization is typically a more relevant objective for private than publicly owned companies, that must trade off productive efficiency against other non-commercial objectives dictated by public interests (De Fraja, 1993; Willner, 2001).

Distortions in a company's objective function have been frequently suggested as a potential explanation to justify a productivity gap and may derive from either desirable or undesirable factors. They may be due to negative interferences, such as rent-seeking and opportunistic behaviour of managers and politicians (Shleifer and Vishny, 1993, 1994) that might exert pressures to force State-owned enterprises (SOEs) to employ excess labour inputs (Boycko et al., 1996) or hire politically connected rather than best qualified people (Krueger, 1990).

However, it is also possible that State-owned firms deviate from profit maximization in favour of socially desirable objectives, providing a solution to market failures, taking social welfare and wealth redistribution into account (Atkinson and Stiglitz, 1980), targeting employment objectives (Shleifer, 1998; Dewenter and Malatesta, 2001) or bearing higher expenditures for research and development (Sterlacchini, 2012).

Nevertheless, more recent contributions have suggested that public ownership is not necessarily associated with worse economic outcomes. Christiansen and Kim (2014) provide evidence of the increasing role of public enterprises and compare the performance of SIEs and non-SIEs in five sectors (air transportation, electricity, mining, oil and gas, and telecommunications), showing that over the last ten years SIEs have generally displayed a better economic performance compared to private companies. Concerning the telecom sector, SIEs enjoyed higher returns in all of the indicators considered: EBITDA (Earnings Before Interest, Taxes, Depreciation and Amortization) margin, gross and profit margin, returns to capital employed, returns to total assets and returns to shareholder funds.

Among the studies supporting the competitiveness of modern State-owned companies, Florio (2014), using a sample of the Forbes 2000 top corporations, shows that SOEs display better financial performance than their private counterparts. Similar results are found by Clò et al. (2015a), which prove that large public enterprises on a global scale display a comparable performance with private ones, if not even higher in some specific sectors.

In the last years this strand of literature widely focused on China, where privatization reforms began to take place. Sun et al. (2002) showed that State-participation has a positive influence on partially privatized SOEs but this relationship shows an inverted U-shape, with extensive or little government control being detrimental for firm performance. Yu (2013) found that government ownership is superior to dispersed ownership, suggesting that this is 'due to the benefits of government support and political connection' (Yu, 2013, p. 75).

In general, the estimation of the impact of privatizations either on prices and consumers' satisfaction or on firms' performance implies some relevant methodological issues. As made clear in Chapter 1 of the present volume, privatization reforms cannot simply be captured by the change of a specific signal but imply a change in the institutional setting: summarizing the effect of privatization reform packages using a single indicator variable may lead to what was classified as a 'conceptual error'. Indeed, defining as a reform indicator what is in fact an 'outcome' variable, for example, the ownership type of a company, may give rise to serious interpretation problems if such an outcome is not directly linked to the reform itself and might be the result of other factors at work. This issue will be overcome in the empirical analysis that follows by accounting for suitable control variables.

The chapter is organized as follows. Section 5.2 provides a detailed list of the major SIEs active in the European telecommunications industry, specifying the identity of the public shareholders and the percentage of shares they hold, and highlights the relationship between parent companies and their subsidiaries. Section 5.3 describes the data used in the analysis and gives the relevant summary statistics. The empirical investigation is performed in Section 5.4, which presents the econometric model to be estimated and regression results. Conclusions are drawn in Section 5.5.

5.2 MAJOR TELECOM SIEs IN EUROPE

As already mentioned, the first country implementing privatization reforms in Europe was the UK in 1984. Since then, the privatization wave gradually hit, with different intensity, other European countries starting from the early 1990s, turning monopolistic markets dominated by State-owned incumbents into mixed oligopolies, where private and SIEs coexist.

Modern SIEs are often controlled by governments through minority stakes and operate in a competitive and international environment, as confirmed by their active participation in the international market for corporate control (Clò et al., 2015b). Nowadays, the most important European SIEs in the telecommunications sector are Swisscom, Telenor, Belgacom, Lattelecom and Telekom Slovenije, with State-participation exceeding 50 per cent, and Deutsche Telekom, Orange (ex-France Télécom), TeliaSonera, Hellenic Telecommunications Organization (OTE), Telekom Austria and S.E.S., where the State holds from 10 to about 40 per cent of the shares.

In turn, these large SIEs own (partially or fully) a number of subsidiaries, especially in Eastern Europe, which, therefore, turn out to be indirectly controlled by foreign governments.

Table 5.1 provides an exhaustive list of the major telecom SIEs, in terms of operating revenues, included in the analysed sample, reporting the name of the corresponding public shareholder and the percentage of its shares. Parent companies are marked in bold.

Table 5.1   Major telecom SIEs in Europe

Company	Country	Public shareholder	Share (%)
1. PROXIMUS SA	Belgium	Etat Belge	53.3
BELGACOM ICS	Belgium		53.3
2. SWISSCOM AG	Switzerland	Government of Switzerland	51
SWISSCOM ENTERPRISE SOLUTIONS	Switzerland		51
FASTWEB SPA	Italy		51
3. TELENOR ASA	Norway	Government of Norway	54
TELENOR A/S	Denmark		54
TELENOR BULGARIA EAD	Bulgaria		54
TELENOR MAGYARORSZAG	Hungary		54
TELENOR NORGE AS	Norway		54
TELENOR SVERIGE AKTIEBOLAG	Sweden		54
4. LATTELECOM SIA	Latvia	Government of Latvia +TeliaSonera	51 + 49
5. TELEKOM SLOVENIJE DD	Slovenia	Republika Slovenija	62.5
6. DEUTSCHE TELEKOM AG	Germany	Federal Republic of Germany (FRG)	31.7
TELEKOM ROMANIA MOBILE	Romania		
HT-HRVATSKI TELEKOMUNIKACIJE	Croatia		
T-MOBILE AUSTRIA GMBH	Austria		
T-MOBILE CZECH REPUBLIC AS	Czech Republic		
T-MOBILE POLSKA SA	Poland		
T-SYSTEMS LIMITED	Germany		
MAGYAR TELEKOM	Hungary		
SLOVAK TELEKOM AS	Slovakia		
7. TELEKOM ROMANIA COMMUNICATIONS SA	Romania	Government of Romania + FRG	46 + 31.7
8. HELLENIC TELECOMM. ORGANIZATION (OTE)	Greece	Government of Greece + FRG	10 + 31.7
COSMOTE MOBILE TELECOMMUNICATIONS	Greece		

Table 5.1   (continued)

Company	Country	Public shareholder	Share (%)
9. **ORANGE SA**	France	Government of France	23
ORANGE ESPAGNE SA	Spain		
ORANGE POLSKA SA	Poland		
ORANGE ROMANIA SA	Romania		
ORANGE SLOVENSKO AS	Slovenia		
10. **TELEKOM AUSTRIA AG**	Austria	Government of Austria	28
A1 TELEKOM AUSTRIA	Austria		
S1.MOBIL TELEKOMUNIKACIJSKE S.	Slovenia		
MOBILTEL EAD	Bulgaria		
VIPNET DOO	Croatia		
11. **TELIA COMPANY AB**	Sweden	Government of Sweden + Finnish State	37 + 3
SONERA MOBILE NETWORKS OY	Sweden		
STOFA A/S	Denmark		
TELIA EESTI AS	Estonia		
TELIASONERA FINLAND OYJ	Finland		
TELIASONERA MOBILE NETWORKS AB	Sweden		
TELIASONERA SVERIGE AB	Sweden		
TEO LT AB	Lithuania		
UAB OMNITEL	Lithuania		
LATVIJAS MOBILAIS TELEFONS SIA	Latvia		
12. **SES SA**	Luxembourg	Luxembourg State	33
13. **CYTA**	Cyprus	Government of Cyprus	n/a

Source: Author's elaboration from Orbis data.

5.3 DATA

Using the Orbis online Database, maintained by Bureau Van Dijk, a sample of 144 telecom companies from 30 European countries (EU28 Member States plus Norway and Switzerland) was built. The selection process adopted was the following: the top five enterprises by operating revenues were selected for each country, with the exception of Malta (top three) and Cyprus (the largest one only).

After dropping companies with missing financial or ownership information, the number of companies in the list was reduced to 120, among which 72 (60 per cent) are private and 48 (40 per cent) are State-invested. The time span covered ranges from 2006 to 2014, with a total of almost 900 observations. Company distribution across countries is shown in Table 5.2.

Table 5.3 shows that private companies are on average larger than SIEs in terms of total assets, value added and operating revenues, while the opposite holds when the number of employees is considered. However, as shown by the high *p*-values, the differences between sample means are not statistically significant.

Finally, it can be noticed that the share of SIEs listed in the stock exchange is almost identical to the corresponding share of private companies, suggesting that modern SIEs are highly involved in financial markets.

Figure 5.1 illustrates the time-trends of total assets, value added and operating revenues, revealing that the differences found hold over almost the entire period 2006–14. However, these average data hide some important heterogeneity within the two subsamples: some State-invested companies like Deutsche Telekom AG (Germany), Orange SA (France), TeliaSonera AB (Sweden), Telenor ASA (Norway) and Swisscom AG (Switzerland) have an extremely large dimension, even bigger than most of the private companies included in the sample (for example, they all rank within the top 18 companies by operating revenues). On the other hand, within the SIEs' subsample there are small companies like SES SA (Luxembourg), CYTA (Cyprus) and Lattelecom SIA (Latvia).

The same holds in the private subsample, where there can be found giants like Vodafone Plc (UK), Telefónica (Spain) and British Telecom (UK) but also small companies like Go Plc (Malta), UAB Bite Lietuva (Lithuania) and Bulsatcom EAD (Bulgaria). The asymmetric distribution of companies' characteristics within the two different ownership subsamples explains the non-statistically significant differences between sample means.

Similar considerations can be extended to the labour force employed (Figure 5.2). The number of employees is always larger in SIEs except in 2006 and 2011, supporting the hypothesis that they tend to hire more

Table 5.2 Companies' distribution across Europe

Country/Frequency	Total	Private	SIEs
Austria	5	2	3
Belgium	5	3	2
Bulgaria	4	2	2
Croatia	4	2	2
Cyprus	1	0	1
Czech Republic	3	2	1
Denmark	4	2	2
Estonia	2	1	1
Finland	4	2	2
France	5	4	1
Germany	5	4	1
Great Britain	5	5	0
Greece	4	2	2
Hungary	5	3	2
Ireland	4	3	1
Italy	5	4	1
Latvia	3	1	2
Lithuania	4	2	2
Luxembourg	5	4	1
Malta	2	2	0
Netherlands	5	5	0
Norway	3	0	3
Poland	4	1	2
Portugal	4	4	0
Romania	5	2	3
Slovak Republic	4	2	2
Slovenia	2	0	2
Spain	5	4	1
Sweden	5	1	4
Switzerland	5	3	2
Total	120	72	48

labour than private companies in order to target employment objectives (Shleifer, 1998). However, once again the average value masks relevant heterogeneity among companies with the same ownership type.

As far as the economic performance is concerned, it appears clearly from Table 5.3 that SIEs have achieved superior results in all of the indicators considered: EBIT (Earnings Before Interest and Taxes) margin, EBITDA margin and ROA (Return on Assets).[3] Moreover, Figure 5.3 shows that, as for the size variables discussed above, the difference holds for the entire

Table 5.3   Summary statistics

	Full sample	SIEs	Private	*p*-value for means difference
Size				
Total assets (million)	1.090	9.401	11.900	0.154
Value added (million)	3.477	3.293	3.589	0.618
Operating revenues (million)	5.397	4.999	5.648	0.410
No. employees	17.198	17.833	16.790	0.727
Economic performance				
EBIT margin	11.32	14.23	10.90	0.000***
EBITDA margin	28.36	32.43	25.62	0.000***
ROA	6.18	7.61	5.28	0.000***
Listed	30.25%	29.93%	30.46%	

Note: *** significance at 1 per cent level.

Source: Author's elaboration from Orbis data.

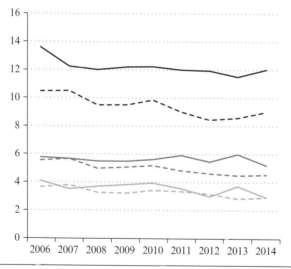

Source: Author's elaboration from Orbis data.

Figure 5.1   Trends of operating revenues, total assets and value added (million euros)

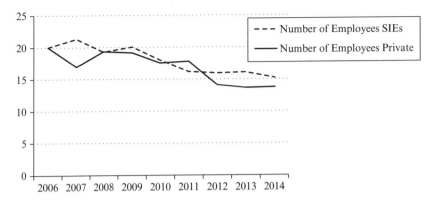

Source: Author's elaboration from Orbis data.

Figure 5.2   Number of employees (thousand)

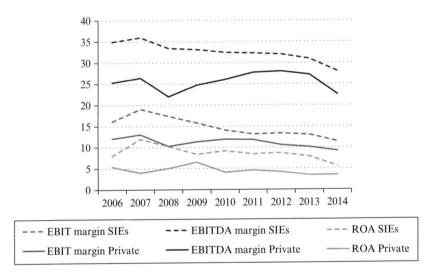

Source: Author's elaboration from Orbis data.

Figure 5.3   Trends of EBIT margin, EBITDA margin and ROA (per cent)

time span under analysis. It is worth noting that the t-tests performed on the equality of means strongly reject the null hypothesis (at the 1 per cent significance level).

To summarize, descriptive statistics suggest no statistically significant difference in size between State-invested and private enterprises but provide evidence that the former perform significantly better in terms of profitability. While this result highlights a strong positive correlation between public ownership and economic performance, it says nothing about the existence of a causal link and the role of other relevant factors driving/explaining such a relationship. To clarify this issue, an econometric analysis is performed in the following section. The aim is to understand whether public ownership is still positively associated with profitability when controlling for potential confounding factors.

5.4 EMPIRICAL ANALYSIS

5.4.1 Econometric Model

Does public ownership still have a positive impact on profitability when other relevant determinants of firm performance are accounted for? To answer this question, the following model is estimated:

$$y_{it} = \beta_0 + \beta_1 public_{it} + \beta_2 X_{it} + \beta_3 GDP\_growth_{ct} + \beta_4 ETCR_{ct} + \delta_t + \gamma_c + \varepsilon_{it} \tag{5.1}$$

where y_{it} is a performance indicator, either the EBIT margin or the ROA.[4] $Public_{it}$ is either a dummy variable, taking value 1 if the company is a SIE and 0 otherwise, or a continuous variable indicating the percentage of shares held by a government or a public authority. The use of a simple dichotomic variable to describe firms' ownership clearly leads to a shrink of statistical variability. Moreover, despite the widely accepted definition of SIEs suggested by Christiansen and Kim (2014) it is clear that companies with limited State-participation may be intrinsically different from fully SOEs. Therefore, also using a continuous specification of the ownership variable is an important way to validate and generalize the estimation results.

X_{it} is a vector of firm-level controls which includes: (1) size variables (since firm dimension may affect performance, for example, via economies of scale), specifically total assets when the performance indicator is the EBIT margin and operating revenues when it is the ROA;[5] (2) a dummy variable taking value 1 if the company is listed on the stock exchange and 0 otherwise.

GDP_growth_{ct} is the yearly GDP growth rate[6] of the country where the company has its seat and allows control of idiosyncratic shocks. $ETCR_{tc}$ is the *aggregated* OECD-ETCR (Energy, Transport and Communications

Regulation) telecommunications indicator.[7] As explained in the first chapter of this book, ETCR indicators summarize regulatory provisions in network industries and are extracted from the ETCR Database which tracks reforms in the Member States in the form of normalized yearly scores given by experts. They are assigned values ranging from 0 to 6, with higher scores associated with more regulated markets.

Finally, δ_t and γ_c are time and country fixed-effects, respectively, accounting for all the variability not explicitly modelled by the regression, while ε_{it} is a random error term.

In case of indirect State-participation, that is, when a given company is in turn held by a State-invested parent company, the following procedure is adopted in order to define the percentage of publicly owned shares to be assigned to the controlled company. If the subsidiary is fully held by the parent company, then it is assigned the same State-participation: for example, Orange Slovensko, which is fully held by Orange SA, is assigned 23 per cent of government shares.

If the parent company partially owns its subsidiary, the percentage of State-owned shares of the parent company is multiplied by the percentage of shares held in the controlled company, which the resulting percentage is assigned to. For example, Deutsche Telecom, whose 31.7 per cent of shares are State-owned, holds a 59 per cent participation in Magyar Telecom. Therefore, Magyar Telekom is assigned (31.7*59)% = 18.7% of State-owned shares. If, in addition to the indirect State-participation, there is also a direct State-participation, then the two participations are summed. For example, Deutsche Telecom holds a 40 per cent participation in OTE, which also records a 10 per cent direct participation held by the Government of Greece. Therefore, the percentage of State-owned shares assigned to OTE is (40*31.7)% + 10% = 22.8%.

5.4.2   Estimation Results

Regression results are shown in Tables 5.4 and 5.5. Columns (1) and (2) report the estimated coefficients when the ownership variable is a dummy, while columns (3) and (4) show the coefficients of the model specifications where public ownership is described by a continuous variable (percentage of public share).

The number of observations is consistently smaller when the ETCR indicator is included in the regressions. However, performing the empirical analysis on this reduced sample, results shown in columns (1) and (3) are qualitatively unaffected.

The regression results confirm that, even when conditioning to the set of covariates included in equation (5.1), public ownership still has a positive

Table 5.4 Influence of public ownership on the EBIT margin

	(1) EBIT margin	(2) EBIT margin	(3) EBIT margin	(4) EBIT margin
SIE	3.848***	3.653***		
	(3.46)	(2.67)		
Public share (%)			0.065***	0.088***
			(2.68)	(2.88)
Total assets (billion)	0.015	0.005	0.018	0.003
	(0.95)	(0.27)	(1.19)	(0.20)
GDP growth	0.126	0.207	0.124	0.201
	(0.93)	(0.97)	(0.91)	(0.95)
Listed	6.623***	8.285***	6.782***	8.646***
	(6.62)	(7.36)	(6.71)	(7.57)
ETCR Telecom		10.79***		10.72***
		(2.66)		(2.69)
Country F.E.	yes	yes	yes	yes
Time F.E.	yes	yes	yes	yes
Cons	18.21***	7.593**	16.95***	5.468
	(8.30)	(3.20)	(8.09)	(1.84)
R^2	0.227	0.253	0.218	0.251
N	871	617	865	615

Note: F.E. is fixed-effects; t-statistics in parentheses; standard errors clustered by country and year; ** $p < 0.05$, *** $p < 0.01$.

and statistically significant impact on company profitability, measured either by the EBIT margin or the ROA. This finding holds for both the discrete and continuous definition of the ownership variable. Specifically, other variables being constant, SIEs display an average profitability bonus of 3.8–3.7 points (depending on whether the ETCR variable is included or not) in terms of EBIT margin and 1.6–1.9 points as far as the ROA is concerned. Looking at the discrete specifications, a unitary increase in the percentage of shares held by a government or public authority results in an average increase of 0.07–0.09 points of the EBIT margin and 0.05–0.06 points of the ROA. Other relevant determinants of company performance are the likelihood of being listed on the stock exchange and market regulation, measured by the ETCR indicator.

Focusing on SIEs, these findings can be interpreted as follows. The probability that a SIE is listed on the stock market is likely to positively affect its performance because it forces the management to satisfy the interests not only of the public but also the private shareholders.

The reform of network industries

Table 5.5   Influence of public ownership on the ROA

	(1) ROA	(2) ROA	(3) ROA	(4) ROA
SIE	1.637*	1.868*		
	(1.93)	(1.79)		
Public share (%)			0.045**	0.060**
			(2.18)	(2.51)
Revenues (billion)	–0.070***	–0.092***	–0.070***	–0.098***
	(2.90)	(3.54)	(2.97)	(3.82)
GDP growth	-0.037	0.074	-0.041	0.068
	(0.38)	(0.57)	(0.42)	(0.53)
Listed	1.666**	2.595***	1.751***	2.839***
	(2.47)	(3.58)	(2.58)	(3.96)
ETCR Telecom		9.595***		9.653***
		(3.62)		(3.67)
Country F.E.	yes	yes	yes	yes
Time F.E.	yes	yes	yes	yes
Cons	4.970***	–19.34***	18.23***	–25.35**
	(4.05)	(2.61)	(8.43)	(3.48)
R^2	0.220	0.240	0.220	0.243
N	884	634	878	632

Note: F.E. is fixed-effects; t-statistics in parentheses; standard errors clustered by country and year; * $p < 0.1$, ** $p < 0.05$, *** $p < 0.01$.

Market regulation has a positive influence on company profitability since a deeply regulated environment may help previously State-owned incumbents to retain high market shares, preserving their stronger market position. However, the size of the ETCR coefficient should be interpreted with caution. As outlined in Chapter 1, ETCR indicators are 'artificial' variables, for which no natural unit of account exists. In particular, the aggregated ETCR index is a mixture of qualitative and quantitative variables aiming to capture the progress of the reforms, whose normalization in a unique scoring system may be problematic to accurately measure a policy reform framework.

5.5   CONCLUSIONS

The present chapter has provided a detailed description of the major State-invested companies currently active in the European telecommunications industry and empirically investigated the differences in profitability with private enterprises. The analysis was performed on a sample of 120 companies from 30 European countries (EU28 plus Norway and Switzerland) whose financial and ownership information was extracted from the Orbis Database and covered the period 2006–14.

The first interesting finding is that, despite the privatization process which occurred in the sector starting from the 1980s, SIEs are still widespread in the European telecom industry: 40 per cent of the companies in our sample are State-participated. Moreover, an in-depth analysis of the ownership relationship linking such companies shows the existence of a thick network of domestic and foreign subsidiaries, suggesting strong participation of SIEs in the market for mergers and acquisitions (see Alonso et al., 2013).

Descriptive statistics showed strong heterogeneity in size within the SIEs' subsample (as well as in the private one) but, on average, companies belonging to different ownership type have no statistically different dimension. On the other hand, balance-sheet data revealed that modern SIEs have achieved higher profitability margins. However, this finding may be driven by several firm- and country-specific characteristics.

To understand whether this result holds when controlling for potentially relevant confounding factors, an econometric analysis was carried out. The aim was to test whether the positive association between public ownership and company profitability still exists when conditioning on additional determinants of performance. The EBIT margin and the ROA were chosen as measures of company profitability.

Regressions results confirmed the positive and statistically significant role of public ownership on both the indicators considered. Other relevant determinants of performance turned out to be the probability of being listed on the stock exchange and the degree of market regulation.

Overall, these findings suggest some considerations about the economic performance of modern SIEs and the quality of their management. Modern SIEs emerged from the processes of liberalization and privatization that took place in Europe over the last three decades. Following market liberalization, even when they are still public, previous incumbents are today no longer monopolists but operate in a mixed oligopoly where they have to compete with private companies in an increasingly international environment.

The competitive pressure exerted by these new market conditions forced governments to appoint qualified management, making it possible that the corporate governance of SIEs is nowadays no less effective than the governance of private companies. The econometric analysis performed suggests that this can be partly explained and confirmed by the fact that a consistent fraction of the European telecommunications SIEs are currently listed on the stock exchange, pushing their management to satisfy the interests not only of the public but also the private shareholders.

It is also likely that SIEs took some benefit in terms of higher market shares from their past monopolistic position and the consequent status of incumbents. For example, they can have benefited from a deep knowledge of the needs and profitability of customer segments, customer loyalty and learning economies.

Indeed, according to regression results, more regulated markets may provide a competitive advantage to former incumbents, preserving their strong market position and thus leading to superior economic achievements.

NOTES

1. This section partly draws from Castelnovo (2016).
2. Following Christiansen and Kim (2014), the term State-invested enterprises (SIEs) is used to denote companies where a share of 10 per cent or more is ultimately owned by the State.
3.

$$EBIT\,margin = \frac{earnings\,before\,interest\,and\,tax}{operating\,revenues}$$

$$EBITDA\,margin = \frac{earnings\,before\,interest,\,tax,\,depreciation\,and\,amortization}{operating\,revenues}$$

4. To limit the influence of outliers the bottom and top 1.5 per cent of each indicator distribution has been trimmed.
5. A specification where the number of employees was also included as a control for firm size was initially considered. However, since the inclusion of this additional covariate gave qualitatively identical results but caused a sample reduction of about 100 observations (because of missing values), it was subsequently dropped from the analysis.
6. This information is obtained from the World Bank Database (http://databank.worldbank.org/data/home.aspx).
7. Source: https://stats.oecd.org/Index.aspx?DataSetCode=ETCR.

REFERENCES

Alonso, J., Clifton, J., Díaz-Fuentes, D., Fernández-Gutiérrez, M. and Revuelta, J. (2013). 'The race for international markets: were privatized telecommunications incumbents more successful than their public counterparts?', *International Review of Applied Economics*, **27**(2), 215–36.

Atkinson, A.B. and Stiglitz, J.E. (1980). *Lectures on Public Economics*, London: McGraw-Hill.

Bacchiocchi, E., Florio, M. and Gambaro, M. (2011). 'Telecom reforms in the UE: prices and consumers' satisfaction', *Telecommunications Policy*, **35**(4), 382–96.

Boardman, A.E. and Vining, A.R. (1989). 'Ownership and performance in competitive environments: a comparison of the performance of private, mixed, and state-owned enterprises', *Journal of Law and Economics*, **32**(1), 1–33.

Boycko, M., Shleifer, A. and Vishny, R. (1996). 'A theory of privatization', *Economic Journal*, **106**(435), 309–19.

Boylaud, O. and Nicoletti, G. (2001). 'Regulation, market structure and performance in telecommunications', *OECD Economic Studies*, **32**(1), 99–142.

Castelnovo, P. (2016). 'State-invested enterprises in the European telecommunications industry: are they competitive players?', *Economia Pubblica/Italian Journal of Public Economics*, **43**(3), 219–40.

Christiansen, H. and Kim, Y. (2014). 'State-invested enterprises in the global marketplace: implications for a level playing field', OECD Corporate Governance Working Paper No. 14, doi: 10.1787/5jz0xvfvl6nw-en.

Clò, S., Ferraris, M. and Florio, M. (2015a). 'Public enterprises in a global perspective in the last decade', *L'industria*, Società editrice il Mulino, **1**, 111–38, doi: 10.1430/79718.

Clò S., Ferraris, M., Florio, M., Vandone, D. and Fiorio, C. (2015b). 'Public enterprises in the market for corporate control: recent worldwide evidence', *Annals of Public and Cooperative Economics*, **86**(4), 559–83.

De Fraja, G. (1993). 'Productive efficiency in public and private firms', *Journal of Public Economics*, **50**(1), 15–30.

Dewenter, K. and Malatesta, P. (2001). 'State-owned and privately owned firms: an empirical analysis of profitability, leverage and labour intensity', *American Economic Review*, **91**(1), 320–34.

Florio, M. (2013). *Network Industries and Social Welfare, The Experiment that Reshuffled European Utilities*, Oxford: Oxford University Press.

Florio, M. (2014). *Applied Welfare Economics. Cost-benefit Analysis of Projects and Policies*, London: Routledge.

Galperin, H. (2007). *New Television, Old Politics: The Transition to Digital TV in the United States and Britain*, Cambridge: Cambridge University Press.

Gasmi, F., Maingard, A., Noumba, P. and Vito, L. (2013). 'The privatization of the fixed-line telecommunications operator in OECD, Latin America, Asia, and Africa: one size does not fit all', *World Development*, **45**, 189–208.

Krueger, A. (1990). 'Government failure in development', *Journal of Economic Perspectives*, **4**(3), 9–23.

Shleifer, A. (1998). 'State versus private ownership', *Journal of Economic Perspectives*, **12**(4), 133–50.

Shleifer, A. and Vishny, R.W. (1993). 'Corruption', *Quarterly Journal of Economics*, **108**(3), 599–617.

Shleifer, A. and Vishny, R.W. (1994). 'Politicians and firms', *Quarterly Journal of Economics*, **109**(4), 995–1025.

Sterlacchini, A. (2012). 'Energy R&D in private and state-owned utilities: an analysis of the major world electric companies', *Energy Policy*, **41**, 494–506.

Sun, Q., Tong, W. and Tong, J. (2002). 'How does government ownership affect firm performance? Evidence from China's privatization experience', *Journal of Business Finance and Accounting*, **29**(1), 1–27.

Willner, J. (2001). 'Ownership, efficiency, and political interference', *European Journal of Political Economy*, **17**(4), 723–48.
Yu, M. (2013). 'State ownership and firm performance: empirical evidence from Chinese listed companies', *China Journal of Accounting Research*, **6**(2), 75–87.

6. National public missions, diversity of operators and competition: postal services in the European Union

Philippe Bance

6.1 INTRODUCTION

Over the past decades, postal services have been radically transformed in a context where markets have been progressively opened to competition and the core activity of mail has contracted. The aim of this contribution is to analyse the characteristics of these changes by examining how national operators with a wide range of characteristics – most being in the public domain – have adapted to this new environment. This chapter also contains a study of how the public service obligations assigned to operators by national authorities are defined and put into action.

The analysis is divided into seven sections and is mainly based on statistical data from a survey by WIK-Consult which took place in 2013 for European authorities (WIK, 2013), and also upon the Organisation for Economic Co-operation and Development Regulation in Energy, Transport and Communications (ETCR) Database indicators of regulation in non-manufacturing sectors (OECD, 2013). Having first set out the initial characteristics of the postal sector (Section 6.2), the chapter subsequently analyses the institutional transformations which have taken place over the last decades and the European policy of market liberalisation in a context where the sector's core activity has been reducing (6.3). Subsequently, there is analysis of developments in the way the sector is managed since the creation of postal companies (6.4), in order to characterise the different natures and strategies of European national operators and the diversity of national markets in Europe (6.5). The following section concerns an analysis of the differences between countries and the development of the boundaries of national public service obligations, which reveal a wide diversity of national conceptions (6.6). We conclude in Section 6.7.

6.2   A GENERAL INTEREST ACTIVITY CARRIED OUT ORIGINALLY WITHIN AN ADMINISTRATIVE FRAMEWORK

The postal service has several old specificities which spring from the public service missions assigned to it. These postal missions started in the seventeenth century in Europe, with most nation states taking responsibility for postal administration, having decided that the service offered by the private sector did not provide sufficient guarantees of reliability for a service which was seen as essential. Postal administrations were subsequently set up across Europe and then across the world as service providers with an extensive public service remit, notably to cover entire national territories at low costs. Tariff equalisation became common practice and inter-customer transfers or cross subsidies between the different types of activity allowed unprofitable productions to be financed.

In the nineteenth century and a good part of the twentieth century, postal services contributed to the overall access to services and to economic development. Any reference to a competition-based model was thus excluded, according to a logical outline which defined a monopoly as the way of providing the best services to the population and nations.[1] It was initially a question of socialising the poorest and most isolated users, guaranteeing that social links could be maintained in rural areas, binding the national territory together and contributing to economic development.

This interventionist approach of taking into account the general interest was called into question after the Washington Consensus of the 1980s, driven notably by the reforms carried out by certain European Union (EU) countries and by the EU itself, which opened the postal sector up to competition.

6.3   A EUROPEAN PROCESS OF POSTAL LIBERALISATION WITH DIFFERENT NATIONAL TRAJECTORIES AND CARRIED OUT IN A CONTEXT OF REDUCTION IN THE CORE ACTIVITY

The policy driven by the EU advanced via a conception whose aim was to open public services – or more precisely according to European terminology, Services of General Economic Interest (SGEI) – up to competition, which can be described as teleological. It was thus a question of progressively liberalising these sectors and, in this case, 'to complete the EU's internal market for postal services and to ensure, via an appropriate regulatory framework, that the general public are permanently provided with reliable and good quality postal services at affordable prices' (Directive 97/67/CE). Three postal directives in fact set the rhythm of the liberalisation agenda. The first (97/67/CE) set up the regulatory framework which defined the minimum characteristics for a universal postal service: common limits for reserved areas (excluded from competition); applicable pricing principles; quality standards; harmonisation mechanisms; creation of independent national regulatory bodies. The second directive (2002/39/CE) set out the stages for the progressive opening of the market by progressively setting the limits of the reserved areas which concerned: letters weighing less than 100 grams and costing less than three times the base rate until 1 January 2003; letters weighing less than 50 grams and costing less than two-and-a-half times the base rate until 1 January 2006. Finally, Directive (2008/6/CE) carried out the last stage of abolition of all reserved areas, which was complete on 1 January 2012.[2]

Although the EU accorded a relaxation of the time limits involved, each Member State had a duty to apply the European reforms according to EU specifications. The national regulatory bodies were set up, in accordance with European rules, to ensure that free and fair competition was upheld. They delivered licences to operators but also specific public service obligations as set out in national legislation.

OECD (2013) indicators of regulation in non-manufacturing sectors show that regulatory barriers restricting entry, displayed in the 'Entry'[3] column, have almost completely disappeared due to the European reforms (Table 6.1). On a scale of 0 to 6, with 0 signifying the absence of any regulatory barriers to entry, all countries were at the lowest possible level in 2013, apart from Italy and Portugal who were at level 1. However, national characteristics and trajectories differed across different countries. From 1975 to 1990, the level of entry barriers was initially very high (4–6) in a majority of current EU countries. During the same period, other countries had much lower levels, reflecting the existence of different national options, which were more liberal: Spain 1; Austria, Greece, Netherlands and Sweden 2; United Kingdom 3 (1975–79), then 2; Belgium and Ireland 3.

Differing trajectories were also observed in the pace of the reforms carried out in the 1990s and 2000s. For some countries (France, Hungary, Italy, Poland, Portugal), the entry indicator decreased significantly under the effect of European reforms, but with a desire to take time in order to adapt historical operators. Other countries, in contrast, saw their indicators fall very rapidly, such as Finland which went from 4 in 1994 to 0 in 1995 and Germany from 6 in 1989 to 2 in 1990. Yet for other countries, the lowering of regulatory barriers occurred very early: Sweden was the pioneer country where the sector was fully liberalised by 1994 ('Entry':

Table 6.1 Regulation indicators in network sectors (energy, transport and communication) and post in 2013

Country	Level per country and criteria					Difference with the EU average level				
	All sectors	Post				All sectors	Post			
	Overall	Overall	Entry	Public ownership	Market structure	Overall	Overall	Entry	Public ownership	Market structure
Austria	1.55	1.70	0.00	3.11	2.00	-0.55	-0.66	-0.07	-0.99	-0.94
Belgium	1.84	1.67	0.00	3.00	2.00	-0.26	-0.69	-0.07	-1.10	-0.94
Bulgaria	2.45	3.00	0.00	5.00	4.00	0.35	0.64	-0.07	0.90	1.06
Croatia	2.75	2.00	0.00	5.00	1.00	0.66	-0.36	-0.07	0.90	-1.94
Cyprus	2.64	3.00	0.00	5.00	4.00	0.54	0.64	-0.07	0.90	1.06
Czech Republic	2.01	2.00	0.00	5.00	1.00	-0.09	-0.36	-0.07	0.90	-1.94
Denmark	1.61	1.53	0.00	1.60	3.00	-0.49	-0.83	-0.07	-2.50	0.06
Estonia	2.40	3.00	0.00	5.00	4.00	0.30	0.64	-0.07	0.90	1.06
Finland	2.47	3.33	0.00	4.00	6.00	0.37	0.97	-0.07	-0.10	3.06
France	2.51	2.67	0.00	5.00	3.00	0.41	0.31	-0.07	0.90	0.06
Germany	1.27	1.67	0.00	2.02	3.00	-0.83	-0.69	-0.07	-2.08	0.06
Greece	2.55	2.87	0.00	4.60	4.00	0.45	0.51	-0.07	0.50	1.06
Hungary	1.73	3.00	0.00	5.00	4.00	-0.37	0.64	-0.07	0.90	1.06
Ireland	2.21	2.67	0.00	5.00	3.00	0.11	0.31	-0.07	0.90	0.06
Italy	2.01	3.33	1.00	5.00	4.00	-0.09	0.97	0.93	0.90	1.06
Latvia	2.66	2.00	0.00	4.00	–	0.56	-0.36	-0.07	-0.10	–
Lithuania	2.02	3.00	0.00	5.00	4.00	-0.08	0.64	-0.07	0.90	1.06
Luxembourg	2.73	2.33	0.00	5.00	2.00	0.63	-0.03	-0.07	0.90	-0.94
Malta	2.28	1.00	0.00	0.00	3.00	0.18	-1.36	-0.07	-4.10	0.06
Netherlands	1.57	0.67	0.00	0.00	2.00	-0.53	-1.69	-0.07	-4.10	-0.94

Poland	2.34	2.00	0.00	5.00	1.00	0.24	-0.36	-0.07	0.90	-1.94
Portugal	2.18	3.00	1.00	5.00	3.00	0.08	0.64	0.93	0.90	0.06
Romania	1.97	1.67	0.00	4.00	1.00	-0.13	-0.69	-0.07	-0.10	-1.94
Slovak Republic	1.88	2.33	0.00	5.00	2.00	-0.22	-0.03	-0.07	0.90	-0.94
Slovenia	2.90	3.33	0.00	5.00	5.00	0.80	0.97	-0.07	0.90	2.06
Spain	1.59	2.33	0.00	5.00	2.00	-0.50	-0.03	-0.07	0.90	-0.94
Sweden	1.87	2.63	0.00	3.40	4.50	-0.23	0.27	-0.07	-0.70	1.56
United Kingdom	0.79	2.33	0.00	5.00	2.00	-1.31	-0.03	-0.07	0.90	-0.94
Average EU	2.10	2.36	0.07	4.06	2.94	0	0	0	0	0

Source: OECD, ETCR Database and author's computations based on ETCR indicators.

0), Austria was at 1 by 1991, the Netherlands at 1 by 1996, the United Kingdom, which reached 2 in 1981, was at 1 in 1999. These countries committed earlier and more clearly to the liberalisation process.[4]

However, being a pioneer in terms of opening the market does not necessarily mean that a country has the most competitive market. As the OECD 'Market Structures' indicator[5] shows in Table 6.1, Sweden was at level 4.5 in 2013 although it was still at 6 in 2009. Austria, the Netherlands and the United Kingdom, who were at 2 in 2013 (that is, not at a level much lower than the EU average of 2.94) were, respectively, at 4.5 in 2000, 4 in 2002 and 4.5 in 2010. The opening of the market does not therefore necessarily mean that competitors will enter it, especially if they are concerned about being in competition with well-established competitors. Other countries have a market structures indicator which has risen in recent years, such as Hungary which went from 3 to 4 in 2011 or Ireland which went from 2 to 3 in 2010; this shows that a move towards re-concentration cannot be ruled out.

The liberalisation process also needs to be put into a general context of a significant reduction of the postal sector's core activity, namely, mail. WIK, carried out for the EU, provides some highly illuminating data on this point. The 'Volume Development' index (VDI, indicator of letter post volume) of selected Universal Service Providers (USPs) (Austria, Denmark, France, Germany, Netherland, Sweden, United Kingdom) quickly decreased (between 10 to 35 per cent) from 2007 to 2012 (WIK, 2013, final report, p. 205).

The large-scale and almost generalised reduction in the core activity of mail, ultimately connected to the development of the competition (substitution by electronic communications) can, however, be differentiated across various zones and countries. The VDI evolution is, on average, to –3.9 per cent across countries in the west, to –6 per cent across those in the south and to –8 per cent in the east of the EU. In the west, it is much more pronounced for Denmark, the Netherlands and Norway (less than –6 per cent). In the south, only Portugal and Italy saw a low reduction in activity with other countries being above –6 per cent (and in some cases by a very clear margin). In the east, the situation is highly disparate but the reduction was very high (–8 and up to –11 per cent) for the three Baltic countries, Bulgaria and Romania (WIK, 2013, final report, p. 169).

However, this reduction in mail activity is compensated by the development of package delivery activities, which is itself driven by new information technology and online ordering and it has become highly competitive due to a high level of presence in the sector (notably of UPS and TNT for express delivery). But this development is spread very unevenly over the different zones and countries in question. The number of parcels per capita is four times higher in countries in the west of Europe than in the south and ten times higher than in the east. The situation is also very disparate from one country to another. The number of parcels per capita is particularly high in Denmark and the United Kingdom (more than twice the European average) but also in Austria, with France being close to the average of the 28 countries in question and the others being significantly below the average (WIK, 2013, final report, pp. 224–5).

In this institutional context, the organisations in charge of postal activity have seen transformations in the way their productive activity takes place, with the creation of public enterprises being a necessary preliminary step.

6.4   A GENERALISED CORPORATISATION AND A PRIVATISATION PROCESS INITIALISED BY CERTAIN COUNTRIES

The liberalisation process required postal activity to be removed from administrative management in order for reforms to be correctly implemented (OECD, 2001). While postal companies needed to be created in order for the sector to be opened to competition, there was also a requirement to remove productive postal and telecommunications services from the old administrations which were in charge of both. This process of corporatisation, before being initiated into the European regulatory framework, was put in place by the Netherlands where, in 1986, the postal administration was broken up in order to open to competition.

Driven by the EU, the wider idea was to rapidly create telecoms companies in order to liberalise a market which was in the middle of a technological revolution and thus subject to huge development (only Luxembourg kept a company which was in charge of both postal and telecom activities). For postal activity, the corporatisation process often took place in a much less prescribed fashion such as in France, via transitory legal measures with adoption, first, of public establishment status before proceeding to company status. This was also a means of avoiding hostile reactions or the worry which can be created by the privatisation conferred by company status.[6]

In terms of management methods, the public enterprise with the state as majority shareholder is the most widespread management method in Europe. WIK (2013, country reports) provides useful information in this area about state holdings in EU national postal companies (mostly relating to 2012, sometimes to 2011, occasionally to 2010). The results show that 19 (out of 28 companies) are public enterprises, which are 100 per cent owned by the national state. The Swedish and Danish postal companies can be added to this number as they are also 100 per cent public but held by two different states. Other postal companies are majority public holdings (directly or indirectly). From highest public holdings to lowest, these are the postal company of Greece (90 per cent), Romania (75 per cent), Austria (52.8 per cent), Belgium (50 per cent). According to WIK, the postal companies of the Netherlands and Malta (sold in 2002 and 2008, respectively) were privately held in 2012 with no public holdings. However, in 2013, the United Kingdom sold shares in Royal Mail in 2013 and 2015, reducing its holding from 100 to 30 and then to 13 per cent of social capital (with the aim of relinquishing all shares). The German postal company is in fact mainly privatised, with the government retaining only 21 per cent of the capital, although it remains the biggest shareholder due to high number of small shareholders. As things stand, the privatised companies belong to countries which (Malta excepted) view the liberalisation process as an opportunity to roll their national companies out on an international scale to put them among the biggest operators in the world. The logic behind this is based on the idea that operators which are subject to liberalisation and then privatisation will be more efficient. These countries are also among those, as we will see, which have the least stringent (or in Germany's case few) public service obligations, as such obligations obviously appear as possible obstacles to business efficiency. The German postal company displays a very proactive approach to expansion into international markets far beyond simple postal activities.

Future privatisation, specifically the purchase of national postal companies by large-scale European operators who benefit from big economies of scale, should not be ruled out, notably as a result of financial strife undergone by states (such as Greece or even Italy). However, two aspects limit the scale of this. The first is a certain reluctance on the part of private capital to take on mail activities which are undergoing strong reductions and public service obligations which make it difficult to justify the level of investment required. The second aspect is that public authorities want to keep control of companies which are widely present in their countries as they are big employers and important in society.

The OECD 'Public Ownership' indicators[7] (Table 6.1) confirm that in 2013 there is strong public control over the postal sector but also a variety of national conceptions. Public control is indeed situated at a high average level of 4.1 for EU countries (still using a scale of 0–6),[8] 17 EU countries are still at level 5, one at 4.6 and three at 4. Exceptions to these general characteristics are Austria, Belgium and Sweden, which are between 3 and 4; Germany at 2; Denmark at 1.6; Malta and the Netherlands at 0. The characteristics of postal companies are diverse and thus require more precise analysis.

6.5   NATIONAL COMPANIES WITH VERY DIVERSE CHARACTERISTICS ON NATIONAL MARKETS WHICH ARE STILL FRAGMENTED

Despite the will of European authorities to open markets up to competition, these remain highly partitioned and dominated by national companies created by 'historical administrations'. These companies have very different sizes according to the markets they serve: in 2012, still according to WIK data, companies' revenues went from 31 million euros for the smallest of them (the Cyprus postal company) to 31 billion euros for the largest; the German Deutsche Post is in second position, the French and Italian postal companies close together with 21.7 billion, in fourth, and some way behind, the British Royal Mail with 11 billion and the Danish and Dutch postal companies with nearly 4.4 billion. In terms of the workforces, these are between a few hundred (around 600 employees for the Maltese postal company) to over 472 000 (Deutsche Post). Yet national companies are all dominant on the highly partitioned domestic mail markets: concerning the 24 countries for which the information is available, 14 cover 95 to 100 per cent of activity, 8 between 90 and 95 per cent, with the other two at 87 per cent (Czech Republic) and 80 per cent (Croatia).

A big disparity can also be observed in the geographical position and the revenue structures of these companies. Concerning the 21 companies for which data is available, eight make all of their revenue on the domestic market and seven make 90 to 99 per cent. But some companies have much lower levels, showing that they have expanded internationally:[9] Royal Mail (84 per cent), Österreichische Post (73 per cent), PostNL (63 per cent), and most particularly Deutsche Post (30 per cent).[10]

These disparities also spring from the distribution of the companies' activities. A distinction can be made between companies whose activity essentially consists of mails and parcels (Courier, Express and Postal – CEP) and those which have diversified significantly, especially into banking and insurance, logistics and transport or retail. Concerning the 23 EU companies for which useable data is available,[11] the largest number can be found in the first category: more than three-quarters of their revenue comes from letters and parcels for 13 of these companies. But other companies have a very different profile. Financial services make up 75 per cent of revenue for Poste Italiane (including insurance), 40 per cent for Poste Romana, 31 per cent for Magyar Post, 20 per cent for La Poste, 17 per cent for Elta (Greece). Freight transportation and logistics represent 52 per cent of Deutsche Post's revenue, 35 per cent for Itella's (Finland). Finally, retail accounts for 21 per cent of An Post's (Ireland) revenue and 16 per cent of La Poste's.

Operators' diversification strategies are thus varied. They can be analysed as products of the history of each company, forged by acquisition merger opportunities or demands for intervention by public authorities, and which is translated, as the evolutionary theory shows, by path dependence (Nelson and Winter, 1982).

However, in the postal sector, operators often seek to benefit from proximity relation which comes from the activity to use the company's good name for commercial purposes. Thus French La Poste now provides a range of home services as a complementary option alongside postal delivery workers' activities.[12] The commercial approach, which is taking an ever more important role by selling products alongside postal services, is a way for companies to adapt to the reduction in the core activity and to cover costs in a context of states requiring companies to balance their books (which they usually manage to do)[13] and in which state subsidies are strictly controlled by the EU to ensure that they are only given for official public service missions. Some operators, among the most powerful (German, French, Austrian, Dutch), have adapted to this new environment by targeting international expansion, notably driven by states.

However, it must be asked whether the development of multiservice strategies and international expansion have an impact on public service obligations in Europe.

6.6 NATIONAL UNIVERSAL SERVICE BOUNDARIES OF VARIABLE GEOMETRY AND GENERALLY SHRINKING APART FROM THE CENTRAL CORE

The obligations of universal service which apply to the postal sector are more or less spread evenly across all Member States, as WIK (2013, country reports) shows. The WIK report divides the boundary of universal service obligations into seven categories: single-piece letter post; bulk letters; bulk advertisements; newspapers, magazines; non-priority correspondence; single-piece parcels; bulk parcels. The report also considers that each category includes three duties: ensured, price regulated, service standards as shown in Table 6.2. This thereby provides, for each country, 21 operating criteria which can have a positive response, a negative response or no response at all about its provision. In addition to this data, there is other information about the number of days of mail and parcel services, which establishes where the country stands regarding the minimum number of service days (five) stipulated by European regulation.

*Table 6.2   Universal service boundary for all EU countries per nature of
provision*

Services	Number of YES	Number of NO	No Answer	YES/ All criteria	YES/ Answers
Single-piece letter post (fastest standard category)					
Ensured	28	0	0	100%	100%
Price regulated	28	0	0	100%	100%
Service standards	28	0	0	100%	100%
Total	84	0	0	100%	100%
Bulk letters					
Ensured	15	13	0	54%	54%
Price regulated	15	6	7	54%	71%
Service standards	11	11	6	39%	50%
Total	41	30	13	49%	58%
Bulk advertisements					
Ensured	10	18	0	36%	36%
Price regulated	11	12	5	39%	48%
Service standards	6	15	7	21%	29%
Total	27	45	12	32%	38%
Newspapers, magazines, etc.					
Ensured	12	16	0	43%	43%
Price regulated	11	11	6	39%	50%
Service standards	6	15	7	21%	29%
Total	29	42	13	35%	41%
Non-priority correspondence					
Ensured	15	13	0	54%	54%
Price regulated	16	5	7	57%	76%
Service standards	12	6	10	43%	67%
Total	43	24	17	51%	64%
Single-piece parcels					
Ensured	28	0	0	100%	100%
Price regulated	28	0	0	100%	100%
Service standards	18	10	0	64%	64%
Total	74	10	0	88%	88%
Bulk parcels					
Ensured	12	16	0	43%	43%
Price regulated	11	10	7	39%	52%
Service standards	6	17	5	21%	26%
Total	29	43	12	35%	40%

Source: Author's computations based on WIK country reports (2013), B4 Scope of
Universal Service, for each EU country.

This information primarily allows the general characteristics of universal service in Europe to be established.

This presentation and these calculations show that it is possibly to categorise a 'universal service universally delivered' in all European countries for two of the categories and for five duty criteria (with 100 per cent 'yes' answers on its provision for all EU countries): single-piece letter post (ensured – price regulated, service standards) and single-piece parcels (ensured – price regulated). Outside this central core of universal services, the results are very disparate for the other criteria: the achievement rate reaches just over 50 per cent of the criteria for bulk letters and non-priority correspondence; it is just over 40 per cent for bulk parcels and newspapers-magazines, and weaker (36 per cent) for bulk advertisements.

The unequal geographical distribution of the universal service can be more precisely analysed via a country-by-country examination of the criteria ratios which are fulfilled. This allows three groups of countries to be identified: those with an extended universal service boundary (Table 6.3), a middle one (Table 6.4) and a restricted one (Table 6.5).

The first group of ten countries with a wide boundary, presented in Table 6.3, is diverse: it consists of 'northern EU countries' (Austria, Belgium, Denmark and France), but also of 'southern and eastern' countries (Greece, Hungary, Malta, Portugal, Romania and Slovakia). Our interpretation is that in these countries the public service tradition and the affinity of the population with their postal services have led to wider legislation. For four of these countries, Belgium, France and Malta as well as Denmark for letters only, this extensive conception of public service has meant that the service is provided six days a week, which is above the European minimum. The universal service obligations are therefore set well above the minimum level set by the 1997 European Directive. This has also led to high standards of quality in the universal service and the setting up, such as in France, of a 'postal service compensation fund' to deal with any shortfall in revenue from universal services. Beyond these universal service postal missions, other missions are also specified by law in France and they are connected to three different areas: covering territory with a dense spread of 'contact points' across the country; distribution of the political press to ensure pluralism; financial services including the provision of universally accessible bank accounts thanks to La Banque Postale (Bance and Rey, 2015; Borsenberger and Joram, 2016).

The second group of countries, with a middle boundary, is also made up of apparently diverse members as shown in Table 6.4 (from the 'west': Germany, Ireland, Luxembourg; from the 'south' Cyprus, Spain, Italy; from the 'east' Croatia, Latvia), which are difficult to consider as a singular set due to the proportions of their replies being different and fairly

Table 6.3   Countries with extended boundary of universal service

	Austria	Belgium	Denmark	France	Greece	Hungary	Malta	Portugal	Romania	Slovakia
Number of YES	17	18	17	16	15	14	18	16	16	19
Number of NO	2	3	2	5	6	0	1	3	5	2
No answer	2	0	2	0	0	7	2	2	0	0
Answers/all criteria	90%	100%	90%	100%	100%	100%	90%	90%	100%	100%
Rate of YES/all criteria	81%	86%	81%	76%	71%	67%	86%	67%	76%	90%
Rate of YES/answers	89%	86%	89%	76%	71%	67%	95%	67%	76%	90%
All items: differential/EU of YES	+25%	+30%	+25%	+20%	+16%	+11%	+30%	+20%	+20%	+35%
Answers: differential/EU of YES	+25%	+22%	+25%	+12%	+7%	+3%	+31%	+20%	+12%	+26%
Days per week: letters	5	5	6	6	5	5	6	5	5	5
Days per week: parcels	5	5	5	6	5	5	6	5	5	5

Source: Author's computations based on WIK country reports (2013), B4 Scope of Universal Service, for each EU country.

Table 6.4   Countries with a middle boundary of universal service

	Croatia	Cyprus	Germany	Ireland	Italy	Latvia	Luxembourg	Spain
Number of YES	9	11	9	10	11	13	10	12
Number of NO	4	9	5	5	10	8	6	6
No answer	8	1	7	6	0	0	5	3
Answers/all criteria	62%	52%	67%	71%	100%	100%	81%	86%
Rate of YES/all criteria	43%	55%	43%	48%	52%	62%	48%	57%
Rate of YES/answers	69%	95%	64%	67%	52%	62%	59%	67%
All items: differential/EU of YES	−13%	−3%	−13%	−8%	−3%	+6%	−8%	+1%
Answers: differential/EU of YES	+5%	−9%	0%	+3%	−12%	−2%	−5%	+3%
Days per week: letters	5	5	6	5	5	5	5	5
Days per week: parcels	5	n/d	6	5	5	5	5	5

Source: Author's computations based on WIK country reports (2013), B4 Scope of Universal Service, for each EU country.

weak for half of them (only Italy and Latvia provided full replies to the questions in hand). The intermediary position of these countries, however, appears to be the result of an attempt by public authorities to implement reforms which will facilitate the opening of the postal sector to competition in a context (except for Spain) where the reduction of core activity is somewhat less marked than for the last category of countries.

The third category, which is made up of the final ten EU Member States, stands out due to a very restricted boundary of universal service (Table 6.5). It is made up of countries from the west (Finland, Netherlands, Sweden, United Kingdom) and from the east (Bulgaria, Czech Republic, Estonia, Lithuania, Poland, Slovenia). This group appears to be fairly homogeneous and characterised by countries which have made the most radical choice in terms of using reforms of the postal sector to renounce public control over an extended boundary of universal service.

This is notably the case for Eastern European countries which are inclined towards radical reforms but also for countries from the west. In the west, in the United Kingdom and particularly in the Netherlands where liberalisation was initiated, public service missions have been reduced to the bare minimum, with universal service applying only to single-piece letters and parcels (the United Kingdom but also Finland extending this to non-priority correspondence). All the Eastern European countries in this category (apart from Slovenia) also display a universal service which applies only to single-piece letters and parcels in addition to non-priority correspondence (Croatia, which is in the second category could also fit into this one).

However, public missions must be compensated for the portion of the net cost of the universal service obligations (calculated on the basis of a 'profitability cost approach'), either from general tax revenues or from a compensation fund financed by mandatory contributions from postal service providers. If compensation funds were created in several countries of the EU during the last years, they do not play a significant role to finance public missions (WIK, 2013, final report, pp. 153–4), and tax revenues miss financing public mission obligations in a context of reducing public deficits. In these conditions, in conformity with the expectations we could have about the consequences of liberalisation (Bance, 2007), it appears that there is a trend towards a more limited definition of the universal service obligation. Whereas in 2010, 20 Member States included bulk letters in the universal service, only 17 have done so in 2013. For direct mails, the number of Member States fells from 16 to 10; for periodicals, from 16 to 13. In contrast, the number of Member States including bulk parcels in the universal service obligation has increased from 9 to 11 (WIK, 2013, country reports, pp. 130–31).

Table 6.5 Countries with restricted boundary of universal service

	Bulgaria	Czech Republic	Estonia	Finland	Lithuania	Netherlands	Poland	Slovenia	Sweden	United Kingdom
Number of YES	9	5	5	8	7	5	9	9	10	9
Number of NO	8	6	10	13	8	16	12	7	11	12
No answer	4	10	6	0	6	0	0	5	0	0
Answers/all criteria	81%	52%	71%	100%	71%	100%	100%	76%	100%	100%
Rate of YES/all criteria	43%	24%	24%	38%	33%	24%	43%	43%	48%	43%
Rate of YES/answers	53%	45%	33%	38%	47%	24%	43%	56%	48%	43%
All items: differential/EU of YES	−13%	−32%	−32%	−18%	−22%	−32%	−13%	−13%	−8%	−13%
Answers: differential/EU of YES	−11%	−19%	−31%	−26%	−17%	−40%	−21%	−8%	−16%	−21%
Days per week: letters	5	5	5	5	5	5	5	5	5	5
Days per week: parcels	5	5	5	5	5	5	5	5	5	5

Source: Author's computations based on WIK country reports (2013), B4 Scope of Universal Service, for each EU country.

The difficulties in financing extended universal service obligations and the desire on the part of public authorities not to restrict commercial development of companies constitute key factors.

6.7   CONCLUSION

The analysis in this chapter shows the complexity and diversity which currently characterise the 'European postal services market'. This is a market which many consider to be a far cry from the single postal market that the EU wishes to put in place.

National markets remain highly partitioned in the letters sector with operators originating from national administrations still undertaking most of the domestic activity. Although competition does exist with some intensity in some sectors, such as express parcel deliveries, it remains weak in the declining letters market, where national companies of various sizes undertake the lion's share of activities. These companies are, for the most part, entirely publicly owned and have widely nationally defined public service obligations.

However, opening the market to competition has led to the emergence of very large European operators (German Deutsche Post, British Royal Mail, PostNL) which are based on a completely different development model. Put in place with the approval and under the auspices of public authorities, it has led to the privatisation of operators with a view to expanding large national companies on an international scale, notably via external growth into world markets. These companies have clearly distinct approaches: the German company is relying on multiple activities by diversifying well beyond the postal sector (notably into logistics). With this outgoing and adventurous model in mind, other European, publicly owned enterprises (and particularly the largest ones whose room for manoeuvre is greater than small national postal services) are adapting in different ways to this new environment, with multifarious plans. Thus, French company La Poste is expanding internationally by relying on multiservice propositions as well as the synergy between and extension of commercial activities which is linked to an extended public service remit. Poste Italiane remains solely in its national market but with the greatest part of its activity in the financial sector and in insurance.

The reading of these strategies put in place by national operators should be based on differing national histories and cultures of strong public services, whose effects remain in the current day despite the European liberalisation process and the desire to set up a single market. The extent of public service obligations, which each country has defined in accordance with the European regulatory framework, reveals a great deal about this permanence of diversity. Countries which have a vision of extended public service obligations are starkly differentiated from those whose vision of obligations is more restricted. These latter ones reduce the universal service to the minimum boundaries required by the European regulatory framework. Moreover, it must be acknowledged that among the countries whose public service obligations are the least widely extended are those states which have entirely or almost entirely privatised the relevant companies (Netherlands, United Kingdom) or have become minority shareholders (Germany), notably in order to encourage international expansion.

These considerations, in turn, lead to reflections upon the scope of thinking by economists about the 'diversity of capitalisms' (Amable, 2005), which underlines the existence and the permanence of different capitalist models within globalisation. It is then possible to wonder whether the place and the role granted to public services (and even to public property) allow us to differentiate national types of capitalism, yet which in Europe are subject to a common framework of liberalisation.

However, the trajectories taken by the postal sector raise questions about the existence, and the capacity to maintain, of such national models of public services anchored in societal frameworks founded on the culture of public service. The policy of openness to competition has created a general contraction of public service missions in the postal sector, beyond the core of universal postal service. Public missions are difficult to finance in a context of shrinking basic postal activity, depletion of public resources and the weak deployment of national compensation funds for public service obligations. In this context, including the virtues of free and undistorted competition in a European-wide framework is not conducive to the reflection and implementation of future policies based on the introduction of new public missions. Faced with the changes in the sector and the rise of digital technology, it necessary to seek to redefine these missions and their financing conditions in support of policies of social and territorial cohesion and in response to new citizen expectations, in the postal sector as in other public services (CIRIEC, 2004). The idea needs to be held up against other areas of public service.

NOTES

1. Legal formalisation in France was provided by the 'Rolland Laws' based around the principles of equality, continuity, mutability (or adaptability) of the service.
2. Full opening of the market was set for 31 December 2010, but certain Member States obtained a delay until 1 January 2012: Cyprus, Czech Republic, Greece, Hungary, Latvia, Lithuania, Luxembourg, Malta, Poland, Romania and Slovakia.

3. For the OECD, the indicator *entry* is based on legal limitations on the number of competitors allowed.

4. In the Netherlands, by 1989 the post office was turned into a public limited company (KPN) and, in 1989, KPN saw reserved areas limited to letters up to 500 grams (Larcher, 2003) followed by full opening to competition in 2006. In the United Kingdom, the government opened the postal sector to competition in 2000 and Royal Mail was fully opened to competition on 1 January 2006.

5. A low-level indicator for *market structure* is based on the market share of new entrants in each of the services covered by the indicator to gauge the extent to which existing regulations actually succeed in promoting competition.

6. For the first time in France, a citizens' vote was organised on 3 October 2009 along the lines of a referendum and by a national committee which opposed postal privatisation. There were ten thousand polling stations in the country and over two million people voted.

7. For OECD, indicators for *public ownership* record the extent of government control in the sector.

8. By comparison with other sectors, the indicator in 2013 is close to 5.1 for railways, 3.5 for electricity, 2.5 for air transport and 1.3 for telecoms.

9. Among the largest operators, La Poste, for which WIK does not provide data, is at 79.1 per cent of turnover made in France in 2015, according to the group's own figures. In contrast, the Italian postal company shows a rate of 100 per cent.

10. According to the group's 2016 figures, the breakdown of turnover is as follows: Germany (29.5 per cent), Europe (32.1 per cent), Americas (17.4 per cent), Asia/Pacific (17 per cent) and others (4 per cent).

11. Luxembourg's PST is excluded from this as most of its revenue (64 per cent) comes from telecommunications.

12. These services are reading water, gas or electricity meters, delivery of shopping including medicines, collection of paper, installation of TV boxes, contact with isolated people, driving instructors, meal deliveries.

13. All EU postal companies are making a surplus in the same survey year (2012 or 2011) with two exceptions: Poste Romana (EBIT of –4.2 per cent) and Slovenska Posta (–2.3 per cent).

REFERENCES

Amable, B. (2005), *Les cinq capitalismes. Diversité des systèmes économiques et sociaux dans la mondialisation*, Paris: Seuil.

Bance, P. (2007), 'Les services postaux', in *Les services publics face aux mutations économiques et sociales*, Les Cahiers français, La documentation française, July–August.

Bance, P. and Rey, N. (2015), 'La Poste: Emblème du service public à la française ou futur groupe public européen', in CIRIEC, L. Bernier (ed.), *Public Enterprises Today: Missions, Performance and Governance*, Brussels: Peter Lang, pp. 335–65.

Borsenberger, C. and Joram, D. (2016), 'La contribution de La Poste à la cohésion économique', in P. Bance (ed.), *Quel modèle d'Etat stratège en France?*, Mont-Saint-Aignan: PURH, pp. 349–68.

CE, Directive 97/67/EC, 15 December 1997, Première Directive postale, Eur-lex, available at http://eur-lex.europa.eu/legal-content/fr/ALL/?uri=CELEX:31997L0067 (accessed 9 August 2017).

CE, Directive 2002/39/EC, 10 June 2002, Seconde Directive postale, Eur-Lex,

available at http://eur-lex.europa.eu/legal-content/en/ALL/?uri=celex%3A32002L
0039 (accessed 9 August 2017).

CE, Directive 2008/6/CE, 20 February 2008, Troisième Directive postale, Eur-
Lex, available at http://eur-lex.europa.eu/legal-content/FR/TXT/HTML/?uri=
CELEX:32008L0006 (accessed 9 August 2017).

CIRIEC (2004), 'Contribution of Services of General Interest to Economic, Social
and Territorial Cohesion', for the European Commission – DG Regio, available
at http://www.ciriec.ulg.ac.be/wp-content/uploads/2015/12/dgregio_2004-en.pdf
(accessed 9 August 2017).

Larcher, G. (2003), *La Poste: le temps de la dernière chance*, Information report,
French Senate, No. 344, available at https://www.senat.fr/rap/r02-344/r02-344.html
(accessed 9 August 2017).

Nelson, R. and Winter, S. (1982), *An Evolutionary Theory of Economic Change*.
Cambridge, MA: Belknap Press of Harvard University Press.

OECD (2001), 'Revue sur le droit et la politique de la concurrence, Promotion de la
concurrence dans les services postaux', Volume 3 – 2001/1, Paris.

OECD (2013), ETCR Database, Regulation in network sectors (Energy, Transport
and Communications), Paris.

WIK-Consult (2013), *Main Developments in the Postal Sector (2010–2013)*, Study
for the European Commission, DG for Internal Market and Services. Final
Report and Country Reports available at Sector Studies 2013, https://ec.europa.
eu/growth/sectors/postal-services/studies_en (accessed 9 August 2017).

PART II

Empirical evaluations

7. Does public ownership provide affordable and reliable electricity to household customers? Case studies of electricity sector reforms in the UK, France, Germany and Italy

Ajla Cosic, Lea Diestelmeier, Alexandru Maxim, Tue Anh Nguyen and Nicolò Rossetto*

7.1 INTRODUCTION

Since major reforms have taken place in the last 30 years, the electricity industry in Europe today looks significantly different from how it was in the 1980s. At that time, in most of the European countries, electricity was provided by a vertically integrated company owned by the state or by a local government. Such a company was usually shielded from competition thanks to the government's guarantee or the provision of a legal monopoly right. This company controlled the entire value chain, from generation to transmission and distribution to end users. Profit maximisation was generally not the top priority. In such a strategic sector, service coverage, quality improvement, protection of vulnerable consumers and industrial relations were common goals set by the government for the incumbent enterprise.

The situation has changed since then. Today, electricity is often considered as a commodity, traded in markets consisting of numerous buyers and sellers . Borders between national markets have blurred and a single energy market is emerging within Europe. Networks, both transmission and distribution, have been unbundled from generation and supply activities. Independent regulatory authorities have been established to regulate the non-competitive segments of the industry. Moreover, governments have started to step back by selling, partially or fully, their generation and retail companies, while commonly maintaining the control of transmission and distribution networks.

Privatisation of public enterprises in the electricity sector has been justified by the assumption that private companies would be more efficient and provide more innovative solutions, hence reducing costs and providing benefits to customers. The possibility to raise significant revenues from the sale of public companies is also seen as an additional advantage, especially in countries with budget deficits.

Discussions about the merits of privatisation have been rife in the academia and in the public debate. However, contrary to expectations, the impact on consumer welfare has not been so clearly positive, both in terms of prices and quality of the electricity service. Empirical research so far has produced mixed results.

As explained in Chapter 1, assessing a change in the institutional framework of an industry is a daunting task for economists. This chapter aims to contribute to this intellectual endeavour by focusing on the relationship between public ownership of electricity companies and household welfare, as measured by the affordability and the reliability of the electricity service.

The European reform process provides an opportunity to test different hypotheses and perform empirical research. The fact that European legislation is silent with regards to the type of ownership in this sector has allowed European Union (EU) Member States to follow different reform pathways. While some countries like France maintain significant public ownership, others like the UK have almost completely privatised their energy companies.[1] This study carries out a comparative analysis of four EU countries (UK, France, Germany and Italy) with four different pathways and mixtures of ownership. By focusing on the affordability and reliability of electricity supply, this chapter concludes that changes in ownership structure are not necessarily related to improvements in household consumer welfare.

7.2 LITERATURE REVIEW ON THE LINK BETWEEN PUBLIC OWNERSHIP AND CONSUMER WELFARE

Electricity was traditionally considered a public service whose production was not trusted in the hands of private entities and the vagaries of free markets so as to ensure the maximisation of social welfare. On the one hand, the importance of electricity for both households and firms and its relatively inelastic demand function increase the possibility for producers to exert market power on consumers and to cause allocative inefficiencies. On the other hand, the natural monopoly characteristics of electricity production (high fixed costs for the construction of long-lived and rather specific physical assets, and the relevant economies of scope between generation, transmission and supply) also create the risk of destructive competition and inadequate service expansion.

Since the beginning of the twentieth century, public authorities in developed economies have reacted to these features of electricity either by regulating privately owned companies or establishing publicly owned enterprises, vested with the task of supplying electricity to the public within a given jurisdiction, be it a municipality, a region or an entire country. The former option has been the preferred one in North America, while the latter has been most frequently adopted in Europe, especially after the Second World War.

However, since the 1970s and 1980s this traditional paradigm has been progressively challenged in terms of economic efficiency and political desirability. Direct involvement of the state in the electricity sector has been questioned, usually by arguing that: (1) competition can provide better results than a regulated monopolistic setting, provided that network operation is unbundled from potentially competitive segments of the supply chain (generation and supply); (2) private firms can deliver electricity at lower costs and with higher quality than public enterprises. Beginning with Chile (1983) and the UK (1989), industry restructuring has taken place in many countries of the world, based on the normative assumption that it would benefit customers and the whole economy.

Despite the diffusion of these ideas in the policy debate, for several years positive theoretical research and empirical testing of the hypotheses behind the reform process have been scant or have provided mixed results. Before the beginning of the restructuring wave, empirical research had been conducted mainly with reference to the US case, where the fragmentation of the electricity industry, especially with regard to distribution, allowed a comparison between the economic results of privately and publicly owned electric utilities.[2] The latter, usually municipal companies managing distribution and retailing, appeared to set prices at a lower level than their private counterparts subject to regulation (Moore, 1970). They also tended to adopt a smaller number of different rate schedules and to adjust them less frequently. Such reduced recourse to price discrimination has been interpreted as one of the reasons explaining the lower average sale of electricity per customer (Peltzman, 1971). Unwilling to upset their principal, that is, the local government, with allegations of price discrimination, public utilities would prefer to set uniform prices, with possible allocative distortions more than compensating the benefits accruing to customers due to lower average prices.

However, in terms of productive efficiency, early studies on US electric utilities did not provide clear results. On the one hand, public utilities showed a lower ratio of peak demand to total capacity, suggesting the possibility that they overinvested (Moore, 1970), but on the other hand, labour productivity was not statistically lower than that observed for private utilities (Di Lorenzo and Robinson, 1982). One study even maintained that production costs of public utilities were actually much lower than those incurred by private utilities (Pescatrice and Trapani, 1980).

More recently, the retreat of the state from its leading role between the 1990s and the early 2000s has provided new data for economists to assess. Indeed, the analysis of the impact of privatisation on consumer welfare has become an important topic after the disappointment recorded in several countries. Retail prices have increased, especially in Europe, where household customers are not benefiting from the decline in wholesale prices observed in the last few years (European Commission, 2016).[3]

The issue of energy poverty, almost not existent in developed economies until ten or twenty years ago, is becoming a major concern, both because energy prices are on the rise and disposable income for large parts of the population is stagnant (Miniaci et al., 2014). Finally, especially during the first few years of reform implementation, a number of blackouts occurred,[4] offering ground to the fears that privatisation and liberalisation of the industry would have led to service quality deterioration.

Dissatisfaction of electricity customers in Europe is confirmed by consecutive Eurobarometer surveys. Research on the subjective assessment by customers in the old Member States (EU 15) suggests that satisfaction with electricity prices did not increase with the implementation of industry reforms (liberalisation and privatisation). More specifically, customers seemed to be happier when there are both public ownership and competition (Fiorio and Florio, 2011).

Focusing on the electricity prices and their affordability for household customers, recent literature shows that public ownership of generation and retail companies is not necessarily associated with higher prices. Evidence from Finland suggests that local companies owned by municipalities can produce electricity efficiently and offer lower retail prices than private companies (Lehto, 2011). Another study, covering EU 15 for a relatively long period of time (1978–2007), concludes that public ownership of the largest electricity company is correlated to lower residential net of tax prices, while liberalisation has a smaller and more uncertain impact on prices (Fiorio and Florio, 2013). Indeed, the study is important because it tries to disentangle the effects of the two policy dimensions, that is, liberalisation and privatisation, which often occur together without being mutually necessary. By estimating the separate effect of the two dimensions, the research confirms that public companies can better protect consumers, especially when the institutional framework is strong (solid tradition in effective management of the public sector, low levels of corruption and so on). As a result, privatisation is not necessarily the best solution for every country. This conclusion is even more apparent if the new Member States of Central and Eastern Europe (EU 12) are taken into consideration. Restructuring of the industry in those countries during the 1990s and the 2000s has led to a significant increase in electricity prices, often worsening problems of affordability for households (Bacchiocchi et al., 2015). The implementation of privatisation in a context characterised by poor competition and weak regulatory institutions is likely to have a negative impact on consumers, suggesting that geographical differences should be taken into account when developing policies at the European level. Looking beyond Europe, an analysis covering 30 countries belonging to the Organisation for Economic Co-operation and Development (OECD) over a long period of time (1975–2011) finds that, once the effects of liberalisation are separately considered, privatisation has a negligible impact on the economic performance of the electricity sector and it may even lead to an increase in prices (Polemis, 2016). Competition and sound industry regulation seem to be more effective in improving market functioning and protecting customers.

Unfortunately, only a handful of researchers so far have looked at the impact of public ownership on service quality in the electricity sector. If quality is interpreted in terms of continuity of supply, there is a common belief that publicly owned companies may invest more in capacity and hire more personnel, thereby ensuring a more reliable service. Managers of public companies are likely to care more about continuity of supply, because they will gain less from pursuing profit maximisation through cost minimisation and lose more from the occurrence of blackouts and public outrage. If this is correct, privatisation of electric utilities, especially if coupled with the introduction of price or revenue capping, could lead to excessive cost cutting and progressive quality degradation.

A study conducted on the Italian electricity distribution sector looked at this issue and showed that partial or full privatisation does not necessarily have a negative impact on service reliability. However, the impact is not positive either. Competition in complementary markets and the existence of an incentive regulation that rewards investment in service quality seem to be more relevant and able to induce electric utilities to take into consideration the qualitative aspects of the service they offer to household customers (Fumagalli et al., 2007).

7.3 METHODOLOGY

The overarching research question addressed in this chapter is: 'Does public ownership benefit household welfare in the EU electricity sector?'

The issue is approached by focusing on the affordability and the reliability of the service for household consumers.

Therefore, we consider two different time series and try to provide an answer to two specific questions. The first looks at the relationship between public ownership and service affordability: 'Is public ownership beneficial for household customers in terms of service affordability?' The second question examines the relationship between public ownership and service reliability: 'Is public ownership beneficial for household customers in terms of service reliability?'

'Affordability' is a vague concept and differs from mere low prices. Fairly speaking, prices are a good proxy of affordability, but they do not tell the whole story about the ability to pay for electricity bills. As employed in Winkler et al. (2011), EBRD (2003) and Frankhauser and Tepic (2005), we decided to address the proportion of household customers' electricity bill out of their real disposable income. Therefore, affordability is measured through a proxy indicator, the share of income spent on electricity (SISE) computed as follows:

$$SISE = P_{el}*Cons_{el}/Income \qquad (7.1)$$

where P_{el} is the electricity price for domestic consumers at constant prices, $Cons_{el}$ is the annual residential consumption of electricity per capita (national average) and *Income* is the net disposable income of households per capita at constant prices (national average).

Measurements of service quality vary in the literature due to availability of data and purpose of research. Since it is not easy to assess commercial quality, we decided to focus our attention on the reliability of supply, that is, on the capability of a system to provide energy to the customers when requested. 'Reliability' is usually assessed through a combination of indicators. The two most common are System Average Interruption Frequency Index (SAIFI) and System Average Interruption Duration Index (SAIDI). The first shows how frequent service interruptions were over a given period of time, while the second provides an idea of how long, on average, those service interruptions were (CEER, 2015).

In order to have a synthetic measure, we combine the two indicators and create a compound 'unreliability of electricity service' indicator. This is calculated as an average of the SAIDI and SAIFI values expressed as an index, where 100 per cent is the value of the first year for which data is available. By using this approach, the absolute values for each country are not taken into consideration in the comparison. However, this does not represent a major issue, given that the initial SAIDI and SAIFI values do not vary significantly among the four markets. The calculation of the indicator for year t and country c was performed using the following formula:

$$Unreliability_{(t,c)} = (SAIDI_{t,c}/SAIDI_{0,c})*0.5 + (SAIFI_{t,c}/SAIFI_{0,c})*0.5$$
$$(7.2)$$

where $SAIDI_{t,c}$ and $SAIFI_{t,c}$ are the values of SAIDI and SAIFI for year t in country c, while $SAIDI_{0,c}$ and $SAIFI_{0,c}$ are the values of SAIDI and SAIFI for the first year of the sample in country c.

Our control variable, that is, public ownership in the electricity sector, is derived from the OECD Database on Regulation in Energy, Transport and Communications (ETCR). For the electricity sector, the ETCR public ownership is evaluated on the basis of the ownership structure (private, mostly private, mixed, mostly public or public) of the largest company in the generation, transmission, distribution and supply segments (OECD, 2016). A summary of the sources adopted is provided in Table 7.1.

In order to provide an answer to the two specific questions highlighted above, we separately investigate the relationship between public ownership and the other two relevant variables by analysing the trends of each variable across countries.

A by-country time series regression analysis was originally proposed to further advance the discussion on the issue of how public owner-ship affects EU consumers in the electricity sector. However, given the

Table 7.1   Data set and sources used in the research

Indicator	Unit of measure	Period covered	Source
Electricity price for domestic consumers (taxes and levies not included)	Euro/kWh	1990–2015	Eurostat (2016)
Annual residential consumption of electricity	GWh	1990–2014	
Net disposable income of households	Euro at current prices	1995–2014/15	
Population	Inhabitants	1990–2015	
Consumer Price Index	–	1990–2015	World Bank (2016)
SAIDI	Minutes	1999/2006–2013	CEER (2015)
SAIFI	No. of interruptions	1999/2006–2013	
Public ownership (PO)	PO rating according to OECD (2016)	1990–2014	OECD (2016)

limited availability of key data – between seven and 20 data points exist for each dependent variable – and the plurality of possible additional control variables to consider, the generation of a time series model is not recommended.

7.4   NATIONAL ELECTRICITY SECTOR REFORMS AND IMPACTS ON CONSUMER WELFARE

As mentioned in the introduction, current European legislation merely prescribes the unbundling of generation and supply companies from transmission and distribution operators. Apart from that, discretion is left to the Member States regarding the ownership structure of the energy company, which could be public or private, or in between. Consequently, electricity sector reforms vary across the EU with regards to ownership structures. This chapter specifically analyses the reform processes in four countries and their impact on consumer welfare, which is composed of 'affordability' (SISE) and 'reliability' (availability of the electricity service). A concise description of the different reform pathways undertaken by the four countries is provided in Table 7.2.

Table 7.2   Developments in the four Member States

	Ownership unbundling	Open wholesale market	Retail market (customer choice)	Privatisation of electricity companies
UK	1989*	1990 (spot market)	1999	1989*
France	No**	2001	2007	No
Germany	2010*	2005 (exchange)	1998	Partial privatisation during the 1990s of municipal companies, currently re-municipalisation
Italy	2005	2004 (power exchange establishment)	2007	1999*

Note: * Beginning of the process; ** since 2013 there is an Independent Transmission Operator.

7.4.1 Public Ownership and Market Share

Before depicting the empirical findings on ownership regimes and variables on consumer welfare, this subsection outlines the setting of the electricity market of the four countries regarding the largest electricity company (generation and/or supply). One of the main aims of liberalisation and subsequent unbundling of vertically integrated electricity utilities is to introduce a competitive market setting. By identifying the biggest electricity company in relation to the level of public ownership, we analyse whether or not public ownership of electricity companies facilitates a competitive market setting. Figure 7.1 illustrates the relationship that may exist between public ownership and the market share of the biggest electricity company (as a proxy indicator of market power).

The liberalisation-to-privatisation market reform model in the UK dramatically brought down public ownership in the electricity sector in the early 1990s. The sale of state-owned unbundled electricity companies allowed entry and growth of private companies. Since then, the market has been controlled by 'the big six' of which the biggest company is British Gas which supplies about one quarter of the electricity market (2015). Since 2000, its market share has not dropped below 20 per cent with the peak of over 50 per cent in 2012. Barely any effort has been made by the government to introduce any further competition into this oligopolistic market.

According to EDF's (Électricité de France) financial statement for 2015 (EDF, 2016), 85 per cent of the shares of EDF – by far the largest electricity supplier in France, with a market share of around 90 per cent – are held by the French state. EDF is consequently considered a publicly owned company. Due to the fact that electricity distribution has a long tradition as 'public service', the task of distributing electricity is subject to a concession regime. The concession is granted by local authorities for a defined territory. Under that regime, EDF is responsible for about 90 per cent of electricity distribution (EDF, 2015).

Germany shows a less clear-cut picture of public and private ownership than the UK and France. The supra-regional level is controlled by four large electricity companies. E.ON SE is a private company (E.ON, 2016), RWE AG is to a large extent privately owned but about 15 per cent of its shares are held by cities and municipalities located in the federal state of North Rhine-Westphalia (RWE, 2011). EnBW AG is owned by the federal state Baden-Württemberg, and Vattenfall is owned by the Swedish state. The 'big four' have a cumulative market share of about 60 per cent (2014). At the local level various small municipal electricity companies (Stadtwerke) were privatised during the 1990s. However, currently, a re-municipalisation is taking place as many of the contracts with private

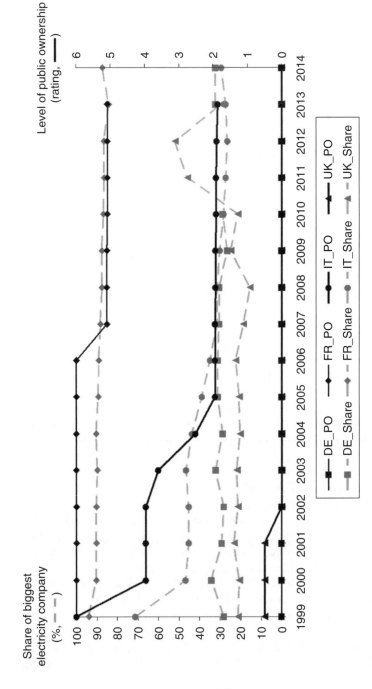

Share of biggest
electricity company
(%, — —)

Level of public ownership
(rating, ——)

DE_PO ■ FR_PO ◆ IT_PO ● UK_PO ▼
DE_Share ■ FR_Share ◆ IT_Share ● UK_Share ▲

Source: Adapted from OECD (2016).

Figure 7.1   Market share of the largest electricity company and evolution of the level of public ownership in Germany,
France, Italy and the United Kingdom

companies (concession contracts) are not renewed and municipalities are regaining control.

The electricity market in Italy is still dominated by the incumbent electricity company Enel, established in 1962 after the nationalisation of the pre-existing private electricity companies. Enel was corporatized in 1992 but only in 1999 did a partial sale of its shares begin. Since then, the electricity market in Italy has been subject to a gradual increase in private participation due, on the one hand, to the gradual decline of the market share of Enel and, on the other hand, to a decrease in the shares of Enel owned by the Italian state (Enel, 2016). However, in the last years the market share of the incumbent has stabilised at around 25–30 per cent and the Italian state has interrupted the sale of its shares (about 30 per cent of the company is still owned by the Italian state directly or indirectly).

7.4.2 Public Ownership and Affordability

Affordability is a complex concept to measure and accurately reflect in empirical research (Kessides et al., 2009). Also, from a legal perspective ambiguities exist in its interpretation (Pront-van Bommel, 2016). This chapter defines affordability as the 'share of annual household expenditure that is spent on electricity'. The SISE indicator employed in the analysis is presented in Section 7.3 and Equation 7.1. Affordability is one of the two variables comprising the concept 'consumer welfare' which is at the heart of this research. Essentially, the question is, whether and to what extent the nature of ownership affects consumer welfare across EU countries.

The question of 'which type of ownership is most beneficial and results in higher consumer surpluses' has been discussed for a long time in the literature (De Fraja, 1993). On the one hand, a typical argument is that under competition privatised companies generate higher efficiency reflected in lower prices for the consumer than publicly owned companies. On the other hand, the contrary can be argued as publicly owned companies bring a more efficient output and lower prices to consumers than private oligopoly markets. Yet another standpoint specifically focusing on the electricity sector stipulates that partly privatising companies neither necessarily worsens nor improves the situation for households. The overall findings of the four countries under investigation confirm the last observation that no significant changes in affordability occurred after changes in the type of ownership (apart from the UK).

The most significant increase of share of income spent on energy happened in the UK. With full privatisation in 2003, the share of income spent on energy increased from 1.2 per cent to 1.6 per cent. Meanwhile, in France only little change occurred in the type of ownership. It is relevant to mention that in 2007, when customers gained the freedom to choose among electricity suppliers, the share of income spent on energy increased. This could be explained by the fact that the creation of competitive retail markets incurs additional costs of marketing and legislation, which are then passed on to the consumers. Nevertheless, other explanations are possible as well, like the fact that in those same years international prices for energy commodities (oil, gas and coal) were on the rise. The share of income spent on energy in Germany merely shows small variations. In Italy, gradual privatisation of electricity companies did not necessarily lead to an increase in the share of income spent on energy. Figure 7.2 depicts the evolution of the level of public ownership of the largest electricity company and the SISE as a proxy for the affordability of electricity supply.

7.4.3 Public Ownership and Service Reliability

Reliability of the electricity service is the second variable composing the concept of consumer welfare. Two indicators are typically used for defining reliability of electricity supply, namely SAIDI and SAIFI (see section on methodology).

The type of ownership may affect the reliability of the electricity service. It is normally assumed that quality of service depends on investments in electricity assets and maintenance of power plants and supply lines. Private companies under pressure of reducing costs may not prioritise continuous investment in the system. In turn, this may lead to lower supply reliability. Some studies available in the literature show that privatisation does not necessarily lead to improvements, neither to quality deterioration of output in the electricity sector (Fumagalli et al., 2007). Figure 7.3 shows the trend in the level of public ownership of the largest electricity company and the unreliability of the electricity service for the four countries considered.

In the UK, the reliability of the electricity service has fluctuated slightly since 2002, with a negative evolution especially in 2003 and 2007. However, since then, the reliability of the system stagnated and even slightly improved. In France, the opening of the retail market in 2007 is correlated with a sharp increase in the reliability of the electricity service. Yet, this improvement only lasted a short period, as service reliability deteriorated in 2008–10. Although the situation improved by 2011, recent figures suggest that the situation may be worsening again. Unfortunately, data on Germany is partly incomplete. The data available shows a significant improvement in the reliability of the electricity service in 2007. After 2012, reliability appears to worsen again. Data on the reliability of the electricity service for Italy shows a steady improvement in reliability during the

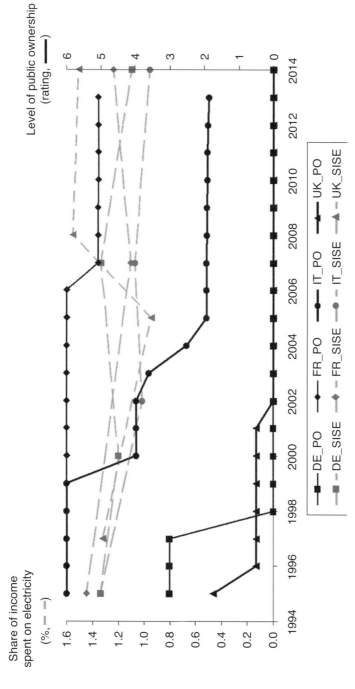

Share of income
spent on electricity
(%, — —)

Level of public ownership
(rating, ——)

Source: Adapted from Eurostat (2016), OECD (2016), World Bank (2016).

Figure 7.2   *Share of the income spent by households on electricity and the evolution of the level of public ownership of the largest electricity company in Germany, France, Italy and the United Kingdom*

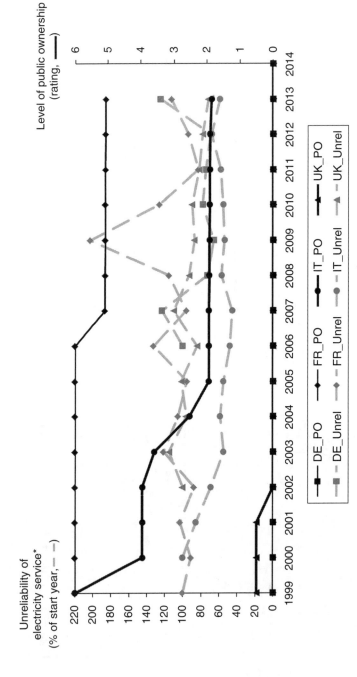

Unreliability of
electricity service*
(% of start year, — —)

Level of public ownership
(rating, ———)

Note: * Higher "Unreliability" figures indicate a reduction of service reliability compared to the start year.

Source: Adapted from CEER (2015) and OECD (2016).

Figure 7.3 *Unreliability of the electricity service and the evolution of the level of public ownership of the largest electricity company in Germany, France, Italy and the United Kingdom*

period 2000–03. With the introduction of ownership unbundling in 2005, the level of reliability did not worsen; however, it also did not show a significant improvement. Since 2012 the data shows a slight improvement in the level of service reliability.

7.4.4   Affordability of Electricity by the Poorest Quintile of Household Consumers

Besides affordability and reliability of electricity supply, it is relevant to consider the poorest household income group per country and assess whether this group experienced an increase or a decrease of the share of income spent on energy. This assessment represents the overall goal to make electricity available to all consumers. Affordability is a relative concept, meaning that access to power could be cheap for high-income households while being expensive for the low-income households. Therefore, in order to assess if the current electricity bill is truly affordable for all, it is more appropriate to look at how affordable it is for low-income households. Since data on electricity expenditure by income class is not easily accessible for the four countries considered, we take energy costs as a proxy of the actual level of electricity bills.

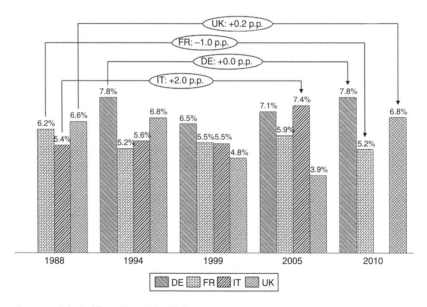

Source: Adapted from Eurostat (2016).

Figure 7.4   Share of income spent on energy by the poorest quintile of households in Germany, France, Italy and the United Kingdom

As Figure 7.4 shows, in the UK, the share of income spent on energy increased by 0.2 percentage points in the period 1988–2010 for the poorest quintile of household consumers. In France, the share spent on energy decreased by 1 percentage point. In Germany, the gap in this cost for different household income groups remained unchanged and there has been no significant difference between 1994 and 2010. In Italy, the share for the poorest quintile of households increased by 2 percentage points.

7.5 CONCLUSION

The liberalisation of the electricity sector often implied partial or total privatisation of the state-owned incumbent companies. While transfer of ownership is commonly believed to improve household welfare, this chapter suggests that the story is more nuanced. First, the share of electricity expenditure for low-income household customers did not clearly decrease in the period considered. Similarly, reliability of electricity supply after strong improvements in the 1990s seemingly stagnated in recent years.

As public ownership has been consistently reduced during the liberalisation process in the UK, France, Germany and Italy, service quality and affordability perceived by consumers did not improve. We cannot exclude the relevance of other factors, such as the unbundling of distribution grids, the price of fossil fuels on international markets or the prolonged economic stagnation that affected Europe in the last decade.

While at the beginning of this millennium European households appeared to be better off, subsequent developments as shown in empirical evidence cast doubts that ownership transfers from public to private entities are significantly linked to such improvements. The emergence of the prosumer – that is, a network user who is both consumer and producer – in addition to the digitalisation of the energy industry and other recent developments add further complexity to this picture and may reduce, in the future, the relevance of the ownership structure of the incumbent for the welfare of household customers.

NOTES

*   The authors would like to thank Liselotte Gijzemijter, Bruno Peretti and Ilias Tsagas, who contributed to the early research for this chapter. The authors would like also to thank Stefano Clô and Massimo Florio, as well as the other anonymous reviewers, for reading, commenting and providing valuable input to the initial versions of this chapter.
1.   The Treaty on the Functioning of the European Union (TFEU) strictly excludes the

option for European policies to specify ownership regimes (Article 345 states that 'the Treaties shall in no way prejudice the rules in Member States governing the system of property rights'). The EU Directive establishing rules on the internal market for electricity (EC/2009/72) merely prescribes the ownership unbundling of generation and supply companies from transmission system operators.

2. Viscusi et al. (2005) provide an overview of this first stream of literature on the comparison between private and public enterprises in the electricity sector.

3. The European Commission notes that prices for households have grown more than prices for industrial customers. It also highlights that the increase in prices is due to a large extent to increases in network costs, taxes and levies. The energy component of the final price has actually decreased since 2008.

4. Limiting the focus to advanced economies, major blackouts occurred in California between 2000 and 2001, in Ontario and part of the USA in August 2003, in Italy in September 2003, and in Central and Western Europe in November 2006.

REFERENCES

Bacchiocchi, E., Florio, M. and Taveggia, G. (2015), 'Asymmetric Effects of Electricity Regulatory Reforms in the EU15 and in the New Member States: Empirical Evidence from Residential Prices 1990–2011', *Utilities Policy*, **35** (August), 72–90.

CEER (2015), *CEER Benchmarking Report 5.2 on the Continuity of Electricity Supply*. Data update Ref. C14-EQS-62-03, accessed 25 June 2016 at http://www.ceer.eu/portal/page/portal/EER_HOME/EER_PUBLICATIONS/CEER_PAPERS/Electricity/Tab4/C14-EQS-62-03_BMR-5-2_Continuity%20of%20Supply_20150127.pdf.

De Fraja, G. (1993), 'Productive Efficiency in Public and Private Firms', *Journal of Public Economics*, **50** (1), 15–30.

Di Lorenzo, T.J. and Robinson, R. (1982), 'Managerial Objectives Subject to Political Market Constraints: Electric Utilities in the U.S.', *Quarterly Review of Economics and Business*, **22** (2), 113–25.

Directive (EC) No. 2009/72 concerning Common Rules for the Internal Market in Electricity and repealing Directive 2003/54/EC, *Official Journal of the European Union*, L 211/55.

E.ON (2016), *2015 Annual Report*, accessed 29 June 2016 at http://www.eon.com/content/dam/eon-com/ueber-uns/publications/EON_Annual_Report_2015_EN.pdf.

EDF (2015), *2014 Facts and Figures*, accessed 29 June 2016 at http://www.edf.fr/sites/default/files/documents/faits_et_chiffres/2015/F%26F_EDF_2014_VA.pdf.

EDF (2016), *Consolidated Financial Statements at 31 December 2015*, accessed 29 June 2016 at http://www.edf.fr/sites/default/files/contrib/groupe-edf/espacesdedies/espace-finance-en/financial-information/publications/financialresults/2015-annual-Results/fy_2015_consolidated_financial_statements.pdf.

Enel (2016), *Annual Report 2015*, accessed 29 June 2016 at http://www.enel.com/engb/Documents/FinancialReports/report2015/Annual_Report_2015.pdf.

European Bank for Reconstruction and Development (EBRD) (2003), *Can the Poor Pay for Power? The Affordability of Electricity in South East Europe*, London: EBRD and IPA Energy.

European Commission (2016), *Report from the Commission to the European*

Parliament, the Council, the European Economic and Social Committee and the Committee of the Regions – Energy Prices and Costs in Europe, 30 November, COM(2016) 769 final, Brussels.

Eurostat (2016), *Structure of Consumption Expenditure by Income Quintile*, accessed 29 June 2016 at http://ec.europa.eu/eurostat/data/database.

Fiorio, C.V. and Florio, M. (2011), 'Would You Say that the Price You Pay for Electricity is Fair? Consumers' Satisfaction and Utility Reforms in the EU15', *Energy Economics*, **33** (2), 178–87.

Fiorio, C.V. and Florio, M. (2013), 'Electricity Prices and Public Ownership: Evidence from the EU15 Over Thirty Years', *Energy Economics*, **39** (September), 222–32.

Frankhauser, S. and Tepic, S. (2005), 'Can Poor Consumers Pay for Energy and Water? An Affordability Analysis for Transition Countries', EBRD Working Paper, No. 92, May.

Fumagalli, E., Garrone, P. and Grilli, L. (2007),'Service Quality in the Electricity Industry: The Role of Privatization and Managerial Behavior', *Energy Policy*, **35** (12), 6212–24.

Kessides, I., Miniaci, R., Scarpa, C. and Valbonesi, P. (2009), 'Towards Defining and Measuring the Affordability of Public Utility Services', World Bank Policy Research Working Paper, No. 4915, April.

Lehto, E. (2011), 'Electricity Prices in the Finnish Retail Market', *Energy Policy*, **39** (4), 2179–92.

Miniaci, R., Scarpa, C. and Valbonesi, P. (2014), 'Verso la definizione e la misurazione dei concetti di *affordability* nei servizi elettrici', in Alberto Clô, Stefano Clô and Federico Boffa (eds), *Riforme elettriche tra efficienza ed equità*, Bologna: il Mulino, pp. 453–76.

Moore, T.G. (1970), 'The Effectiveness of Regulation of Electric Utility Prices', *Southern Economic Journal*, **36** (4), 365–75.

OECD (2016), Regulation in Energy, Transport and Communications, accessed 27 June 2016 at http://www.stats.oecd.org/Index.aspx?DataSetCode=ETCR.

Peltzman, S. (1971), 'Pricing in Public and Private Enterprises: Electric Utilities in the United States', *Journal of Law and Economics*, **14** (1), 109–47.

Pescatrice, D.R. and Trapani, J.M. (1980), 'The Performance and Objectives of Public and Private Utilities Operating in the United States', *Journal of Public Economics*, **13** (2), 259–76.

Polemis, M.L. (2016), 'New Evidence on the Impact of Structural Reforms on Electricity Sector Performance', *Energy Policy*, **92** (May), 420–31.

Pront-van Bommel, S. (2016), 'A Reasonable Price for Electricity', *Journal of Consumer Policy*, **39** (2), 141–58.

RWE (2011), 'RWE Sells Majority Shareholding in German Transmission Systems Operator Amprion', accessed 24 June 2016 at http://www.rwe.com/web/cms/en/113648/rwe/press-news/pressrelease/?pmid=4006512.

Viscusi, W.K., Harrington, J.E. and Vernon, J.M. (2005), *Economics of Regulation and Antitrust*, Cambridge, MA: MIT Press.

Winkler, H., Simões, A.F., La Rovere, E.L., Alam, M., Rahman, A. and Mwakasonda, S. (2011), 'Access and Affordability of Electricity in Developing Countries', *World Development*, **39** (6), 1037–50.

World Bank (2016), 'Consumer Price Index', accessed 25 June 2016 at http://data.worldbank.org/indicator/FP.CPI.TOTL?page=5.

8. Telecommunications policies in Europe: past, present, future and impact on citizens

Serena Marianna Drufuca, Regina Maria Hirsch, Manto Lampropoulou and Rogelio Pesqueira Sánchez*

8.1 INTRODUCTION

Since the early 1980s, the telecommunications sector has been at the forefront of network industries reform, steadily shifting towards greater liberalization and privatization. The post-war pattern of vertical monopolies has gradually given place to competitive markets, and new regulatory models have been introduced across European Union (EU) countries. At the same time, the form and the scope of government intervention in the Services of General Economic Interest (SGEI) markets have significantly changed.

This chapter contributes to the current debate on telecommunications reform by providing an overview of the key developments in the EU telecommunications sector during the past two decades. The policy mix of the ongoing reforms is a combination of corporatization, liberalization and privatization. In the analysis that follows, we aim to map the reform agenda in the EU area and to assess the impact of the telecommunications policies on market-related variables as well as on citizens. In addition, the current status and the major challenges of the telecommunications sector are discussed.

The chapter is structured as follows. In the next section the recent developments in the telecommunications and ICT (information and communications technology) industries are briefly described. In Section 8.3 the critical drivers that determine the price and quality of the telecommunications services are identified. Section 8.4 presents the main policy reforms that have been promoted by the EU and adopted by the Member States in the last two decades. Section 8.5 focuses on the variations observed in the reform patterns across EU countries. Section 8.6 provides empirical evidence on the impact of the reforms on citizens/consumers in a social and economic perspective. In the concluding section the key findings are summarized.

8.2 DEVELOPMENTS IN THE TELECOMMUNICATIONS INDUSTRY

Starting in the nineteenth century, the telecommunications sector went through two hundred years of development. Historically, the first phone calls were made in the second half of the nineteenth century via the Public Switched Telephone Network (PSTN). A century later, in the 1980s, the shift from analogue PSTN to the Integrated Services Digital Network (ISDN) took place in Europe. Meanwhile, mobile telecommunications services became commercially available. Consumers received this new technology with open arms, and in the last decades especially, mobile telecommunications services have experienced impressive growth in demand throughout the world. Banerjee and Ros (2002, p. 1) indicate that 'between 1990 and 2002, the International Telecommunication Union (ITU) estimates that the number of mobile subscribers worldwide grew from 11 million to 1.15 billion – a compounded annual growth rate of almost 47 percent. In 2002, the number of mobile subscribers worldwide surpassed the number of fixed main lines ...'.

However, fixed telephony did not cease to exist and it will not do so in the near future since its infrastructure is a requirement for mobile telephony and the Internet, as emerged in the 1990s. The Internet completely changed the means of telecommunication. In fact, its expansion led to the digital revolution that influenced all areas of human life. Moreover, it contributed to the modernization and emergence of (new) economic sectors, the transformation of consumer behavior and the change in media use in private and economic environments (Banerjee and Ros, 2002).

The ever-increasing demand from consumers for better quality services in telecommunications resulted in the development of new ICT technologies that enable faster (broadband) and wireless (Wi-Fi) Internet connection, both of which revolutionized the industry yet again. However, it is hard to determine whether innovations emerged because of market pull or technology push. Furthermore, it has to be kept in mind that in the past, consumers could not have even uttered current demands because they were not yet conceivable. Today, research is already being conducted on the fifth generation network and consumers demand free-of-charge Internet in public places and also more bandwidth for Wi-Fi. Florio (2013) emphasizes that the relatively quiet life of the telecommunications industry has been shaken by a series of technological shocks since the 1980s.

8.3   THE FORCES AT STAKE: PRICE AND QUALITY DRIVERS

The technological changes mentioned above, the presence of substitutes for traditional operators and the substitute services determine price and quality of service in the telecommunications industry:

1. Technological change. When new technologies are introduced, the price is initially high but later on the increased demand helps to lower prices. For example, the shift from analogue to digital telephony not merely lowered the costs for the operators but eventually also lowered the prices for the consumers. Due to the development of mobile voice technology, the costs decreased again and this allowed services to be offered for a much cheaper price (Evans, 2004).
2. The presence of substitute operators. Privatized companies created competition in the market and lowered the prices for the consumer. For example, fixed telephony used to be costly because there was no substitute service for it. Florio (2013) asserts that the policy reforms of privatization and liberalization of the telecommunications sector together contributed towards reducing the prices of local calls.
3. Substitute service providers. Over-The-Top (OTT) providers serve as a substitute to traditional telecommunications services and are a substitute for the whole telecommunication value chain. Since the 1990s, OTT providers such as Netflix, YouTube and Amazon have changed the sector tremendously. In addition, the free-of-charge telephony services (for example, WhatsApp and Viber) lower the price for telecommunications. They drive competition, but they also improve the service quality. Finally, OTT services can be run independently from physical infrastructure. If the network enables Internet signals, then any service can be organized on this infrastructure. It is possible to develop a service in a small start-up company and enter the global market. A decade ago, this opportunity did not exist. The OTT brought into question the traditional roles of the infrastructure operators, the value added service providers and the service reseller (Picot, 2016).

Currently, prices for telecommunications services are stable but differ between European Member States. This fact probably reflects different competitive market situations. Generally, prices for broadband connection have fallen as demand has increased. Yet the prices per end user for tele-communications increased again because other (different) services are bundled in a package with mobile voice telephony, for example, Internet and television.

8.4   MAIN POLICY REFORMS AT THE EU LEVEL

Each of the above-mentioned drivers raises new questions for the telecom-munications industry and the policy makers. As Florio (2013) argues, the importance of the telecommunications sector is that this is the core labora-tory for network industries.

There are several kinds of telecommunications policy reforms which often have different aims: protecting the consumers, ensuring adequate infrastructure investments (mainly roll-out of broadband), creating a strong network, promoting competitive behavior, obtaining lower prices, increasing the service quality, allowing the portability of the number, fight-ing against roaming charges, easing access for the consumer, achieving neu-trality of the European network[1] or regulating entrant barriers of the offers.

Traditionally, in the telecommunications sector the different policy reforms choose one of the different possible combinations as an outcome: public ownership/private ownership of the industry, free entry/oligopoly/monopoly of the market and regulation/liberalization of the industry (Florio, 2013). Hence, the regulatory regimes can be categorized accord-ing to ownership, level of competition and the presence of regulation. There are vertically integrated public monopolies; privatized, but still vertically integrated monopolies, without any price regulation; price-cap regulated privatized monopolies; and different steps of liberalization from unbundling to unregulated oligopolies to full market entry.

When we study policy reforms in telecommunications, it is important to stress that the process of technological change implies that regulators and lawmakers have to frequently adjust their views because of entirely new developments (Newbery, 2000). The telecommunications sector is not homogeneous as it presents different kinds of services and tariffs structure, subscription rates, connection charges and rental prices of equipment (see Bacchiocchi et al., 2011). Therefore, it is very difficult to directly compare one product with another. Dynamic models should be used because a particular policy reform can take time to apply for reasons of contractual obligations (Picot, 2016).

The EU offers something near to a natural experiment. On the one hand, there is one policy actor, the European Commission, who pushes towards a well-defined reform package, basically embodied in telecom directives.

On the other hand, there are the Member States that more or less are in compliance with the EU legislation and which show notable differences in reform design, sequencing, timing and market structure (Bacchiocchi et al., 2011).

The most important reforms in the telecommunications sector promoted by the EU aim at establishing a single market in Europe and creating a single European regulator. Concrete measures to achieve this objective were approved in the legislative package of the European Commission on 11 September 2013 (MEMO /13/779) with the following aims: (1) creating four or five major operators providing services across the EU; (2) creating common and simple rules; (3) eliminating roaming charges; (4) removing surcharges on international calls; (5) providing rights to telecommunications consumers; (6) promoting network neutrality.

A major recent development in the telecommunications sector promoted by the EU is network neutrality. This reform was adopted on 27 October 2015 and stipulates that Internet traffic should be treated equally for all 'general services' (browsing, emails), but not for 'specialized services' (Internet protocol television services, high definition online video conferencing). In addition, this law opens the door to 'zero-rating' (excluding some applications to the data consumption rate of the consumer). Furthermore, the rule allows operators to prioritize traffic (not just in the case of network congestion). Thus, some independent observers and academics affirm that this regulation does not provide network neutrality at all – prompting fierce debate.

Another important point to note is the EU policy goal to deploy broadband to all citizens. The 2020 European Strategy underlines the importance of broadband deployment (see Table 8.1 showing the European broadband coverage at the end of 2012) in order to promote social inclusion and competitiveness in the EU. Therefore, the digital agenda established the following goals: (1) coverage for all European citizens of basic broadband (accomplished); (2) coverage for all European citizens of fast broadband in 2020; (3) coverage for 50 percent of European citizens of ultra-fast broadband in 2020.

Table 8.1   Achievements of EU telecommunications policy

Basic broadband coverage achieved by EU at the end of 2012	
Fixed (ADSL, VDSL, optical fiber, copper)	96.1%
Mobile (2G, 3G, 4G)	99.4%
Satellite (148 satellites)	100%

Source: http://europa.eu/rapid/press-release_IP-13-968_en.htm (accessed 7 April 2017).

8.5   DIFFERENT REFORM PATTERNS ACROSS EUROPE

The reform paths in the telecommunications sector vary largely among and within EU countries. The process of European integration and the common market prerequisites have worked as strong drivers for delineating national policies in the network industries and the domestic regulatory frameworks have tended to converge since the 1990s (Thatcher, 1999, 2006). In the same way, the diffusion of liberal policies and the impact of globalization and Europeanization have directly affected the regulatory and policy patterns in the telecommunications sector (Bartle, 2005; Rodine-Hardy, 2013). However, the picture does not correspond to a uniform policy framework and notable differences are observed across the national reform programs.

Policy patterns can be discerned according to vertical and horizontal criteria. Drawing on the existing literature and empirical research (Levi-Faur, 2004; Thatcher, 2006; Schneider and Werle, 2007; Florio, 2013; Rodine-Hardy, 2013; Szcepanski, 2013; European Commission, 2015; ITU, 2015), some key differences are summarized in Table 8.2.

In a cross-country perspective, empirical evidence illustrates significant

Table 8.2   Telecommunications reform patterns: key differences

Policy and regulation-related variables	Market and sector-related variables
Role of the State	Corporatization of State-owned enterprises
Degree of privatization, liberalization and deregulation	Ownership and organization status of incumbents
Type and volume of Europeanization	Framework of consumer protection
Type and methods of privatization	Public service and universal service obligations
Pace and timing of the reforms	Research and development framework
Policy diffusion mechanisms	Market-related variables (degree of market opening, market structure, unbundling techniques, pricing, licensing measures, net neutrality etc.)
Delegation/allocation of authority and regulatory powers	Technical issues (fees, spectrum sharing/ allocation)
Degree of institutional adjustment	Technology used/technological adjustment and modernization

Source: Levi-Faur (2004), Schneider and Werle (2007), Thatcher (2006), Florio (2013), Rodine-Hardy (2013), Szcepanski (2013), European Commission (2015), ITU (2015).

variations, indicating that telecommunications policies and markets in the EU are far from full harmonization. Regarding State ownership, after about 30 years of privatization policies, the share of the State in telecom corporations ranges from 0 percent (UK, Italy, Ireland, Netherlands, Spain) to 100 percent (Luxembourg, Cyprus) (OECD, 2013). Mixed ownership ranges between 20 and 53 percent in Austria, Belgium, Estonia and France, while in Denmark, Greece and Finland the State holds minority shares in telecommunications companies (< 10 percent) (OECD, 2013). Hence, despite the successive reforms, State ownership to a certain degree seems to survive. The structure of the market and the degree of competition also vary. For instance, new entrants' market share in Fixed Broadband Lines in 2014 was relatively small in Luxembourg, Cyprus, Portugal and Italy (21–50 percent), medium in Spain, Greece and France (53–60 percent) and large in the UK, Romania, Poland and Bulgaria (67–77 percent) (European Commission, 2014, p.9, COCOM data). Regarding the research and development expenditure in the telecommunications sector, public funding is remarkably high in Sweden, slightly above the EU average in the UK, Italy and the Netherlands and relatively low in France, Cyprus, Portugal and Malta (European Commission, Joint Research Centre, 2013).

Further variations and divergences are observed in the particular reform paths within the EU. Britain adopted more radical reforms at an earlier stage compared with other European countries and is considered to be a pilot case of the EU liberalization process[2] (Thatcher, 1999). The adopted strategy on industrial activities and public utilities prioritized market forces and was characterized by a clear orientation towards liberalization, deregulation and privatization (Hulsink, 1999; Clifton et al., 2006; Stern, 2014). The pattern may be briefly described as 'regulated competitive markets' (Thatcher, 2006) and is steadily progressing towards competitive markets and the delegation of activities to the private sector.

Contrary to the British paradigm, the French pattern is more 'State-controlled' oriented, as the government has an active role, both in entrepreneurial and administrative terms, and still embeds protectionist and interventionist elements (Hulsink, 1999). In addition, France was a latecomer to reforming the ICT sector and certain delays were observed in the regulatory adjustment process (OECD, 2003; Thatcher, 2006). A key feature of the French case is the greater importance that is attributed to public service concerns, which often conflicts with the rules of the competitive market (Bauby, 2002; Valin, 2007).

The Dutch model was oriented towards international trends of liberalization, privatization and deregulation, but the country adopted a more moderate approach and a gradual implementation pace compared with the UK and the USA (Hulsink, 1999). The 'pro-liberalization' Dutch model

(Levi-Faur, 1999) to a certain degree was inspired by the telecommunications pattern of Britain (Hulsink, 1999, p. 293), and these two countries can be differentiated from the 'pro-regulatory' ones that are mainly supported by France and Germany (Natalicchi, 2001[3]). In a similar way to France, especially in the early stages of the EU liberalization process, Germany and Italy adopted a defensive and protectionist approach to their national monopolies before initiating the required institutional modifications in the late 1980s and 1990s (Thatcher, 1999).

8.6 REFORMS IMPACT ON CONSUMERS

The past reforms in the telecommunications sector have introduced elements of competition and moved the market from predominantly State-controlled monopolies to a privatized/liberalized one. The question is whether privatization and liberalization, beyond their effects on investment and efficiency, have benefited European consumers by increasing choice, lowering prices and introducing high quality and innovative services. According to the existing literature, consumers benefited more from increases in competition and technological developments than privatization (Bacchiocchi et al., 2011).

Competition has been promoted first, with some positive effects on consumer welfare through price reduction. The implementation of the EU law[4] has been a main driver for the price drop between 2000 and 2010, mostly for national long-distance calls and international calls.

According to the literature, policy reforms have different impacts on prices: the introduction of number portability has a negative impact on mobile call prices (Grzybowski, 2005); prospective and effective competition both reduce the price of all telecommunications services (Boylaud and Nicoletti, 2001); privatization of the incumbent telecom operator increases prices while the establishment of an independent regulatory authority decreases them (Estache et al., 2006); and privatizations increase prices in developing countries while they have no effect on developed economies (Gasmi and Virto, 2010). The cross-country study by Bacchiocchi et al. (2011) on the impact on consumer prices of European telecommunications privatization and liberalization of telephony markets shows that prices of international and national phone calls were reduced significantly by an increase in the number of mobile phone users and by higher levels of investment and increases in competition (liberalization) – while the change from public to private ownership (privatization) made no significant difference.

Overall, it is very difficult to assess how a policy reform impacts telecommunication prices.[5] Along with studies assessing the effect of privatization on prices, Banerjee and Ros (2000), Gutierrez (2003), Fink et al. (2002), Ros (2003) and Li and Xu (2002, 2004) report that privatization reduces unmet demand in developing countries.

In addition, Eurobarometer surveys, which analyse citizens' opinions on telecommunications services, should also be considered in order to address satisfaction with reforms (Clifton et al., 2005; Clifton et al., 2010; Bacchiocchi et al., 2011; Fiorio and Florio, 2011). Two main dimensions can be considered: consumer satisfaction with telecommunication prices and satisfaction with quality. The perception of quality is important: it must be assessed whether, with market liberalization, citizens have ended up with lower quality services (CEEP and ETUC, 2000). Paired with unfair prices and restricted access to service, this has consequences for equity and social cohesion (Clifton et al., 2011). Bacchiocchi et al. (2011), using the Eurobarometer data on opinions, find that regulation variables have a significant effect on the probability of being satisfied. Public ownership has a negative impact on satisfaction, suggesting that consumers are more likely to express dissatisfaction with prices the further the reform process has gone. Entry regulation, instead, positively affects satisfaction with prices. As for what concerns perception of quality, the same study finds no significant effect of privatization, while legal conditions regarding competition have a negative impact on the perception of higher quality. A negative and significant effect is obtained by considering the market structure indicator, as the perception of the quality of the service becomes higher when the market becomes more open. In addition to these results, Clifton et al. (2011), focusing on the UK and Spain, showed that the citizens who expressed higher levels of dissatisfaction with telecommunications services are those more potentially vulnerable as consumers, for instance, the unemployed, the elderly and the less educated.

Moreover, competition enforcement was a challenge for incumbents that were forced to protect their domestic market positions, such as Deutsche Telekom, Slovak Telekom, Telefónica of Spain and Telekomunikacja Polska.

However, the increase in competition in the telecommunications sector does not necessarily guarantee consumer rights protection. Further measures are necessary in order to safeguard consumer privacy and to ensure affordability and universal access to essential telecommunications services. Hence, emphasis has been placed by EU institutions on ensuring access to services, fair pricing, provision of relevant information on services subscribed and privacy of personal information.[6]

Finally, investments in broadband networks supporting high-speed Internet have been promoted at the EU level together with investments in the development and diffusion of wireless technologies.[7] In 2014, the special Eurobarometer report *E-Communications and Telecom Single Market Household Survey* was released, containing results of an extensive survey conducted at the EU level on household access to telecommunications services. Concerning the issue of accessibility, nearly all EU households have telephone access, either fixed and/or mobile.[8] The overall proportion of households that have Internet access at home is around 65 percent, most of which is represented by broadband access, with dial-up access only remaining significant in a small number of countries.[9]

8.7 CONCLUSION

The above-described reforms in the EU telecommunications sector indicate a major policy shift towards privatization and liberalization, which has significantly changed the dynamics and the rules of the game for the whole sector. During the past two decades, a certain degree of convergence in domestic telecommunications policies occurred as a result of the common EU regulatory framework and the Europeanization process. However, notable variations in the reform patterns across countries are still observed.

The opening of the market has led to more consumer choice, lower prices and a better quality of service, while the privatization effect per se is not clear. In addition, accessibility and affordability have been improved for consumers in all traditional telecommunications services. What remains to be done is to provide consumers with services of higher quality, such as access to high technology broadband connection.

Despite the positive effect of policy reforms on consumers, the main drivers of welfare increase have been technological advancements and innovations. The massive increase in telecommunications consumption all over the world and the appearance of new smart technologies will be the main demand drivers. Today, things are changing as OTT services enter the market and operate independently from the rules and infrastructures of the traditional telecommunications industry, also questioning the role of the infrastructure operators and the regulators.

NOTES

*   The authors would like to thank Armen Ghalumyan for his contribution to an initial version of this chapter presented in the EUsers Summer School – 'Performance and Governance of Services of General Interest. Critical Perspectives on Energy, Telecommunications, Transport and Water Reforms in the EU', 27 June–1 July 2016, Palazzo Greppi, Milan.

1. Network neutrality is the principle that neither the content nor the quality of the connections may be affected by the commercial interests of Internet service providers (ISPs) or other companies.
2. A 'reform frontrunner', in Florio's words (2013, p. 36).
3. Nattalicchi (2001) cited by Heritier (1999, p. 41).
4. See Directive 2002/21/EC of the European Parliament and of the Council of 7 March 2002 on a common regulatory framework for electronic communications networks and services ('framework directive').
5. From a theoretical point of view, the impact of privatization and liberalization on prices is ambiguous a priori. A positive effect of privatization and liberalization on prices can be expected if they have been set artificially low by public-owned (monopoly) enterprises. The reasons behind such behavior can be found in its rationale, for example, political reasons. In this case, the effect on consumer welfare is expected to be negative, as the reform process leads to higher tariffs, in a perspective of financial sustainability (Foster et al., 2004). However, as stressed by Florio (2013), telecommunications providers were profitable across EU countries and often independent of transfers from the government. Changes in price structure can also occur. In many cases, public telephone monopolies have cross-subsidized between local and long-distance calls, which are usually not sustainable in a competitive framework. Instead, if enterprises have been inefficient in the case of public ownership or in the case of private monopolies, reforms will probably lead to tariff reductions as consumers benefit from the improved efficiency if they offer more potential space for competition. Yet, while there have been great advances in telecommunications services in the last decades, there is still debate whether privatization is the only possible source of efficiency increases and consequently of consumer prices decreases. Borghi et al. (2016) suggested that the negative effect on the productivity of public-owned firms can be reduced (or reversed) if the quality of institutions (regulatory quality, government quality and effectiveness) is high.
6. Misleading Advertising Directive: Council Directive 84/450/EEC relating to the approximation of the laws, regulations and administrative provisions of the Member States concerning misleading advertising. The Distance Selling Directive: Directive 97/7/EC on the protection of consumers in respect of distance contracts. The Unfair Commercial Practices Directive: Directive 2005/29/EC concerning unfair business-to-consumer commercial practices in the internal market. Regulation on cooperation in consumer protection within the European single market: Regulation (EC) 2006/2004 on cooperation between national authorities responsible for the enforcement of consumer protection laws (the Regulation on consumer protection cooperation).
7. See also https://ec.europa.eu/digital-single-market/node/118 (accessed 7 April 2017).
8. Penetration rates in Europe range from 100 percent in ten Member States to 94 percent in Portugal, Romania and Slovakia.
9. Most Member States in eastern and southern areas generally have broadband penetration of 56 percent or less, with the lowest levels recorded in Italy (41 percent) and Portugal (43 percent).

REFERENCES

Bacchiocchi, E., Florio, M. and Gambaro, M. (2011), 'Telecom reforms in the EU: prices and consumers' satisfaction', *Telecommunications Policy*, **35** (4), 382–96.
Banerjee, A. and Ros, A.J. (2000), 'Telecommunications privatization and tariff rebalancing: evidence from Latin America', *Telecommunications Policy*, **24** (3), 233–52.
Banerjee, A. and Ros, A.J. (2002), 'Drivers of demand growth for mobile telecommunications services: evidence from international panel data', accessed

6 February 2017 at http://www.nera.com/content/dam/nera/publications/archive1/DriversofDemandGrowth_Banerjee_Ros.pdf.

Bartle, I. (2005), *Globalization and EU Policy-making: The Neo-liberal Transformation of Telecommunications and Electricity*, Manchester: Manchester University Press.

Bauby, P. (2002), 'L'Europe des services publics: entre libéralisation, modernisation, régulation, évaluation', *Politiques et Management Public*, **20** (1), 15–30.

Borghi, E., Del Bo, C. and Florio, M. (2016), 'Institutions and firms' productivity: evidence from electricity distribution in the EU', *Oxford Bulletin of Economics and Statistics*, **78** (2), 170–96.

Boylaud, O. and Nicoletti, G. (2001), 'Regulation, market structure and performance in telecommunications', *OECD Economic Studies*, **32** (1), 99–142.

CEEP and ETUC (2000), 'Proposal for a Charter of Services of General Interest, Brussels', 15 June, accessed 7 February 2017 at https://www.etuc.org/documents/etucceep-proposal-charter-services-general-interest#.WJmKPtKLTcs.

Clifton, J., Comín, F. and Díaz-Fuentes, D. (2005), 'Empowering Europe's citizens? On the prospects for the Charter of Services of General Interest', *Public Management Review*, **7** (3), 417–43.

Clifton, J., Comín, F. and Díaz-Fuentes, D. (2006), 'Privatizing public enterprises in the European Union 1960–2002: ideological, pragmatic, inevitable?', *Journal of European Public Policy*, **13** (5), 736–56.

Clifton, J., Comín, F. and Díaz-Fuentes, D. (2010), 'Evaluating EU policies on public services: a citizens' perspective', *Annals of Public and Cooperative Economics*, **81** (2), 281–311.

Clifton, J., Díaz-Fuentes, D., Fernández-Gutiérrez, M. and Revuelta, J. (2011), 'Is market-oriented reform producing a two-track Europe? Evidence from electricity and telecommunications', *Annals of Public and Cooperative Economics*, **82** (4), 495–513.

Council (1984), Council Directive 84/450/EEC of 10 December relating to the approximation of the laws, regulations and administrative provisions of the Member States concerning misleading advertising, OJ L 250, 19.9.1984, p. 17.

Estache, A., Goicoechea, A. and Trujillo, L. (2006), 'Utilities reform and corruption in developing countries', World Bank Policy Research Working Paper 4081, accessed 6 February 2017 at http://www-wds.worldbank.org/external/default/WDSContentServer/IW3P/IB/2006/12/06/000016406_20061206151405/Rendered/PDF/wps4081.pdf.

European Commission (2009), Regulation (EC) 2006/2004 on cooperation between national authorities responsible for the enforcement of consumer protection laws (the Regulation on consumer protection cooperation).

European Commission (2013), MEMO/13/779, 'Commission adopts regulatory proposals for a Connected Continent', Brussels, 11 September.

European Commission (2014), 'Implementation of the EU regulatory framework for electronic communications 2014', accessed 11 November 2016 at https://ec.europa.eu/digital-single-market/en/news/2014-report-implementation-eu-regulatory-framework-electronic-communications.

European Commission (2015), 'Implementation of the EU regulatory framework for electronic communications 2015', accessed 25 June 2016 at http://ec.europa.eu/transparency/regdoc/rep/10102/2015/EN/10102-2015-126-EN-F1-1.PDF.

European Commission, Joint Research Centre (2013), 'The EU ICT sector – R&D expenditure', accessed 6 February 2017 at https://ec.europa.eu/jrc/sites/default/files/jrc-infographic-eu-ict-sector-rd-expenditure_en.pdf.

European Parliament and Council (1997), Directive 97/7/EC of the European Parliament and of the Council of 20 May 1997 on the protection of consumers in respect of distance contracts ('The Distance Selling Directive'), http://europa.eu.int/comm/consumers/policy/developments/dist_sell/dist01_en.pdf.

European Parliament and Council (2002), Directive 2002/21/EC of the European Parliament and of the Council of 7 March 2002 on a common regulatory framework for electronic communications networks and services ('Framework Directive'), http://eur-lex.europa.eu/legal-content/EN/TXT/?uri=celex:32002L0021.

European Parliament and Council (2005), Directive 2005/29/EC concerning unfair business-to-consumer commercial practices in the internal market ('The Unfair Commercial Practices Directive'), http://eur-lex.europa.eu/LexUriServ/LexUriServ.do?uri=OJ:L:2005:149:0022:0039:en:PDF.

Evans, L. (2004), 'A force for market competition or market power?', in P. Drysdale (ed.), *The New Economy in East Asia and the Pacific*, London: Routledge, pp. 210–25.

Fink, C., Mattoo, A. and Rathindran, R. (2002), 'An assessment of telecommunications reform in developing countries', World Bank Policy Research Working Paper 2909, http://citeseerx.ist.psu.edu/viewdoc/download?doi=10.1.1.20.1167&rep=rep1&type=pdf.

Fiorio, C.V. and Florio, M. (2011), 'Would you say that the price you pay for electricity is fair? Consumers' satisfaction and utility reforms in EU15', *Energy Economics*, **22** (2), 178–82.

Florio, M. (2013), *Network Industries and Social Welfare: The Experiment that Reshuffled European Utilities*, Oxford: Oxford University Press.

Foster, V., Tiongson, E.R. and Ruggeri Laderchi, C. (2004), *Poverty and Social Impact Analysis: Key Issues in Utility Reform*, Washington, DC: World Bank.

Gasmi, F. and Virto, L. (2010), 'The determinants and impact of telecommunications reforms in developing countries', *Journal of Development Economics*, **93** (2), 275–86.

Grzybowski, L. (2005), 'Regulation of mobile telephony across the European Union: an empirical analysis', *Journal of Regulatory Economics*, **28** (1), 47–67.

Gutierrez, L.H. (2003), 'The effect of the endogenous regulation on telecommunications expansion and efficiency in Latin America', *Journal of Regulatory Economics*, **23** (3), 257–86.

Heritier, A. (1999), *Policy-making and Diversity in Europe: Escaping Deadlock*, Cambridge: Cambridge University Press.

Hulsink, W. (1999), *Privatisation and Liberalisation in European Telecommunications: Comparing Britain, the Netherlands and France*, London and New York: Routledge.

ITU (International Telecommunication Union) (2015), *Trends in Telecommunications Reform 2015: Getting Ready for the Digital Economy*, Geneva: ITU.

Levi-Faur, D. (1999), 'Governing Dutch telecommunications reform: state-business interactions in the transformation of national policy regimes to (European) embedded policy regimes', *Journal of European Public Policy*, **6** (1), 102–22.

Levi-Faur, D. (2004), 'On the "net impact" of Europeanization. The EU's telecoms and electricity regimes between the global and the national', *Comparative Political Studies*, **37** (1), 3–29.

Li, W. and Xu, L.C. (2002), 'The political economy of privatization and

competition: cross-country evidence from the telecommunications sector',
Journal of Comparative Economics, **30** (3), 439–62.

Li, W. and Xu, L.C. (2004), 'The impact of privatization and competition in the
telecommunications sector around the world', *Journal of Law and Economics*,
47 (2), 1–36.

Natalicchi, G. (2001), *Wiring Europe: Reshaping the European Telecommunications
Regime*, Lanham, MD and Boulder, CO: Rowman & Littlefield.

Newbery, D. (2000), *Privatization, Restructuring and Regulation of Network
Utilities*, Cambridge, MA: MIT Press.

OECD (2003), *Reviews of Regulatory Reform. Regulatory Reform in France:
Regulatory Reform in the Telecommunications Sector*, Paris: OECD Publishing.

OECD (2013), *OECD Communications Outlook 2013*, Paris: OECD Publishing,
accessed 12 January 2017 at http://www.keepeek.com/Digital-Asset-Management/
oecd/science-and-technology/oecd-communications-outlook-2013_comms_outlo
ok-2013-en#.WJmNGdKLTcs.

Picot, A. (2016), 'Telecommunications in the European Union' (PowerPoint slides),
accessed 6 February 2017 at http://users.unimi.it/eusers/wp-content/uploads/6_
Picot_A_28.06.2016.pdf.

Rodine-Hardy, K. (2013), *Global Markets and Government Regulation in
Telecommunications*, New York: Cambridge University Press.

Ros, A.J. (2003), 'The impact of the regulatory process and price cap regulation in
Latin American telecommunications markets', *Review of Network Economics*, **2**
(3), 270–86.

Schneider, V. and Werle, R. (2007), 'Telecommunications policy', in P. Graziano and
M. Vink (eds), *Europeanization: New Research Agendas*, Basingstoke: Palgrave
Macmillan, pp. 266–80.

Stern, J. (2014), 'The British utility regulation model: its recent history and future
prospects', Centre for Competition and Regulatory Policy (CCRP), Working
Paper 23, City University, London.

Szcepanski, M. (2013), 'Towards a European single market for telecoms', Briefing
– European Parliamentary Research Service, 25.11.2013.

Thatcher, M. (1999), 'The national politics of European regulation: institutional
reform in telecommunications', Paper presented at the 6th biennial conference of
the European Community Studies Association, Pittsburgh, June.

Thatcher, M. (2006), 'Europe and the reform of national regulatory institutions: a
comparison of Britain, France and Germany', Paper for Council of European
Studies 15th Conference, Chicago, 29 March–1 April.

Valin, S. (2007), *Services publics: un défi pour l'Europe. Approches nationales et
enjeux communautaires*, Paris: Charles Léopold Mayer.

9. The changing nature of railways in Europe: empirical evidence on prices, investments and quality

Giovanni Esposito, Julia Doleschel, Tobias Kaloud and Jadwiga Urban-Kozłowska*

9.1 INTRODUCTION

Network services such as electricity, natural gas, telecommunications, transport and water are crucial factors of economic well-being as they offer society the opportunity to coordinate, over time and space, large and complex flows of essential goods, people or services (Florio, 2013). Until the 1980s, these services in Europe were mainly provided by vertically integrated state-owned monopolies. Then, following the wave of New Public Management (NPM) reforms in the organization of national public sectors, many governments dismantled stated-owned enterprises:

> Europe has been at the forefront of change. Elsewhere, in the USA, Latin America, Asia, and in formerly planned economies, there have been similar reforms, but perhaps nowhere have they been so consistently implemented as in the European Union. In the past two decades, first in the UK, then subsequently in all the other EU member states, governments have increasingly moved away from the direct provision of public services, from ownership of utilities, and from franchised monopolies. Ministries and independent regulators have shown a greater reliance on market mechanisms, and now consider the network service providers as market players ... In Europe, the critical mass for the policy shift was achieved in the 1980s, after the social and political upheavals of the 1970s and the severe oil shocks that destabilized public finances. (Florio, 2013, pp. 5–8)

At the European Union (EU) level, policies aimed at creating a well-functioning internal market have played a key role in the restructuring of national network industries. In fact, for many decades an exclusion clause subscribed in the Treaty of Rome (1957) by the six founders of the European Community (Belgium, France, Italy, Germany, Luxembourg and the Netherlands) allowed them to exclude services such as telecommunications, transport, energy and water from some common market rules. Then, since the 1980s the EU's efforts to create a unique internal market for those services intensified and, in 2009, the Lisbon Treaty abandoned this exemption by introducing competition rules and forbidding state aid, except under special circumstances to be notified and approved by the European Commission.

Within this context, over the last 20 years many changes have occurred in the structure, regulation and performance of European network industries. Florio (2013) provides a detailed analysis of how public ownership, vertical integration, entry regulation and market concentration have evolved across the EU 15's network industries over the last two decades. Firstly, telecommunications, electricity and airlines, despite some differences, experienced an almost effective process of regulatory convergence from the standard industrial organization (state-owned monopoly) towards the NPM model: this is particularly evident in the telecommunications sector. Secondly, when looking at postal services and gas over the last two decades, in both sectors there is no clear convergence as countries show very different regulatory settings. Finally, the rail sector represents a *sui generis* case as only few countries have actually modified the initial state-owned monopolistic structure of the industry. Indeed, only the UK showed a mostly fully liberalized and privatized industry, with Denmark, Sweden, Germany and the Netherlands midway or fairly advanced in the reform process. Despite little progress, remaining countries still show the fundamental features of the traditional industrial organization of the rail sector.

The Organisation for Economic Co-operation and Development (OECD, 2016) data about entry regulation, public ownership, vertical integration and market concentration provide detailed insights about the change process experienced by network industries over the last 20 years. Firstly, as to entry regulation, the data show that the rail sector has shown great resistance in improving terms and conditions of third party access (TPA), whereas all other sectors have been more accepting. Secondly, the OECD's information on public ownership reveals that, except for telecommunications, all other network industries have shown some resistance in reducing the shares owned – either directly or indirectly – by the government in the largest firms in the sector. As far as vertical integration is concerned, telecommunications and – to a smaller extent – rail are the sectors demonstrating improved degrees of vertical separation among the different segments of the industry. Finally, concerning the market structure, telecommunications is the sector where network provision has evolved the most towards more competitive states of the market. In the majority of the other sectors, the market share of the largest company in the sector is between 50 per cent and 90 per cent. More specifically, rail and – to a smaller extent – gas industries are characterized by the highest number of countries where the market share of the largest company in the sector is above 90 per cent.

The considerations above show that rail is among the sectors that have resisted the most to the changes the NPM paradigm has introduced in the organization and management of state-owned enterprises. This chapter thus focuses on the transformations of the rail sector over the last two decades and is organized in two sections. Section 9.2 describes the change by providing a historical overview of the reform context and referring to the main aspects of the organizational change experienced by the European rail industries in the last decades; it also outlines the most important regulatory innovations introduced by the EU in this sector. Section 9.3 assesses change by empirically investigating the way regulatory innovations have influenced the price, investment and quality of European rail services, using OECD's data from 1996 to 2013. We conclude this chapter (Section 9.4) by offering reflections on the development of railways in Europe.

9.2 REFORM CONTEXT

Over the last decades, European public sectors and state-owned enterprises have experienced a profound process of organizational change in which private sector managerial tools and principles have spread across many countries with the aim of improving effectiveness, efficiency and economy (Aucoin, 1990; Hood, 1991, 1995; Stewart and Walsh, 1992; Walsh, 1997; London, 2002; Esposito et al., 2017). This change occurred between the 1970s and 1980s when the striking international trend of NPM reforms introduced a new paradigm for the organization and management of public sectors:

> These reforms sought to reduce the role of the State in production, as well as in service delivery and to encourage the deregulation of public enterprises. The emphasis was on maintaining macro-economic stability, lowering inflation, cutting deficit spending, and reducing the scope and cost of government. (United Nations, 2001, p. 32)

In the wake of NPM-style restructuring of national public sectors, many European network industries evolved from vertically integrated state-owned monopolies to market-friendly and competitive organizational schemes.[1]

9.2.1 Rail Sector: Industrial Organization in Transition

The traditional organizational structure of most European railways in the post-war period was that of a vertically integrated state-owned monopoly. During this period, the rail sector was managed as a natural monopoly because of the high fixed costs associated with providing infrastructure and the importance of offering affordable and attractive public transport to all income groups (Drew and Ludewig, 2011). Nevertheless, in the 1950s the market share of most railways began to decrease in many countries as they were unable to compete with roads and airways. Many rail companies – particularly their freight branches – ran into traffic decline and financial difficulties. According to Drew and Ludewig (2011), two reasons were behind these competitiveness shortcomings. Firstly, railways were traditionally managed as part of a government ministry with few incentives for managers to meet market requirements. Secondly, politicians expanded railway infrastructures and services without necessarily paying for them but rather by accumulating debt. These two characteristics of the railway sector – politically driven management and debt-based investments – were the major causes that represented the driving force behind the reform process of this sector in the 1990s.

The EU has played a key role in this reform process by promoting several regulatory instruments (Directive 91/440 and four railway packages in 2001, 2004, 2007 and 2016) aimed at: (1) establishing in the member states rules allowing for open access to railway infrastructure and fair competition between railways, undertakings for freight and international passenger services, in the context of a single European market for railways; (2) ensuring the financial viability of companies operating in the rail sector. The European Commission (1996, p. 3) highlighted both issues in the white paper, 'A Strategy for Revitalising the Community's Railways', stating that:

> the railways have been largely insulated from market forces. Governments have a certain responsibility in that as they often did not allow sufficient managerial independence and imposed obligations without compensating fully for the costs involved; they also failed to set clear financial objectives but subsidized losses or let debt pile up … A new kind of railway is needed. It should be first and foremost a business, with management independent and free to exploit opportunities, but answerable for failure. For this it should have sound finances, unencumbered by the burden of the past. It should be exposed to market forces in an appropriate form which should also lead to a greater involvement of the private sector. A clear division of responsibilities is required between the State and the railways, particularly for public services.

Through the use of regulation, the EU has prompted liberalization policies intended to: (1) allow new entrants to compete with each other and, mainly, with incumbent operators; (2) create the proper market conditions compelling companies to adopt price competition systems. However, beside regulatory instruments, a key role was played by its investment policy in Trans-European Networks (TENs) contributing to the ongoing liberalization process through improved technical harmonization and interoperability across Europe.[2]

It is worth noticing that regulatory instruments and TENs investment policy have been introduced by the EU not only to support liberalization efforts but also to improve competitiveness. On the one hand, the above-mentioned regulation has been aimed at enhancing the business environment of rail sector undertakings and, by doing so, lowering costs. On the other, TENs' policy has prioritized member states' investments in high-speed rail (HSR) systems with the purpose of rendering railway services more competitive than those provided by roads and airways. Before the arrival of HSR services, railways were constantly losing market share in favour of roads (mostly for freight traffic) and air. Then, in 1981 the introduction of HSR services in Europe with the inauguration of the Paris-Sud-Est line was a break point for air, road and rail market share. It paved the way for the modernization of rail transport and favoured the promotion of effective competition between railways, roads and airways in terms of medium and long distance trips. Therefore, supporting the rail mode became one of the main axes of the European transport policies. In 1994, the Trans-European Network – Transport (TEN-T) programme was established and provided the most important EU financial framework to support member states' investments in railway infrastructures and, namely, HSR.[3]

9.2.2   EU Reform Framework: The Railway Packages

The EU's rationale behind the rail sector reforms was to create a single, efficient and competitive market for railways throughout Europe (the so-called 'Single European Railway Area'). In order to achieve this goal, the following key reform aspects were identified and implemented by the European Commission through four legislative packages plus a recast:

(1) unbundling of rail infrastructure and operating activities; (2) liberalization of access rights for railway undertakings; (3) commercialization of the incumbent railway companies; (4) technical standardization and improvement of interoperability; (5) introduction of independent national regulatory authorities (European Commission, 2001).

The First Railway Package, adopted by the European Commission in 2001, was composed of four directives. Directive 2001/12/EC had the objectives of: (1) introducing the 'open access' principle for the international freight services; (2) creating an independent body responsible for guaranteeing fair and non-discriminatory access to rail infrastructure; (3) avoiding cross-financing by imposing mandatory separation of balance sheets as well as profit and loss accounts for the infrastructure managers and train operators; and (4) defining infrastructure charging and licensing. Regarding the separation of infrastructure and operations, the directive allowed member states to achieve this either by creating distinct divisions within a single undertaking (the so-called 'holding company model') or by setting up independent entities charged with infrastructure management (Asmild et al., 2008, p. 5).

Another component was Directive 2001/13/EC, which stipulated the common criteria for granting the license to EU rail operators. The issue of capacity allocation was tackled under Directive 2001/14/EC. The deadline for implementing these legal instruments was 15 March 2003. The objective of Directive 2001/16/EC was to enhance the interoperability of the trans-European conventional rail system.

Together with the previously issued Directive 96/48/EC on the interoperability of the trans-European HSR system, these two legal instruments were designed to ensure a smooth and safe transit of trains from one member state's rail network to another. They focused on crucial technical aspects, such as safety, control systems, signalling, freight wagons and training for staff engaged in international rail transport operations.

In 2002 the European Commission proposed a new set of legal instruments (known as 'the Second Railway Package'), which entered into force on 30 April 2004. It encompassed three directives – scheduled to be implemented by 30 April 2006 – and one regulation.

The aim of Directive 2004/49/EC was to develop a common approach to rail safety.

With a view to clarifying interoperability requirements, Directive 2004/50/EC amended and updated Directive 96/48/EC and Directive 2001/16/EC. As a result, the scope of Directive 2001/16/EC was extended to cover the whole of the European rail network. Such a modification was of great importance as the full liberalization of the rail network to national and international freight transport services was scheduled for January 2007 (Directive 2004/51/EC).

Regulation 881/2004 (amended by Regulation (EC) 1335/2008) created the European Railway Agency (ERA), a body designated to coordinate safety and interoperability efforts. ERA has played a key role in the alignment of technical and safety regulations in different member states and, by doing so, has been a driving force in the modernization of European railways.

The third step towards revitalization of the railways and the enhancement of an integrated European railway area took place in 2007 with the issuing of the so-called 'Third Railway Package'. It was composed of two directives and one regulation. The main objective of Directive 2007/58/ EC was the liberalization of the rail market with regard to international passenger trains. The opening up of the international passenger services within the EU was scheduled for 1 January 2010. As a result, cabotage to international rail services was introduced. Pursuant to Directive 2007/59/EC the European licensing system for train drivers was created: minimum requirements relating to medical fitness, basic education and general professional skills for train drivers were set out. Regulation 1371/2007 stipulated minimum quality standards to be guaranteed to all passengers on all lines. One of its main innovations was the introduction of the compensation system in case of train delay – thanks to this instrument, passengers were granted the right to partial reimbursement of their ticket cost, depending on the extent of delay.

In 2012 the European Commission launched a recast of the First Railway Package in order to simplify and consolidate various existing legal provisions. Directive 2012/34/EU addressed the main shortcomings that had been identified by the European Commission.

As regards competition issues, Directive 2012/34/EU aimed at improving transparency of access conditions in the rail market by requiring, for instance, more detailed network statements and providing better access to rail-related services. The power of national rail regulators was further strengthened through the extension of their competences to rail-related services and ensuring their independence from any other public authority. In order to enhance rail investment, Directive 2012/34/EU called for smarter infrastructure charging rules to be adopted and obliged member states to develop long-term strategies regarding investment in rail infrastructure.

The Fourth Railway Package was introduced in 2016 and consisted of two main parts: the so-called 'Market Pillar' and 'Technical Pillar'. The former has aimed to recast the interoperability (Directive 2016/797) and rail safety directives (Directive 2016/798) as well as strengthen the role of ERA (Regulation 2016/796). The latter will allow for open access for domestic passenger services from 14 December 2020.[4] However, this regulatory package does not impose full institutional unbundling of train operations and infrastructure management. Moreover, the introduction of competitive tendering of public service contracts in the railway sector was only partially achieved, given the numerous derogations to this principle.[5]

Regarding all foregoing considerations, it turns out that not all of the EU's targets have been fully achieved.[6] It is also appropriate to note that most EU legal instruments were adopted in the form of a directive. This means that their transposition into national legal systems is required in order for them to be fully effective. In other words, the practical impact of the EU regulatory innovations has greatly depended on the cooperation of member states[7] in implementing supra-national reform guidelines. With this in mind, we now consider the actual reform implementation in several member states.

9.2.3 Actual Reform Implementation: Rail Passenger Sectors in Italy, France, Germany and Spain

The status of reform implementation is measured by the 'Rail Liberalization' (LIB) Index. It depicts the degree of market opening among the EU member states as well as Switzerland and Norway. Specifically, the LIB Index considers legal entry barriers and practical market access possibilities for railway undertakings. However, it does not take into account market results like prices, quality and the degree of competition. Figure 9.1 reports data from the 2011 LIB Index and shows that the status of reform implementation varies across EU countries. While few member states (UK, Germany, Sweden and Denmark) presented an advanced stage of reform

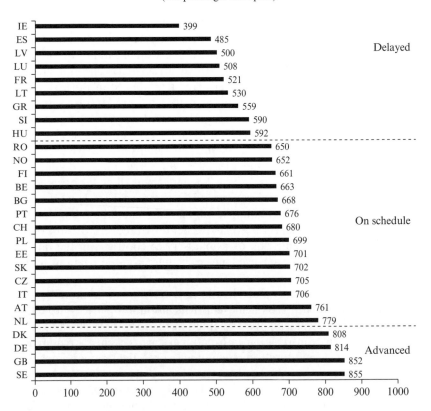

LIB Index 2011
(rail passenger transport)

Figure 9.1   LIB Index 2011 (rail passenger transport)

implementation (ahead of schedule), in the majority of countries reforms were on schedule or delayed. Following the enforcement of the EU's four railway packages, positive achievements have been met with regard to the opening up of national freight and international passenger markets. Nevertheless, progress towards creating an integrated European railway area and a genuine EU internal market for railway services is still needed in the field of the national passenger market.

The OECD's Energy, Transport and Communications Regulation (ETCR) indicator provides additional data to compare the status of implementation of railway reforms across European countries. However, unlike the LIB Index, it only captures differences in terms of regulatory regimes. The overall indicator ranges between 0 (describing a condition of full liberalization) and 6 (describing a condition of non-liberalization) and comprises issues of entry regulation, public ownership, market structure and vertical separation.

In a first step, it is important to observe the correlation between the LIB Index and the ETCR indicator in order to prove that both databases do not provide diverging information and, therefore, are equally reliable. We do find a significant and negative relationship (–0.75). As higher LIB and lower ETCR levels are associated with increased liberalization, we conclude that both statistics yield similar results for our sample.

In order to gain a deeper insight, we narrow the focus of the analysis down to four selected countries: Italy, France, Germany and Spain. We chose these four countries to account for the three different situations of reform implementation status presented in Figure 9.1: advanced status (Germany), on schedule status (Italy) and delayed status (France and Spain). Figure 9.2 shows that between 1996 and 2013 the reform process (as measured by the ETCR index) deepened in the four countries under examination: nevertheless, coherent with the LIB Index, in France and Spain to a smaller extent than in Italy and Germany.

The Italian state-owned company underwent major structural transformations between 1986 and 1992: the workforce was reduced to half and divisions were created to rationalize the management. The company was privatized in 1992 with the creation of Ferrovie dello Stato SpA (FS SpA), a joint stock company. However, the privatization was only formal, since shares were still owned by the Italian government. On 1 June 2000, the company's two main divisions (service and infrastructure) were separated and two different independent companies were created: Trenitalia, responsible for transport service, and Rete Ferroviaria Italiana (RFI), responsible for the management of the rail infrastructure. Both companies are still subsidiaries of FS SpA.

The French company Société Nationale des Chemins de Fer Français

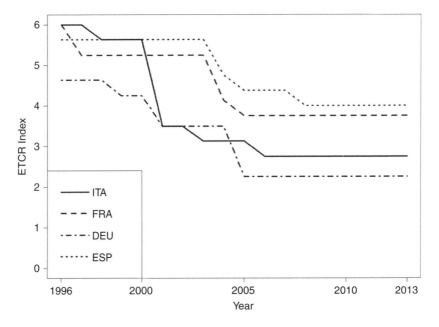

Source: Authors' elaboration on OECD ETCR database (2016).

Figure 9.2   General ETCR index

(SNCF) – backed by national authorities – has shown resistance to the EU process of reform and over the years has intensively lobbied the European Commission to reduce the scope of EU regulation and push back the deadlines to comply with legal requirements (Drew and Ludewig, 2011). The implementation of EU reforms in France has been particularly slow and it was one of the last countries to transpose the European regulation into the national legal system. In fact, the separation between infrastructure management and operation management was introduced in 1997 when Réseau Ferré de France (RFF) was created to manage the rail infrastructure. The legal separation between infrastructure and operations was introduced with an unusual condition according to which RFF was obliged to employ the services of SNCF's technical infrastructure services (Drew and Ludewig, 2011). Moreover, rail freight competition was authorized only at the end of March 2006 and the opening of the international passenger transport market, along with the related cabotage, was introduced in early January 2010. RFF now operates again under the supervision of SNCF. On 1 January 2015, RFF became SNCF Réseau, the operational assets of SNCF became SNCF Mobilités, and both groups were placed under the control of SNCF.

In Spain, in November 2003 the Law 39/2003 was approved by the national parliament and transposed the First Railway Package into legislation. This law set the rules for a new organizational model of the Spanish rail sector, the end of the monopoly held by Renfe and the market opening to competition. It separated the management of transport services from the management of infrastructure and assigned them to two independent organizations, Renfe Operadora and Adif, respectively. The law also defined the conditions regulating the access of railway undertakings to the rail transport market by establishing a licensing system subject to the compliance with certain requirements. According to these legal provisions, service operators should pay Adif a fee for infrastructure usage, as well as for the use of stations and other facilities. Moreover, Law 39/2003 allowed the government to declare of public interest the provision of certain rail transport services financed by debt but necessary to ensure territorial cohesion in Spain. Finally, it establishes the gradual opening of the rail network to new transport companies introducing competition for the first time. From January 2005, national and international freight were liberalized while the market opening for the passenger transport was postponed. In September 2015, Law 38/2015 was released and changed the existing track access charging system, as it was not considered encouraging for newcomers. With the aim of increasing use of the Spanish network, the new regulation abolished the annual access charge – as it was seen as a major entry barrier to competitors – and allowed operators to be charged only for capacity allocation, line usage and use of electrification systems. The law also set financial incentives for Public Services Obligations (PSO), and established separate charges for the use of gauge-changing installations, station and platform tracks, as well as freight terminals and other sidings.

In Germany in 1994, two former state enterprises, Deutsche Bundesbahn and Deutsche Reichsbahn, were transformed into a single business enterprise (Deutsche Bahn AG) which – according to a new article of the German constitution – was to be organized as a joint stock corporation with a privatization option (Drew and Ludewig, 2011). At the same time, German rail transport markets were opened to competition. Open access in both rail freight and passenger transport markets were based on provisions of the 1993 General Railway Act (*Allgemeines Eisenbahngesetz*, AEG), offering open access in all German rail transport markets. Directive 91/440/EEC provided non-discriminatory open access to the network infrastructure, not only for all German railway undertakings, but also for those coming from other EU member states. In April 2005, AEG was comprehensively revised by transposing the Second European Railway Package into the German law, also giving the Federal Network Agency (Bundesnetzagentur, BNA) new scopes of responsibility in the field of railway regulation. In 2010 the Third Railway Package entered into force and provided access rights for international cross-border passenger traffic. It was transposed into German law thanks to the fourth amendment to the General Railway Act, without seeking recourse from the possibility of restricting cabotage, and protecting parallel national public rail services – which are subsidized.

Despite the formal opening of market regulation promoted by EU regulatory effort, the state is still a crucial actor in the four countries under examination (Beria et al., 2010). This is especially true for the rail passenger sector where the state is simultaneously the owner, planner, client and regulator. It follows that the transposition of EU directives often resulted in a formal process of organizational separation (also known as legal unbundling) based on the holding company model.

In Italy, RFI – network manager – and Trenitalia – service provider – both participate in Ferrovie dello Stato, the public holding company of the rail industry. A similar situation occurs in Germany where the federal state holds via Deutsche Bahn both DB Netz and DB Bahn. In France and in Spain – where the domestic market is open to competitors just for cross-border and freight traffic – the situation is the same: the state owns both entities.

In France, as of 1 January 2015 SNCF and RFF merged together (and RFF was renamed SNCF Réseau) to form a single state-owned railway company 'to strengthen and modernize the railway service in France' (Ministère de l'Environnement de l'Énergie et de la Mer, 2013, p. 1). The intention is to have the system ready by 2019, when the network will be opened to competitors, including domestic traffic.

As for planning, in all selected countries the state still represents the key player. Indeed, in all examined countries, investments in maintenance and network development often result from negotiations between the network manager and the public authority, with the latter determining price and investment funding. Germany represents a *sui generis* case as investments concerning the regional network are managed jointly with regions.

Furthermore, in all selected cases, the state is also the client of railway companies. Indeed, regional traffic – which is a PSO – is subsidized everywhere by the states' or regions' budget. States' or regions' authorities negotiate standard service levels and prices with the provider. In Italy, the regulatory framework is stricter than anywhere else as there is no negotiation between regions and service providers about PSO. In this country the region can unilaterally determine the required service level and price that it is going to pay for the service.

As to regulation, there are different arrangements in place between France and Spain, on the one hand, and Italy and Germany, on the other.

Fixing prices for PSO is a prerogative of regional authorities in both Germany and Italy, whereas in France and Spain it is up to the central state. Concerning access of newcomers to the network, while in France and Spain the market is closed to new competitors, in Italy and Germany the state has the right to determine the access rules: particularly in Italy, the licensing rules are clearly in favour of newcomers. In both Italy and Germany, slot allocation rules are still missing due to the fact that traffic congestion only occurs on certain links and never in profitable tracks.

In a nutshell, in-depth insights for the selected countries show that despite formal improvement of market access regulation, the actual organization of the rail industry still relies on state-controlled structures. The state is still a crucial actor and is often the owner, planner, client and, eventually, the regulator. It follows that the EU objective of creating a single and competitive European railway market seems to be barely met by some member states which still prefer to manage rail sector-related services by using state structures instead of market arrangements. Beria et al. (2010) argue that this happens because national governments consider railways as a strategic sector playing a crucial role in the design and implementation of overall national industrial and economic policy. Nonetheless, some improvements are expected with the implementation of the Fourth Railway Package.

9.3   EMPIRICS

In the preceding sections, we have described rail sector transformations and the process of opening up national state-owned monopolies through liberalization policies promoted by the EU. In addition, the regulatory effort through European legislation as part of several reform packages has been outlined in detail. We then focused on the status of reform implementation in Italy, France, Germany and Spain.

The aim of this section is to conduct a quantitative analysis of the relationship between regulatory regimes prevailing in national railway sectors, on the one hand, and the price of rail passenger services, investment level in infrastructures and quality aspects, on the other. Prices and investments are addressed by an econometric strategy outlined below.

9.3.1   Data and Estimation Strategy

We merge several datasets from the OECD, European Commission and DICE Database to analyse the relationship between rail sector regulatory regimes and consumer prices for rail passenger services, as well as railway infrastructure investments.

With regard to our data structure, we created a panel dataset that includes all EU member states (except for Malta and Cyprus as these countries do not have railways). Regarding the time dimension, our unbalanced[8] dataset comprises the years from 1996 to 2013. Formally, we specify the following empirical estimation equation:

$$y_{it} = x'_{it} \beta + \eta_i + \mu_t + \varepsilon_{it} \qquad (9.1)$$

Subscripts i and t denote a country at a specific point in time. While y_{it} depicts the dependent variable (e.g. prices for rail passenger services), x'_{it} is a row vector that captures explanatory variables (e.g. regulation, passenger kilometres, consumer price level and gross domestic product) and β is a column vector of respective coefficients. The country-specific variable η_i summarizes unobserved individual components, μ_t captures time fixed effects and, finally, ε_{it} denotes the independent and identically distributed error term with its usual characteristics. In order to account for time-invariant country-specific factors, we apply the fixed effects estimator by considering the variation within the countries over time (Wooldridge, 2014).

The first dependent variable to take into account is the 'Harmonized Consumer Price' Index for rail passenger services extracted from Eurostat (European Commission, 2016a). This variable is crucial for our analysis as lower prices are commonly expected to be a result of deregulation. It should be pointed out, however, that estimation results relying on this harmonized price index should be interpreted with caution. Firstly, only a small sample of rail products that might not represent the general market is taken into account (European Commission, 2016c). Secondly, railway prices at the regional level are often regulated and therefore largely independent from the degree of market liberalization.

In our second model, railway infrastructure investments at current prices in million euros serve as the dependent variable (DICE Database, 2014). Without question, investments are of central importance as they are necessary for a reliable and competitive railway system and capture the firms' long-term decisions.

Concerning our set of explanatory variables, we are primarily interested in the coefficients associated with the degree of regulation. The OECD's ETCR indicators provide a quantitative measure of the regulatory regime in the railway market. These indicators cover entry regulation, public ownership, vertical integration as well as market structure and range between 0 and 6. Higher values imply tighter regulation (OECD, 2016).

As further covariates, we add billions of travelled passenger rail kilometres, the overall Harmonized Consumer Price Index as well as the gross domestic product at current prices in billions of purchasing power parities

(European Commission, 2016a). While the former variable is included to control for demand effects, the latter two rule out possible endogeneity arising from the overall economic development.

9.3.2   Estimation Results

The aim of our first model is to identify the relationship between state-level regulatory regimes and the price for rail passenger services by including travelled passenger rail kilometres, the overall Harmonized Consumer Price Index as well as the gross domestic product as covariates. Table 9.1 presents our results. While column 1 solely includes dummies for the sample of countries, column 2 also considers time-specific effects.

Table 9.1   OLS estimation of the relationship between regulatory policies and the price for rail passenger services

	Dependent variable:	
	PRICE FOR RAIL PASSENGER SERVICES	
	(1)	(2)
Entry	−2.704***	0.637
	(0.713)	(0.387)
Public Ownership	−2.672**	0.044
	(1.288)	(0.665)
Vertical Integration	−8.183***	−1.860***
	(1.162)	(0.626)
Market Structure	−0.095	0.893**
	(0.825)	(0.414)
Passenger Kilometres	−0.197	−0.355***
	(0.272)	(0.137)
Harmonized Consumer Price Index	0.059	0.035
	(0.046)	(0.024)
Gross Domestic Product	0.040***	−0.005
	(0.010)	(0.006)
Country Fixed Effects	Yes	Yes
Time Fixed Effects	No	Yes
Observations	317	317
R^2	0.492	0.181
Adjusted R^2	0.450	0.059
F Statistic	40.400*** (df = 7; 292)	8.680*** (df = 7; 275)

Note: ** $p < 0.05$, *** $p < 0.01$.

The model presented in column 1 yields significant and negative coefficients for the regulatory variables of entry, public ownership and vertical integration. This implies that a looser regulation in these areas correlates with higher prices for rail passenger services. In addition, rises in the gross domestic product are also associated with price increases.

When not only country- but also time-specific fixed effects are considered, the significance and the magnitude of our coefficients change. Specifically, we find that the indicator for vertical integration drops to around one-quarter of its initial value, while the only other significant regulatory variable to remain is market structure – that positively correlates with the price for rail passenger services. In addition, travelled passenger kilometres are negatively associated with this price index. To summarize, we find no evidence that deregulation in the railway sector is associated with lower prices.

One of the reasons for deregulating European rail sectors was the expectation that more competition would have increased investment expenditures (Kern et al., 2010). Therefore, our second model examines the relationship between railway infrastructure investments and OECD's regulatory indicators as well as our other covariates. Nevertheless, data are only available for the period between 1996 and 2010 (DICE Database, 2014). Table 9.2 summarizes the regression results. Again, column 1 considers country and column 2 country as well as time-specific effects.

The regression results show a similar pattern for both models. Specifically, lower levels of regulation in the fields of vertical integration, as well as market structure, are correlated with higher railway infrastructure investments. Quantitatively, a decrease in these two categories of the regulation index by one unit is associated with a rise in rail investments by around 360 and 175 million euros, respectively. In addition, decreasing overall price levels (columns 1 and 2) as well as a rising gross domestic product (column 2) are also associated with a growth in investments. These results lead to the conclusion that lower levels of regulation are indeed correlated with more investments.

To summarize, this subsection has shown that the relation between regulation in the rail sector and prices for rail passenger services is far from clear, while it demonstrates that deregulation correlates with high levels of infrastructure investments. More importantly, the main finding is that there is no evidence that the regulatory innovations promoted by the EU are correlated with lower prices for final users in the member states.

Table 9.2   OLS estimation of the relationship between regulatory policies and railway infrastructure investments

	Dependent variable:	
	RAILWAY INFRASTRUCTURE INVESTMENTS	
	(1)	(2)
Entry	91.336	70.171
	(60.094)	(61.312)
Public Ownership	139.033	140.720
	(98.519)	(99.101)
Vertical Integration	−355.170***	−364.092***
	(103.631)	(108.375)
Market Structure	−175.849**	−172.576**
	(69.543)	(68.348)
Passenger Kilometres	6.291	10.363
	(24.033)	(23.868)
Harmonized Consumer	−13.343***	−11.500***
Price Index	(3.744)	(3.712)
Gross Domestic Product	0.839	2.143**
	(0.854)	(0.927)
Country Fixed Effects	Yes	Yes
Time Fixed Effects	No	Yes
Observations	276	276
R^2	0.249	0.215
Adjusted R^2	0.174	0.074
F Statistic	11.825*** (df = 7; 250)	9.131*** (df = 7; 233)

Note: ** $p < 0.05$, *** $p < 0.01$.

9.3.3   Quality Aspects

Furthermore, it is important to consider differences in terms of quality of rail services across member states and the relationship between market liberalization and quality. One way of evaluating quality aspects is to measure customer satisfaction of rail services in general as well as actual punctuality and reliability in particular. These data are provided in the Flash Eurobarometer Survey FL382a on 'Europeans' Satisfaction with Rail Services' conducted in 2012–13 (European Union Open Data Portal, 2015). As the Eurobarometer data on satisfaction are limited to the year 2012 the questions of interest can only be analysed in a static framework; however, we are confident that this still provides a useful insight to quality differences across member states.

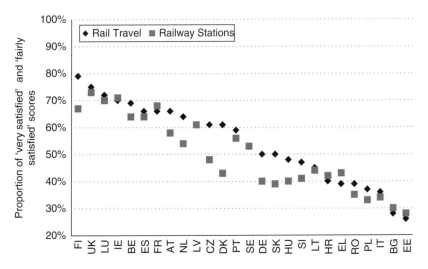

Source: European Union Open Data Portal (2015).

*Figure 9.3a   Satisfaction scores with rail travel and railway stations across
            the EU*

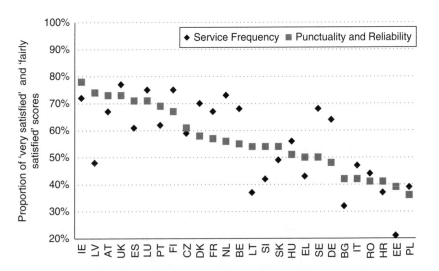

Source: European Union Open Data Portal (2015).

*Figure 9.3b   Satisfaction scores with frequency and punctuality/reliability
            across the EU*

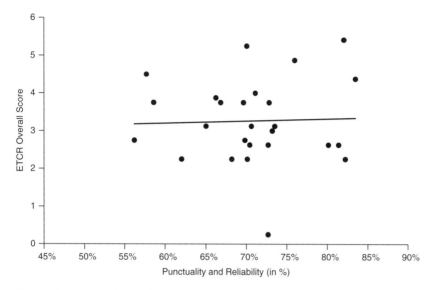

Figure 9.4   Correlation between ETCR and perceived punctuality and reliability

Figures 9.3a and 9.3b depict information on satisfaction with rail travel, service frequency and punctuality/reliability.

On average, approximately half of the respondents report their level of satisfaction with rail travel as 'high' or 'good' (Figure 9.3a). However, one can notice a large variation across member states with Western European countries generally reporting higher levels of satisfaction. Also with respect to punctuality and reliability as well as service frequency, satisfaction scores vary substantially between member states (Figure 9.3b) (European Commission, 2016c).

We also check if it is possible to find any relationship between the perception of quality and the state of market liberalization (Figure 9.4). While perceived punctuality and reliability differ considerably between countries, there is no significant correlation between them and the regulatory regimes as captured in the ETCR score. However, it should be considered that satisfaction levels might differ across countries for other reasons, thus not fully reflecting actual punctuality of train services.

In a next step, we considered the relationship between ETCR indicators and actual punctuality (Figure 9.5), as provided by the European Commission (2014b). Actual punctuality is measured as the percentage of regional and suburban trains with less than five-minute delay in the year 2012. When using data on actual punctuality instead of perceived

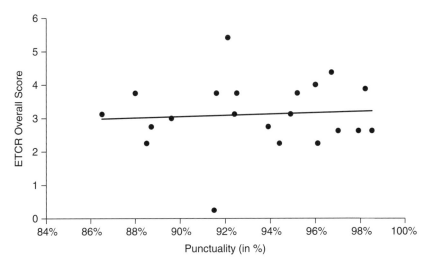

Figure 9.5   *Correlation between ETCR and actual punctuality and*
reliability

punctuality we find a similar relationship between quality and regulation as before. While the variation in actual punctuality across member states is less pronounced than the perceived value, once again we find no clear-cut correlation between punctuality and market-friendly regulatory regimes. It is also worth noticing that the European Commission (2016c) finds that punctuality and reliability rather depend on the size of the country and the number of passengers travelling on the line.

The perception of the evolution of quality of rail services over the past years seems to be ambiguous on the aggregate European level. While 34 per cent of the surveyed persons report that the quality of rail transport has improved, 27 per cent state that there is deterioration during the same time period (European Commission, 2014a). However, this ambiguity may result from the aggregate perspective, as we have seen that quality, and potential changes in quality, differ considerably across countries.

9.4   CONCLUSIONS

This chapter has attempted to explain and assess the process of change European railways have undergone over the last decades. After a brief explanation of the main transformations that occurred in these sectors, Section 9.2 presented the EU regulatory milestones in support of liberalization and offered insights on the implementation status of these reforms in the selected countries. Our major conclusion from this section is that, despite the formal improvement of market access regulation, in several European countries reforms achieved mixed results, as state-controlled structures still play a crucial role in the organization and management of railway industries. However, improvements could be expected for the future when member states will have fully transposed the Fourth Railway Package, adopted in 2016. In Section 9.3 we went a step further and undertook an empirical study of the relationship between regulatory regimes in national railway sectors, on the one hand, and the price of rail passenger services, investment level in infrastructures and quality of the service, on the other.

As far as prices are concerned, our analysis could not find any evidence that liberalization reforms are correlated to lower prices for passengers. This last finding leads to a number of reflections. Firstly, the impact of inefficiencies on the prices of public- or private-led operations is not clear-cut and, drawing on Holmberg et al. (2009) and Florio (2013), one can assume that it largely depends in fact on (a) the quality of governance mechanisms in both environments and (b) the actual role of competition, rather than specific regulatory regimes. Secondly, one can suppose that reforms have not lowered prices because existing TPA regulations are not fully effective. This would be coherent with our findings on reform implementation status showing that, despite the formal improvement of market access regulation, in several countries the state still plays the role of owner, planner, client and regulator. Finally, there is a remark to be made regarding the political dimension of the reforms debated in this chapter, as in the last 20 years they have not resulted in lower prices. Indeed, as noticed by Florio (2013), governments may have good reasons to consider rail services as essential to society and cast doubt on the social desirability and functioning of market mechanisms in the provision of these services. This is especially true for governments committed to ensure that household expenditure for railway services does not exceed a given share of their income. In this case, governments would consider economic accessibility of railway services a crucial political objective to which market logics could be eventually adapted.

As for investments, our findings are coherent with the existing literature and confirm that market-friendly regulatory regimes are correlated with higher investment levels (Kern et al., 2010). Indeed, one of the major problems associated with state-owned monopolies was the low level of investments in the rail network: only when competition and market arrangements were introduced did investment flows experience new positive trends.

Regards quality, because of data limitation, we could only analyse this aspect in a static framework by using 2012 Eurobarometer data on customer satisfaction of rail services as well as on actual punctuality and reliability. Our analysis could not find any significant correlation between these data and ETCR indicators on regulatory regimes. However, it is worth remembering that there might be other factors which influence customer satisfaction more clearly than regulatory regimes do (for example, cultural differences among countries may be associated with different conceptions of satisfaction). The same is true for actual punctuality and reliability, which rather depend on the size of the country and the number of passengers travelling on the line (European Commission, 2016c).

NOTES

* We would like to thank our colleagues from the Department of Economics, Management and Quantitative Methods of the University of Milan who provided insight and expertise that greatly assisted the research. We would also like to show our gratitude to the researchers gathered in Milan at the 2016 summer school on 'Performance and Governance of Services of General Interest' for sharing their pearls of wisdom with us. We are particularly grateful to Raphael Marzahn – from the University of Leipzig – and Marco Mariotti – from DB Schenker Europe GmbH. Finally, we would like to acknowledge that this research was supported by ULg's non-FRIA doctoral scholarship and a grant from the National Science Centre in Poland awarded on the basis of decision no. DEC-2013/11/N/HS5/04234.
1. For the sake of clarity, it is worth noting that NPM reforms and the liberalization of network-related Services of General Economic Interest (SGEI) do not refer to the same thing. While NPM consists of a broad reform paradigm emphasizing the concept that ideas used in the private sector must be successful in the public sector, liberalization of SGEI refers to a specific model of providing network services. More specifically, before liberalization, the predominant model was vertical integration of network supply. Liberalization has allowed new entries in networks' supply markets.
2. See Directives 2016/797, 2014/106/EU, 2014/38/EU, 2013/9/EU 2011/18/EU, 2009/131/EC, 2008/57/EC.
3. This became particularly clear in 2004 when TEN-T investment guidelines funded the realization of 30 priority projects: of these 30 projects, 18 related to rail and, of these 18 projects, 14 specifically to HSR.
4. See Directive (EU) 2016/2370 of the European Parliament and of the Council of 14 December 2016 amending Directive 2012/34/EU as regards the opening of the market for domestic passenger transport services by rail and the governance of the railway infrastructure, OJ L 352, 23.12.2016, pp. 1–17.
5. See Regulation (EU) 2016/2338 of the European Parliament and of the Council of 14 December 2016 amending Regulation (EC) No 1370/2007 concerning the opening of the market for domestic passenger transport services by rail, OJ L 354, 23.12.2016, pp. 22–31, Article 1(5)(b).
6. Compare European Commission, 'White Paper – Roadmap to a Single European Transport Area – Towards a Competitive and Resource Efficient Transport System', COM/2011/0144 and *Report from the Commission to the European Parliament and the Council – Fifth Report on Monitoring Development of the Rail Market*, COM/2016/0780.
7. As regards Directive 2007/58/EC on the opening of the market of international rail passenger transport, none of the member states had notified its transposition on time. As a result, the Commission opened infringement procedures against 19 member states on 31 July 2009 for failing to notify the measures taken to transpose Directive 2007/58/EC. See

Report from the Commission to the European Parliament, the Council, The European and Social Committee and the Committee of the Regions on the implementation of the provisions of Directive 2007/58/EC on the opening of the market of international rail passenger transport accompanying the Communication to the Council and the European Parliament on the Fourth Railway Package, COM/2013/034.

8. As pointed out by Kwak (2011), missing values in a panel dataset could lead to biased and inconsistent results unless absence occurs completely at random. Formally, missing completely at random can be tested with Little's MCAR test (Little, 1988). This test rejects the assumption of completely random absence in our data. Further investigation shows that concerns of non-random missing values arise for the group of countries comprising Bulgaria, Croatia, Czech Republic, Greece, Hungary, Latvia, Lithuania, Romania and Slovenia. Although our general results are robust to the exclusion of these countries, prudence is necessary when applying our estimates on this group of countries. Further results are available upon request.

REFERENCES

Asmild, M., T. Holvad, J.L. Hougaard and D. Kronborg (2008), 'Railway Reforms: Do They Influence Operating Efficiency?', Discussion Chapters, 08-05, University of Copenhagen, pp. 1–28.

Aucoin, P. (1990), 'Administrative Reform in Public Management: Paradigms, Principles, Paradoxes and Pendulums', *Governance*, **3**(2), 115–37.

Beria, P., E. Quinet, G. de Rus and C. Schulz (2010), 'A Comparison of Rail Liberalization Levels Across Four European Countries', MPRA Chapter No. 29142.

Council Directive 96/48/EC of 23 July 1996 on the interoperability of the trans-European high-speed rail system, OJ L 235, 17.9.1996, pp. 6–24.

DICE Database (2014), 'Rail Infrastructure: Investment and Maintenance Spending 1992–2010', Ifo Institute, Munich, accessed 28 June 2016 at http://www.cesifo-group.de/DICE/fb/3HddP52fY.

Directive 2001/12/EC of the European Parliament and of the Council of 26 February 2001 amending Council Directive 91/440/EEC on the development of the Community's railways, OJ L 75, 15.3.2001, pp. 1–25.

Directive 2001/13/EC of the European Parliament and of the Council of 26 February 2001 amending Council Directive 95/18/EC on the licensing of railway undertakings, OJ L 75, 15.3.2001, pp. 26–8.

Directive 2001/14/EC of the European Parliament and of the Council of 26 February 2001 on the allocation of railway infrastructure capacity and the levying of charges for the use of railway infrastructure and safety certification, OJ L 75, 15.3.2001, pp. 29–46.

Directive 2001/16/EC of the European Parliament and of the Council of 19 March 2001 on the interoperability of the trans-European conventional rail system, OJ L 110, 20.4.2001, pp. 1–27.

Directive 2004/49/EC of the European Parliament and of the Council of 29 April 2004 on safety on the Community's railways and amending Council Directive 95/18/EC on the licensing of railway undertakings and Directive 2001/14/EC on the allocation of railway infrastructure capacity and the levying of charges for the use of railway infrastructure and safety certification, OJ L 164, 30.4.2004, pp. 44–113.

Directive 2004/50/EC of the European Parliament and of the Council of 29 April 2004 amending Council Directive 96/48/EC on the interoperability of the trans-European high-speed rail system and Directive 2001/16/EC of the European Parliament and of the Council on the interoperability of the trans-European conventional rail system, OJ L 164, 30.4.2004, pp. 114–63.

Directive 2004/51/EC of the European Parliament and of the Council of 29 April 2004 amending Council Directive 91/440/EEC on the development of the Community's railways, OJ L 164, 30.4.2004, pp. 164–72.

Directive 2007/58/EC of the European Parliament and of the Council of 23 October 2007 amending Council Directive 91/440/EEC on the development of the Community's railways and Directive 2001/14/EC on the allocation of railway infrastructure capacity and the levying of charges for the use of railway infrastructure, OJ L 315, 3.12.2007, pp. 44–50.

Directive 2007/59/EC of the European Parliament and of the Council of 23 October 2007 on the certification of train drivers operating locomotives and trains on the railway system in the Community, OJ L 315, 3.12.2007, pp. 51–78.

Directive 2012/34/EU of the European Parliament and of the Council of 21 November 2012 establishing a single European railway area Text with EEA relevance, OJ L 343, 14.12.2012, pp. 32–77.

Directive 2016/797 of the European Parliament and of the Council of 11 May 2016 on the interoperability of the rail system within the European Union, OJ L 138, 26.5.2016, pp. 44–101.

Directive 2016/798 of the European Parliament and of the Council of 11 May 2016 on railway safety, OJ L 138, 26.5.2016, pp. 102–49.

Drew, J. and J. Ludewig (2011), *Reforming Railways. Learning from Experience*, Hamburg: Eurail Press.

Esposito, G., G.L. Gaeta and G. Trasciani (2017), 'Administrative Change in the EU: A Cross-country Empirical Study on the Contextual Determinants of NPM Reform Rhetoric', *Annals of Public and Cooperative Economics*, **88**(3), 323–344. Available at SSRN: https://ssrn.com/abstract=3018846 or http://dx.doi.org/10.1111/apce.12142.

European Commission (1996), 'A Strategy for Revitalising the Community's Railways', White Paper COM(96)421 final, accessed 24 August 2016 at http://europa.eu/documents/comm/white_chapters/pdf/com96_421_en.pdf.

European Commission (2001), 'White Paper – European Transport Policy for 2010: Time to Decide', COM(2001)370, accessed 24 August 2016 at https://ec.europa.eu/transport/themes/strategies/2001_white_paper_en.

European Commission (2011), 'White Paper – Roadmap to a Single European Transport Area – Towards a Competitive and Resource Efficient Transport System', COM/2011/0144, accessed 24 August 2016 at https://ec.europa.eu/transport/themes/strategies/2011_white_paper_en.

European Commission (2014a), *Special Eurobarometer 422a – Quality of Transport Report*, accessed 29 June 2016 at http://ec.europa.eu/public_opinion/archives/ebs/ebs_422a_en.pdf.

European Commission (2014b), *Fourth Report on Monitoring Development in the Rail Market*, Commission Staff Working Document, accessed 23 September 2016 at http://ec.europa.eu/transport/sites/transport/files/modes/rail/market/doc/swd%282014%29186_final_en.pdf.

European Commission (2016a), Eurostat, accessed 28 June 2016 at http://ec.europa.eu/eurostat/data/database.

European Commission (2016b), *Report from the Commission to the European Parliament and the Council – Fifth Report on Monitoring Development of the Rail Market*, COM/2016/0780, accessed 24 September 2016 at http://ec.europa.eu/transport/modes/rail/market/market_monitoring_en.

European Commission (2016c), *Study on the Prices and Quality of Rail Passenger Services*, accessed 28 December 2016 at https://ec.europa.eu/transport/sites/transport/files/modes/rail/studies/doc/2016-04-price-quality-rail-pax-services-final-report.pdf.

European Union Open Data Portal (2015), 'Flash Eurobarometer 382a: Europeans' Satisfaction with Rail Services/382b: Europeans' Satisfaction with Urban Transport', accessed 7 August 2017 at https://data.europa.eu/euodp/data/dataset/S1111_382A__382B.

Florio, M. (2013), *Network Industries and Social Welfare*, Oxford: Oxford University Press.

Holmberg, S., B. Rothstein and N. Nasiritousi (2009), 'Quality of Government: What You Get', *Annual Review of Political Science*, **12**, 135–61.

Hood, C. (1991), 'A Public Management for All Seasons', *Public Administration*, **69**(1), 3–19.

Hood, C. (1995), 'The "New Public Management" in the 1980s: Variations on a Theme', *Accounting, Organizations and Society*, **20**(2), 93–109.

Kern, H., B. Diewald and S. Sumbalsky (2010), *Regulierung in Österreich*, Vienna: Linde.

Kwak, D.W. (2011), 'Empirical Methods for Unbalanced Panel Data: An Empirical Application to the Effect of Class Size Reduction on SAT Score for Grades in K-3', PhD dissertation submitted to Michigan State University.

Little, R. (1988), 'A Test of Missing Completely at Random for Multivariate Data with Missing Values', *Journal of the American Statistical Association*, **83**(404), 1198–202.

London, R. (2002), 'Tools for Governing: Privatization, Public-private Partnerships and Entrepreneurial Management', *Public Administration Review*, **62**(1), 118–23.

Ministère de l'Environnement de l'Énergie et de la Mer (2013), 'La réforme ferroviaire, renforcer et moderniser le service public ferroviaire', Press release, October, accessed 10 January 2017 at http://www.developpement-durable.gouv.fr/IMG/pdf/13186_argu-ref-ferro-nouveau-SP.pdf.

OECD (2016), 'Sectoral Regulation: Energy, Transport and Communications', OECD Product Market Regulation Statistics, accessed 29 June 2016 at http://dx.doi.org/10.1787/data-00596-en.

Regulation (EC) No. 881/2004 of the European Parliament and of the Council of 29 April 2004 establishing a European Railway Agency, OJ L 164, 30.4.2004, pp. 1–43.

Regulation (EC) No. 1370/2007 of the European Parliament and of the Council of 23 October 2007 on public passenger transport services by rail and by road and repealing Council Regulations (EEC) Nos 1191/69 and 1107/70, OJ L 315, 3.12.2007, pp. 1–13.

Regulation (EC) No. 1371/2007 of the European Parliament and of the Council of 23 October 2007 on rail passengers' rights and obligations, OJ L 315, 3.12.2007, pp. 14–41.

Regulation (EC) No. 1335/2008 of the European Parliament and of the Council of 16 December 2008 amending Regulation (EC) No. 881/2004 establishing a European Railway Agency, OJ L 354, 31.12.2008, pp. 51–9.

Regulation (EU) 2016/796 of the European Parliament and of the Council of 11 May 2016 on the European Union Agency for Railways and repealing Regulation (EC) No. 881/2004, OJ L 138, 26.5.2016, pp. 1–43.

Stewart, J. and K. Walsh (1992), 'Change in the Management of Public Services', *Public Administration*, **70**(4), 499–518.

United Nations (2001), *World Public Sector Report – Globalization and the State*, Department of Economic and Social Affairs. New York: United Nations Publications.

Walsh, K. (1997), *Contracting for Change – Contracts in Health, Social Care, and Other Local Government Services*, Oxford: Oxford University Press.

Wooldridge, J. (2014), *Introduction to Econometrics*, Croatia: Cengage Learning.

10. Local Public Transport services: the efficiency of public enterprises competing with the private sector in the EU Member States

Annalisa Negrelli, Anastasia Roukouni and Angélique Chassy*

10.1 INTRODUCTION

A key success factor for every city is undoubtedly an efficient public transport system. Public transport includes various services that provide mobility to the general public such as buses, metro, light rail, tram, ferries, shared taxi and their variations. Being a basic instrument of mobility for a large percentage of the world's population, it forms one of the driving forces of economic and social life (Polat, 2012). Local Public Transport (LPT) policies generally promote collective sustainable mobility in urban areas. High quality public transport refers to the existence of a relatively fast, convenient, comfortable and integrated service which is able to attract travelers who would otherwise use their private vehicles. In this way, traffic problems such as congestion and environmental pollution can be diminished and consumer welfare (surplus) benefits are produced (Valeri et al., 2011; Litman, 2016).

Critical supply and demand in the LPT sector can be interpreted with the aid of factors related to economics and mobility as well as factors reflecting institutional and geographical characteristics (e.g. level of personal income inequality, type of contracting, existence or not of a center of political decisions in the city and so on) (Albalate and Bel, 2010). An interesting point is that although quality of service certainly affects demand, the level of demand can also have an impact on the level of service (Holmgren, 2013). Moreover, many aspects of modern life currently act and are expected to continue acting as factors that will affect the demand of LPT services in the future. In particular, four factors of this kind are: the urban sprawl phenomenon; the aging of developed societies; the radical technological progress; and the creation of 'sharing economies'.

The term urban sprawl describes a trend towards a low-density outward expansion. First coined as a term in 1937 for the USA, nowadays the phenomenon becomes more and more intense in the European landscape as European cities are experiencing population increases while becoming less dense (Glaeser and Kohlhase, 2004; Christiansen and Loftsgarden, 2011; Oueslati et al., 2015). The second point concerns the aging of developed societies. Metz (2000) claims that the quality of life of elderly people directly depends on their ability to commute and travel. Currie and Delbosc (2010) and Alsnih and Hensher (2003) discuss the peculiar usage of LPT for this category of people, pointing out the necessity of services and facilities expressly suited for them. Moreover, in the last decades, the development and diffusion of information and communications technology (ICT) has drastically changed the variety of services offered and their delivery (Neirotti et al., 2014). While the impact of technology on the production function of LPT is rather intuitive, several works indicate that this change will also modify consumers' behavior and their transport choices. For instance, Dal Fiore et al. (2014) pointed out that, being more informed about the places they could potentially visit, people are more likely to increase their mobility. New technologies have also contributed to enabling the rise of the so-called 'sharing economy'. In the field of transport, 'ride-sharing' or 'shared mobility' is usually defined as a transportation strategy that enables users to gain short-term access to transportation modes on a demand-based basis (Moudon et al., 2005; Baptista et al., 2015; Hamari et al., 2015; Shaheen et al., 2015; Yin et al., 2016).

From the above discussion, it is obvious that public transport is going through a period of continuous and considerable change throughout the world. There is notable variety in the way public transport is organized among countries as well as considerable differences even among cities within the same country (Pedro and Macário, 2016). In many countries within the European Union (EU), reform in the public transport sector is taking place (European Commission, 2005 and 2011). Public transport is gradually being transformed towards a more customer-oriented perspective and service contracts between public authorities and private operators are often used to achieve this purpose. Service contracts set bilateral commitments for the aforementioned parties involved. A tendency to shift towards incentive contracts which rely on qualitative requirements and attempt to achieve social targets is also observed (Hensher and Houghton, 2004; Beirao and Cabral, 2006; Marcucci and Gatta, 2007; Mouwen and Rietveld, 2013). The internationalization of the public transport sector during the last two decades drew attention to the fact that the disparities among countries were sooner or later inevitably going to create legal issues and a debate started within the EU which eventually led to the adoption of a new Regulation by the European Commission in 2007 (Van de Velde, 2008).

In this context, the objective of the present chapter is to critically examine the main policy reforms promoted by the EU and adopted by the Member States in the last two decades regarding the LPT industry. More specifically, this chapter aims to identify the existence of significant variations (if any) in the reform patterns across countries and provides an evaluation of the role of government-owned enterprises. The chapter also investigates whether European citizens have been well served by the evolution of policy reforms in this area and presents positive and negative examples of Member States' policy experiences.

The chapter is structured as follows. Section 10.2 examines the changes of policy frameworks in the EU regarding the LPT sector during the last decades. The section starts with a presentation of preliminary definitions of key terms, a prerequisite in order to help the reader understand the analysis that follows, which includes a discussion of the different policy frameworks that currently exist in a selection of Member States (that are considered as representative examples). Section 10.2 provides an in-depth analysis of the existing EU legal LPT framework and the evolution patterns that lead to its implementation and offers a glimpse on the diversity of capitalism and how this has affected LPT in the EU. A critical comparison of the different policy frameworks among countries is presented in Section 10.3, followed by an examination of existing forms of contracting LPT and the performances of service providers. Section 10.3 also focuses on interpreting the role of government-owned enterprises in the market of LPT and the degree of EU citizens' satisfaction from the provision of LPT services and attempts to reveal how this satisfaction or dissatisfaction is related to the policy reforms that have occurred. The chapter concludes in Section 10.4 with a critical overall analysis and suggestions for further research.

10.2 MEASURING CHANGES OF POLICY FRAMEWORKS IN THE EU

10.2.1 Preliminary Juridical Classifications

The complexity of measuring the policy frameworks in the EU induces us to place some theoretical considerations of the most widespread governances of LPT before the empirical comparison among European countries.

A first juridical classification implies distinguishing between public and private 'ownership' of the enterprises that supply the LPT services, on the one hand, and the 'awarding' procedures, on the other hand.

Beginning from the former distinction, it is necessary to mention that EU legislation gives freedom of choice to the Member States (Article 295 TFUE). Consequently, every national system can opt for different solutions: ownership can be public, private or a combination of the two and may include one or several stakeholders.

As for the second aspect, the awarding procedures for delivering public services can be resumed in two main modalities: (1) 'private awarding' through a competitive tendering procedure (e.g. concessions to private entrepreneurs) and by means of a negotiating procedure to mixed-ownership companies (e.g. public-private partnerships (PPPs), municipal companies); or (2) 'public awarding' (e.g. self-production, in-house providing).

Observing the 'private awarding procedures', Article 5(3) of Regulation (EC) No. 1370/2007 defines the procedural requirements for the competitive tendering of public service contracts. It stipulates that if a competent authority uses a third party, other than an internal operator, to provide public passenger transport services, 'it shall award public service contracts through a fair, open, transparent and non-discriminatory "competitive tendering procedure"'. On the other hand, for the 'public awarding procedures', Article 5(2)(b) of Regulation (EC) No. 1370/2007 allows local administrative authorities to provide public passenger transport services by rail and by road themselves. In this model, a public service contract of LPT, in the presence of certain conditions developed by the European Court of Justice,[1] is directly awarded and competitive tendering procedures are not required. Therefore, the local competent authorities can supply the LPT services in self-production.

10.2.2   Changes of the Policy Framework Within the Member States

The EU Regulation on LPT follows two decades of reforms at the country level. Since the 1980s, many European countries have implemented significant changes in the organizational and regulatory framework of their road and rail transport sectors, especially on bus services. The general approach has been based on the idea that LPT services could be supplied either directly by publicly owned companies without tendering procedures or by private – and likewise public – companies selected through tender (Van de Velde, 1999). Nowadays, three governance models exist depending on the degree of internal market opening: market competition with tendering procedures to private providers; direct commitment to public entities, fully owned by municipalities or local administrations; and hybrid forms of mixed public-private operators in a market competition with residuary regulation.

1. Private providers (with or without competition)

The most important experience is probably the one that occurred in the UK, in which the government, during the last decade of the twentieth century, suddenly fully privatized services, except for London and Scotland. Observing the bus services outside London, the Transport Act of 1985 introduced an important competition between the private operators: they can choose operating procedures, bus lines, links, frequencies and price lists (Amaral, 2009). In this perspective, the Local Transport Authorities (LTAs) are only allowed to support bus services where no commercial service has been provided, through tendering procedures with private operators: 20 percent of bus services outside London are provided in this way. LTAs only own bus companies ('municipal companies') in a few urban areas outside metropolitan areas that operate in the same deregulated free market as elsewhere outside London.

As for the 33 municipalities of Greater London, the management is different. The Greater London Authority (GLA) plans, provides and procures the majority of public transport services, assuring the economic and social development of the sector. In particular, the LPT services are supplied by Transport for London (TfL), an agency of GLA, responsible for the entire transport sector within the area of London and for some suburban transport services (e.g. the overground), which handles the implementation of calls for tenders in the field of road transport and light rail. Private operators answer calls for tender and contracts are awarded through 'gross cost' incentives, connected to their performances.

In spite of the cases of several EU cities (such as London, Stockholm, Barcelona), in which local authorities have chosen geographical fragmentation, horizontal separation or vertical disintegration that implicate the coexistence of several operators (public and private), in France these forms are very uncommon (Yvrande-Billon, 2006; Roy and Yvrande-Billon, 2007). The LPT provisions have been reformed by the *Code des Transports*, enacted in December 2010, and modified in 2015. In particular, according to these provisions – with the exception of the urban area of Paris (Île de France) – the municipalities are responsible for the services of local/urban transport, but frequently (in more than 80 percent of cases) public transport planning and delivery are delegated to the Associations of Authorities that guarantee interurban cooperation (*Communautés urbaines o Communautés d'agglomération*) and operate within a predetermined perimeter (PTU). Furthermore, these laws specify that the competent authorities choose the forms of contracting for the LPT service that can be managed with tendering procedures. The concession of public service with a private operator is the preferred choice in the awarding procedures: 90 percent of urban authorities delegate the supply of public transport services to a single operator with an exclusive right on the territory (Amaral, 2009). The other 10 percent of urban authorities give direct management to a local public company (*régie municipal*), without tendering (e.g. Tolosa, Marsiglia, Nizza, La Rochelle). Finally, as regards the territory of the Île de France, the organization of the LPT is supplied by the Network of the Parisian transports, RATP, SNCF (public operators), plus more than 90 private companies under the supervision of STIF (Syndicate des transports d'Île-de-France).

2. Public-owned companies (with direct awarding or competitive tendering)

In the majority of the other European countries, minimal development of liberalization is observed. Direct award to locally public-owned companies is the most widespread arrangement, otherwise private third parties deal with small and complementary parts of LPT services.

As for the Eastern Europe models, the actual set-up is based on an integrated approach: municipalities, provinces, regions and central governments are usually all involved in ruling, managing and organizing activities of public transport, often without a clear distinction of roles (GUTs Project, 2013). In the Czech Republic, typically, cities have their own integrated transport system, as for instance in the case of the city of Karlovy Vary, where TCKV, a single company owned by the local municipality, supplies urban public transport services in a uniform manner. In Hungary, contract tendering is not applied to public transport providers; in many cases there is no tender at all or only one participant applies, such as Hiànos, the only provider for decades in the city of Sopron. In Poland, most transport companies are private entities owned by the municipalities, with no competition, no separation between regulator and regulated parties and between owner of the infrastructure and the service operator.

In the Italian model, since 2000, local mobility services have been devolved to regional governments and local administrations (Arabia et al., 2004; Bucci, 2006; Ottoz et al., 2009; GUTs Project, 2013). In most large Italian cities, like Rome (ATAC SpA) and Milan (ATM SpA), municipalities have maintained public governance in delivering LPT services, with some exceptions. Particularly relevant is the case of Trieste, which represents one of the few Italian examples where LPT services are actually awarded through competitive tendering procedures. The delivery of the LPT services is guaranteed by a local operator, Trieste Trasporti SpA. This case represents an 'anomaly' in the Italian system because the second shareholder of the company is the international group Arriva (now acquired by Deutsche Bahn), which holds 40 percent of the capital. With regard to Genoa, in 2005 the municipality privatized, albeit only in part, AMT (Mobility and Transport Company), which was a 100 percent publicly owned company supplying the LPT service. In particular, for the first time in Italy, a French private company (Transdev) acquired 41 percent of the share capital of AMT, after a competitive tendering with 'double object'. The opening of the Italian LPT market favored the entrance of a significant number of foreign companies, mainly from France, the UK and Germany, large multinationals specialized in public utilities. This change relates, for instance, to the urban area of Florence (with the French RATP).

Also in Germany, most of the main cities have their own operators to which the services are directly awarded. Some countries and smaller cities sometimes organize the service through their own companies, but not in the majority of cases. In regional and urban road transport, many companies coexist: some are private-owned companies, others are members of international groups, or are very small, operating only on two or three lines. Subcontracting is widespread in the road transport service and about 30 percent of the LPT services are awarded using this procedure through competitive tendering.

The Austrian LPT sector is organized through a nationwide coverage of transport operators, gathered together into eight transport associations, along the German model of the *Hamburger Verkehrsverbund*. The largest LPT companies are fully owned by municipalities (altogether 667 companies in Austria for local and regional public transport in 2003): seven out of nine Länder capitals use the concept of internal operators. Unlike the Italian case, international companies are not involved in the Austrian LPT system. In the largest Austrian cities LPT services are mainly supplied by private operators organized differently from city to city (Hensher, 2003). In Vienna, for instance, the Wiener Linien has been responsible for all LPT service since 1999; a formally independent company under private law and fully owned by the city, it supplies the transport services through direct awarding without tendering. The Wiener Linien provides most of the transport services itself but has also assigned transport services to private enterprises, promoting competitive tendering for 30 percent of local road transport and 50 percent of bus lines.

Similarly, in Switzerland, and in particular in the area of Zurich, since 1990 the urban transport system has been governed by the ZVV (Zürcher Verkehrsverbund), a public authority that operates as a holding company under the governance of the Canton of Zurich, fully financing the eight transport companies and the transport system in the area.

BOX 10.1   PUBLIC OR PRIVATE OWNERSHIP IN TERMS OF
          LPT PROVISION IN THE EUROPEAN MEMBER
          STATES

- Belgium, France, Italy, London, Spain, Eastern Europe: most predominant PUBLIC INITIATIVE

- Austria and Germany: formally MARKET INITIATIVE but dominated by authority-owned companies with exclusive right to serve the market

- UK – outside London: FULL DEREGULATION, open entry market initiative (without exclusive rights) where public authorities just keep a complementary role

- Cities of Paris, Velenje, Barcelona, Scandinavian model: MIXED PUBLIC-PRIVATE OWNERSHIP with coexistence of public and private providers that award the services through competitive tendering procedures

---

3.   Hybrid model: mixed public-private governance with competition between public and private providers

Observing the different systems developed in Europe, as shown in Box 10.1, most European metropolitan areas and large cities make a choice between purely public and purely private forms of delivery. LPT services, by road and by rail are private in almost all cities in England and most cities in France. On the other hand, in most cities in Germany, Italy, Switzerland, Austria, Eastern Europe and Spain – analysed below – the service is provided by public companies. Competition between public and private suppliers is uncommon in European experiences. This latter form of governance has made some headway in a few of the largest cities of Europe, such as London, Paris, Vienna, Scandinavian cities (e.g. Stockholm and Copenhagen) and cities in the Netherlands, which are generally more given to introducing competition in product and services markets (Boitani et al., 2013).

As for the Scandinavian model, the implementation of the European Directive has induced reform of the LPT sector. Traditionally, in the metropolitan area of Copenhagen, Aarhus, Odense and Aalborg, the road transport service was supplied through 'in-house' municipal companies. From 1990, and especially from 2007, structural reform has reorganized the sector with unique legislation, and Copenhagen Transport began to award services through short-term gross cost contracts. Since the reform, in the Eastern areas of Denmark different operators provide services for the local road transport sector (Linjebus). Since 1990 other foreign operators share the Danish market of LPT services: Arriva supplies 41 percent of the local road transport services.

Similar considerations may be observed for the Dutch experience, which has seen substantial developments in transport policies, especially with the imposition of competitive tendering as the governance model for public transport services. The new 'Passenger Transport Law', which came into effect in 2001, forced the public transport authorities, except in the four largest cities, to organize passenger transport services provision through concessions with a maximum length, and to tender out these concessions. Nowadays, the obligation to competitively tender includes the four largest cities, but only three of the four have started the tender process for bus services and one for rail services as well (Veeneman and Van de Velde, 2016).

In Slovenia also, the governance model is based on mixed public-private ownership, in a competitive market with residuary regulation. Public transport services are supplied by concessionaires, based on a PPP: the providers are selected through public procurement procedure, while the municipality sets the conditions for delivering the service.

The most important experience in terms of opening to the market is probably the one that occurred in Barcelona, with a large-scale mixed public-private service organization. In most of the largest Spanish cities, the LPT service is provided by public firms entirely owned by municipalities. However, local transportation in the metropolitan area of Barcelona is a mixed system in which one public operator (Transports Metropolitans de Barcelona, TMB) and several private companies – supplying the transport service in different areas – coexist. TMB is a fully public firm, owned by local governments, absorbing 75 percent of passengers, 62 percent of the length of routes and 70 percent of vehicles; while a group of much smaller private concessionaires, which have increased in recent years, connect the suburban areas with the city center.

10.2.3   The EU Legal Framework

The absence of clear and homogeneous rules at Member State level governing the awarding of LPT services gives rise to legal uncertainty and obstacles to the free provision of local transport services and causes distortions in the function of the internal market. As a result, private transport operators may be deprived of their rights within the internal market, while public authorities may not find the best use of public money. The existence of an adequate, balanced and flexible legal framework for the awarding of LPT would ensure effective and non-discriminatory access to the market to all EU economic operators and legal certainty, favoring public investments in infrastructures and strategic services to citizens.

This is the economic, political and social background in which the EU has intervened. But unlike other sectors, such as electricity and telecommunications, in which EU directives have played a crucial role in the liberalization process, the impact of European legislation on the LPT sector has been restricted on the general principles elaborated by the EU Treaty, about equality of treatment, transparency, proportionality and mutual recognition. Indeed, as seen in Table 10.1, LPT services are neither subjected to EU Services Directive 123/2006, nor to Directive 2014/23/UE.

In this field, the EU Regulation 1370/2007/EU[2] is the main EU source of law. The purpose of the EU law is to define the conditions in which the competent authorities can intervene in the area of public passenger transport (rail and road transport), to guarantee its provision in the context of Services of General Interest (SGI) and to ensure the provision of higher service frequencies, better quality and/or lower fares than the market would otherwise provide. More specifically, it sets out the conditions under which authorities should compensate the service provider, and the mechanisms to be applied by public authorities to award public services contracts to a third party, other than an internal operator, by means of transparent and non-discriminatory competitive procedures which may be subject to negotiation. It establishes that, subject to certain reservations detailed in Article 5 of the Regulation, competent local authorities may provide public transport services themselves or assign them to an internal operator over which they have control comparable to that over their own services.

These provisions seem to reproduce the legislations of some Member States. Indeed, local authorities can produce services themselves (in self-production or in-house option), in which competitive procedures are not required, or decide to contract these out by means of competitive (or negotiated) tendering procedures.

An interesting report of the European Commission published in February 2016, 'Study on economic and financial effects of the implementation of Regulation 1370/2007 on public passenger transport services', demonstrates that the Regulation has affected the approach to service

Table 10.1   Summary of the applicable legal basis for contract awards by type of contractual arrangement and by transport mode

Public passenger services by	(Public) service contracts as defined in Directives 2014/24/EU and 2014/25/EU	Service concessions as defined in Directive 2014/23/EU
Bus and tram	Directives 2014/24/EU and 2014/25/EU	Regulation (EC) No. 1370/2007
Railway and metro	Regulation (EC) No. 1370/2007	Regulation (EC) No. 1370/2007

provision of most Member States, as it can be deduced from Table 10.1. In particular, in a limited number of Member States, the Regulation has allowed a more flexible approach to the award of contracts than was previously the case under the relevant national legislation. For example, in Italy it is now possible to award contracts directly, whereas formerly authorities were obliged to procure services through competitive tender.

10.3 RESULTS OF COMPARISON UNDER A CRITICAL PERSPECTIVE

From the comparison analysis in Section 10.2, it can be said that in the last two decades, market opening reforms promoted by the EU and adopted by the Member States in LPT have impacted most European countries, but it is obvious that there is not 'one' European LPT governance and organization model. At the same time, it is true that many countries and urban areas have introduced competition in the field of LPT services, but this trend has not always been accompanied by consistent reforms of the legislation existing beforehand.

The comparison reveals that LPT systems in the EU now operate under a broad plurality of organizational forms with a high degree of variability in LPT arrangements that vary from public monopolies to open markets. Furthermore, although in principle top-down-regulations in the EU provide Member States with instructions, there are variations not only among countries but also within the same country. These differences mostly affect the legal framework of the LPT service organization and the following main issues arise.

The first one is the issue of multilevel governance: in the public administration perspective, the presence of at least three levels of government (local/municipal, regional/provincial and national), rounded by the European system, implies adopting decisions not in isolation from each other but in a cooperative manner, following a coherent approach (GUTs Project, 2013). This mode of governance can be different according to country and their territory in the management of the LPT and might entail different level of regulation among EU and national regulation and probably federal/regional peculiarity as well.

Secondly, an issue of fragmentation emerges more and more often in the internal market of LPT services. As revealed by recent studies, the provision of many utilities (telecommunications, electricity, water) entails important scale and density economies, which mean that it is more efficient to give the exclusive right to operate the service to a single company. In the case of local bus transportation, however, the literature suggests that the provision of this service does not imply significant scale economies. Therefore, it is possible to split the metropolitan areas of larger cities into separate routes or regions and to award them to different concessionaires. Indeed, no scale benefits seem to be lost when creating several concessions in a large metropolitan area (Franquelli et al., 2004; Hensher et al., 2007; Hensher and Stanley, 2008).

Related to the transport sector, it is necessary to underline two other critical aspects: the compensatory measures of the public services obligations and the public support to infrastructure financing.[3] The award of economic benefits – through public resources – to companies providing public transport services, even at the local level, must comply with European guidelines on State aid. To ensure compatibility with European law it must be proved alternately that: (a) there is not a benefit and it does not constitute State aid, considering the conditions set by the European Court of Justice;[4] (b) the State aid falls under the '*de minimis* parameter', so it is assumed that there is no impact on competition and trade; (c) the State aid complies with the special provisions contained in Regulation (EC) No. 1370/2007, which implements Article 93 TFEU.

According to the provisions of the *Altmark* judgment by the Court of Justice, and considering the legislative lack in this area, the European Commission regulates the sector in a coherent and organic manner. The Commission has adopted two policy packages: the 'Monti-Kroes package', which specifies the conditions under which State aid – in the form of public service compensation – is compatible with the EU Treaties, and the 'Almunia package',[5] which replaces the decision and the statement of the previous Monti-Kroes. With these measures, the Commission has further clarified the basic principles relating to State aid and introduced a more diversified and proportionate approach, with simpler rules for local Services of General Economic Interest (SGEI) and for SGI. In addition, confirming the importance of SGEI for economic growth and social cohesion, the Commission sought to ensure the effective use of public resources for SGEI, also considering the need for public finances consolidation in the Member States.

Fourthly, it is necessary to underline the issue of durable contracts. Observing the Member States' systems, it should be pointed out that concessions are usually long-term and complex arrangements in which the concessionaire assumes responsibilities and risks traditionally borne by the contracting authorities and contracting entities and normally falling within their remit. The length of the contract is an increasingly pressing issue from various points of view (Gagnepain et al., 2013): if the contract is too short, then the private operators will not have any incentive to invest in its business. On the other hand, with long-term contracts it could be very difficult for the local authorities to stop collaboration with inefficient private operators. The European intervention should not be underestimated by the Member States: in order to assure the opening of the market of public services to competition, the EU imposes short-term concessions and attributes the economic risk to the provider, as established by Directive 2014/23/UE about the awarding procedures of concessions of public services.[6]

The fifth aspect to keep in mind is the issue of ownership. As underlined above, the EU is neutral to ownership and treats public and private enterprises as equal entities. Indeed, contracting authorities and contracting entities should be allowed considerable flexibility to define and organize the ownership and the procedure leading to the choice of concessionaire. Many works have attempted to deal with this issue of ownership by investigating the connection between alternative forms of governance in LPT service provisioning and their efficiency (e.g. Karlaftis and Tsamboulas, 2012), as measured in terms of performance, operating cost savings, consumers'/citizens' satisfaction. Most of them focus mainly on the differences between public and private ownership; they compare a number of transport systems categorizing them according to organizational types and use a number of performance indicators to estimate efficiency.

However, the models used in these studies, generally, provide a macroeconomic point of view and do not represent the political, social and economic context of the single territory analysed that varies among the different governance systems of the EU. It could be interesting to evaluate the role of government-owned enterprises in the market from a different perspective that highlights the relationship between the organization of LPT service and the quality of the institutions. In this latter perspective, it also seems relevant to investigate the diversity of capitalism and its effects on LPT. The literature (Amable, 2005) observes that the form of capitalism that rolls out in each country is to be modulated according to the degree of competition and the nature of the public intervention involved. The typologies of capitalism proposed by Amable could result in: Anglo-Saxon capitalism or neoliberal, social democratic capitalism, continental European capitalism and Mediterranean capitalism. Berrou and Carrincazeaux (2005) propose adding another model, specific to Central Europe and Eastern Europe. These different models of capitalism seem to demonstrate the influence of two types of approach: the monopolizing State approach and the trade in the supply of local public services approach. In more practical terms, it may be better to appraise the choice of public authorities between three types of governance according to the degree of openness of the interior market: direct commitment to public entities, fully owned by municipalities or local administrations; market competition with tendering procedures to private providers; and hybrid forms of mixed public-private operators in a market competition with residuary regulation.

Furthermore, to understand the effect of good or bad administration on the efficiency of the LPT service model of governance, it is necessary to investigate the different characteristics of territory of the cities and to contextualize the analysis in a socio-economic and political framework of each urban area. This means that in defining the concept of LPT, it is relevant to distinguish among metropolitan areas with or without metro; passenger transportation by rail or by road; small (urban) or medium (interurban) territorial scale (Zatti, 2012). Also, the modes of transport assume critical relief: road transport on rubber wheels (bus, local or intercity, like transit bus, electric bus); on tram rails (cable car, tram); suburban rail (metro, commuter rail); vehicles for hire (taxicab).

10.3.1 The Role of Government-owned Enterprises in the Market of LPT

The results from the case studies in the European major cities led to the comparison and evaluation of the different structure and organization of the LPT market to ponder the role of government-owned enterprises in the market of LPT.

The widespread public involvement in the ownership of the companies that supply LPT (e.g. in France, Italy, London, Spain and Germany) and the gradual decentralization of strategic, financial and organizational responsibility seem to be corroborated by Regulation (EC) No. 1370/2007. Indeed, this regulation establishes that 'At the present time, many inland passenger transport services which are required in the general economic interest cannot be operated on a commercial basis; the competent authorities of the Member States must be able to act to ensure that such services are provided.'

Even if it is true that regional and local authorities are more sensible and capable of ensuring specific local needs, it is not appropriate to underestimate the potential drawbacks of these policy frameworks. The fragmentation of the governance and the lack of coordination between LPT providers and local authority, combined with the reduction of national public funds to LPT, lead to a limitation to finance the social role of LPT services by the local government (Kostal, 2015). Therefore, it is necessary to investigate if liberalization policies, on the one hand, and the privatizing wave, on the other hand, combined with a necessary budget consolidation, could overcome the risks and achieve these requirements.

More liberalized market structures are seen in major cities located in the UK, outside London, in which a de-integration model has been developed; in France, with a 'medium' degree of liberalization; and in Scandinavia.

Only a few countries have implemented a separation between internal and external actors; conversely, in most countries the local authority influences the provider through ownership and/or financial relations. After all, no strict link between the observed financial problems and the degree of liberalization and privatization is evident.

Mouwen and Van Ommeren (2016) have shown that in the Netherlands, the effect of competitive tendering is completely absent, and this is interpreted by considering that in the country's market the majority of concessions is tendered through competition. The authors also claim that the renewal of long-term contracts is associated with an at least 10 percent reduction of operational costs and moreover with a 7.7 percent rise in public transport ridership. According to Schaaffkamp (2014), there is absence of strong evidence regarding if and how specific contract types can ensure success in the passenger market. Furthermore, the author claims that notwithstanding tendered contracts include strong incentives for cost reduction, they are not very successful in stimulating the operator's interest in addressing the passengers' needs and creating opportunities for the growth of LPT's market share. Finally, Filippini et al. (2015) attempted to identify and evaluate the differences in cost efficiency between bus lines operated under competitively tendered contracts and performance-based negotiated contracts in Switzerland. They applied regression analysis using cross-sectional data and concluded that no statistically significant differences are observed.

However, the private ownership structure model, typical mainly in Great Britain and Sweden, and common in other countries but only for complementary and additional services (such as Austria, Belgium, Germany, Italy, Poland and Spain), reveals increasing involvement of private operators at different levels of the production chain: suppliers of specific functions (cleaning, ticketing, advertising and so on), subcontractors of large monopolistic operators, route or small network providers or even large network providers, service initiators in commercially oriented approaches, partners in long-term PPP models (Kostal, 2015).

Furthermore, as revealed by recent studies on the 'Barcelona model', the growth in the share of routes managed by private companies, coexisting with public ones in the same territorial jurisdiction, shows how privatization is crucial for increasing the competition, allowing more operators to participate and make the competition more effective. This hybrid organizational form, with the presence of private competitors on the LPT market, seems to be a 'credible threat' that may well stimulate improved performance among public managers, thereby escaping the classical public-private dilemma on governance (Albalate and Bel, 2010). Indeed, the Barcelona model presents many advantages in terms of efficiency, as underlined in recent studies (e.g. Albalate and Bel, 2010), which suggests that – if it is true that mixed public-private provisions of bus services may reduce scale economies – it helps to discipline operators: the presence of public operators gives the regulator information about costs and demands that is useful for overseeing private operators, and may also help to protect passengers' interests in areas of demand. Conversely, private companies are useful to identify the inefficiencies of public firms and to moderate the demands of public employees.

As for advantages of this mixed public-private model, through the coexistence of private competitors governments are allowed to pursue different goals: it permits not only comparison of public-private firms' production processes and costs, using benchmarking regulation with positive effects on their performances (Miranda and Lerner, 1995), or to reduce the entry barriers and the costs of regulation (Dalen and Gòmez-Lobo, 2003) but also to increase the number of available service providers in the jurisdiction and thus fosters competition (Ballard and Warner, 2000). Ultimately, as pointed out in the literature, mixed systems can improve efficiency in the local market, avoiding opportunistic behavior by incumbents, provide information on the nature and the costs of the service and ensure government capacity to overreach contract failure (Warner and Bel, 2008).

10.3.2 Citizens' Satisfaction from LPT Services Across the EU and How it is Related to Relevant Policy Reforms

A very important parameter for assessing the outcome of LPT policies is users' satisfaction, as demonstrated by numerous research studies worldwide (e.g. Fiorio et al., 2013; Fellesson and Friman, 2008; Abou-Zeid et al., 2012; Diana, 2012). In 2016, Eurobarometer published a survey regarding the degree of satisfaction of EU citizens about the public transport system of the city where they live. The sample included almost 12 000 inhabitants from 23 EU Member States and the overall result was that although the average percentage of frequent LPT users is not particularly high, the majority of urban dwellers (62 percent) appears to be satisfied with urban public transport. An impressively high percentage is met in Luxembourg (88 percent), followed by Latvia (83 percent), while the lowest appears in Malta (31 percent). Nevertheless, only 39 percent of survey participants claimed to be satisfied with the ticket prices offered by their LPT authority. Cities with a very high percentage of citizens' satisfaction are: Zurich, Vienna, Helsinki and Oslo, while at the opposite end, three Italian cities are placed: Palermo, Rome and Naples, followed by Nicosia. Cities of the European South tend to be more dissatisfied with the LPT service offered to them, compared to cities of Northern and Central Europe (European Commission, 2016).

In an attempt to interpret this phenomenon, it should be taken into account that citizens of Southern Europe tend to distrust the institutional authorities of their countries, due to the (real or perceived) increased levels of corruption. Therefore, it is not always a matter of whether, for instance, competitive tendering is the preferable option followed by the local authorities; the notion is if the citizens could be sure that the bidder who wins the contractual agreement is actually the best objective option according to the established criteria.

Fellesson and Friman (2008) in their study pursue a transnational comparison of the perceived service satisfaction with LPT in nine European cities, namely, Stockholm, Barcelona, Copenhagen, Geneva, Helsinki, Vienna, Berlin, Manchester and Oslo. With the aid of factor analysis, four citizens' satisfaction dimensions were identified as being predominant in the majority of cities: safety/security; system (with supply and reliability items); comfort; and staff behavior. In similar research with a focus on the LPT industry in Greece, Botzoris et al. (2015) suggested the following four main components of user satisfaction: service organization; rolling stock (buses) equipment; bus stops' facilities; and equipment and drivers' capabilities and behavior.

It should be underlined though that the development of accurate and valid measures of service quality, as with all the things that involve perceptions and attitudes, is far from being an elementary task. Quality indicators are hard to define due to the fact that the attributes comprising perceived quality (such as safety and comfort) are mainly intangible and abstract and cannot be easily measured. This has to be taken into account while designing contracts of public transport, which include monitoring of LPT service quality. Therefore, acquiring a better understanding of citizens' perceptions of quality of the service provided by public transport is very important (Beirao and Cabral, 2006).

Mouwen and Rietveld (2013) examined whether competitive tendering can improve customer satisfaction with LPT in the Netherlands. They concluded that in the majority of concession areas, the average trip satisfaction has indeed experienced an increase within a ten-year period; nevertheless, there is still 40 percent of cases in which a deterioration was reported. With a focus outside European cities, recent research by Chunqin et al. (2016) shows the existence of a strong relationship between different organizational forms (e.g. ownership structure and contractual practices) and passenger satisfaction of the public transport service in China. According to the authors, the highest passenger satisfaction is met when public transport operators are franchised to public ownership and are regulated by a management contract.

Fiorio et al. (2013) investigated the degree of correlation between user satisfaction and alternative organizational models of LPT service provision, based on the outcome of a survey conducted in 2009 in 33 European cities. They found that the presence of a single LPT provider is correlated to higher levels of citizens' satisfaction, in contrast with the existence of multiple providers that operate in the same market area.

10.4   CONCLUSIONS AND DIRECTIONS FOR FURTHER RESEARCH

The literature review in combination with empirical evidence indicates that there are no 'magic recipes' for success. Every ownership and governance form has its own benefits and pitfalls, and the successful (or not) implementation of a policy reform is case sensitive, due to the fact that it strongly depends on factors such as the socio-economic context of the city, the 'corruption tradition' of the country and the effectiveness of institutional authorities.

The 'Barcelona model', for instance, which combines public and private provision of service as described earlier in the chapter, appears to be very efficient and seems to be able to contribute to the establishment of some so-called 'win-win situations' between public and private entities, and at the same time it can succeed in keeping citizens satisfied. Nevertheless, this observation should not be translated as 'do it like Barcelona' advice; the analysis conducted in this chapter clearly shows that a successful LPT urban governance model cannot be simply transferred to another city and expect it to be equally successful: place-based policy is the key to success.

Most of the time, people do not seem to be really concerned about the governance form, the institutional settings and the contractual details. They want a LPT system characterized by efficiency, equity, sustainability and feasibility. Local institutional authorities should inspire trustworthiness in their citizens. Establishing a sustainable urban transportation system to meet the changing mobility needs of citizens requires a comprehensive and integrated approach to policy-making and decision-making, with the aim of developing affordable, economically viable, people-oriented and environment-friendly LPT systems. Urban space lies at the core of economic and social dynamics and new approaches and tools are essential to support European cities in facing their demanding futures.

The decision-making process related to transportation planning issues and particularly transportation policy issues – is intrinsically complex due to the fact that, in addition to the large number of factors (both quantitative and qualitative) involved, there are many different stakeholders to be taken into account. According to the latest Urban Mobility Package of the European Commission (2013), citizen and stakeholder engagement should be promoted (Keseru et al., 2015). Therefore, citizens and stakeholders should be given the opportunity to express their own views and aspirations on the topic, but caution should be paid in order to eliminate the so-called 'asymmetry of information'. An interesting direction for future research on the topic is thus to investigate how this engagement could be useful to decision-makers in order for them to gain a better understanding of the relationship between the promotion/implementation of EU policy reforms in the LPT sector and achieving citizens' satisfaction with the LPT service provided

NOTES

*   We are grateful to Professor Massimo Florio and Giovanni Perucca for precious advice and guidance. We are also grateful to Christian Winter and Henrik Burda for their contribution to a preliminary version of this chapter during the EUsers summer school. Sections 10.2, 10.2.1, 10.2.2, 10.2.3, 10.3 and 10.3.1 have been written by Annalisa Negrelli; Sections 10.1, 10.3.2 and 10.4 by Anastasia Roukouni; and by Angélique Chassy on the issue of diversity of capitalism in Section 10.3.

1.   Local authorities have to exercise control over the company concerned similar to that which it exercises over its own departments and, at the same time, that company should carry out the essential part of its activities with the controlling local authorities.
2.   http://eur-lex.europa.eu/legal-content/EN/TXT/?uri=URISERV%3Al24488 (accessed April 2017).
3.   See more at 'Istituzioni e regolamentazione dei trasporti:temi di riflessione', rapporto dell'advisory board (2015), in http://www.autorita-trasporti.it/rapporti-advisory-board/ (accessed April 2017).
4.   European Court of Justice, 24 July 2003, case c-280/00, *Altmark Trans Gmbh and Regierungspräsidium Magdeburg v. Nahverkehrsgesellschaft Altmark GmbH.*
5.   See more in Pesaresi et al. (2012).
6.   Article 18, Directive 2014/23/UE. 'Duration of the concession: 1. The duration of concessions shall be limited. The contracting authority or contracting entity shall estimate the duration based on the works or services requested. 2. For concessions lasting more than five years, the maximum duration of the concession shall not exceed the time that a concessionaire could reasonably be expected to take to recoup the investments made in operating the works or services together with a return on invested capital taking into account the investments required to achieve the specific contractual objectives. The investments taken into account for the purposes of the calculation shall include both initial investments and investments during the life of the concession.'

REFERENCES

Websites last accessed April 2017.
Abou-Zeid, M., Witter, R., Bierlaire, M., Kaufmann, V. and Ben-Akiva, M. (2012),

'Happiness and travel mode switching: findings from a Swiss public transportation experiment', *Transport Policy*, **19** (1), 93–104.

Albalate, D. and Bel, G. (2010), 'What shapes local public transportation in Europe? Economics, mobility, institutions, and geography', *Transportation Research Part E*, **46**, 775–90.

Alsnih, R. and Hensher, D.A. (2003), 'The mobility and accessibility expectations of seniors in an aging population', *Transportation Research Part A*, **37** (10), 903–16.

Amable, B. (2005), *Les cinq capitalismes. Diversité des systèmes économiques et sociaux dans la mondialisation*, Paris: Seuil.

Amaral, M. (2009), 'Modes d'organisation et performances: le cas du transport public urbain en Europe', Thèse pour le Doctoratès Sciences économiques, Université Paris 1 Panthéon Sorbonne.

Arabia, A.G., Gariglio, D. and Rapallini, C. (2004), *La Governance del trasporto pubblico locale*, Milano: Giuffrè.

Ballard, M.J. and Warner, M. (2000), 'Taking the high roads: local government restructuring and the quest for quality', in AFSCME (ed.), *Power Tools for Fighting Privatization*, Washington, DC: American Federation of State, County and Municipal Employees, 6/1–6/53.

Baptista, P., Melo, S. and Rolim, C. (2015), 'Car sharing systems as a sustainable transport policy: a case study from Lisbon, Portugal', in M. Attard and Y. Shiftan (eds), *Sustainable Urban Transport* (Transport and Sustainability), Vol. 7, Lisbon: Emerald Group Publishing, pp. 205–27.

Beirao, G. and Cabral, J.A.S. (2006), 'Enhancing service quality in public transport systems', *WIT Transactions on the Built Environment*, **89**, 837–45.

Berrou, J.P. and Carrincazeaux, C. (2005), 'La diversité des capitalismes et les pays d'Europe centrale et orientale: une analyse statistique', *Les cahiers du GRES*, no. 18.

Boitani, A., Nicolini, M. and Scarpa, C. (2013), 'Do competition and ownership matter? Evidence from local public transport in Europe', *Applied Economics*, **45** (11), 1419–34.

Botzoris, G., Galanis, A., Profillidis, V. and Eliou, N. (2015), 'Commuters perspective on urban public transport system service quality', *WSEAS Transactions on Environment and Development*, **11**, 182–92.

Bucci, O. (2006), *Il trasporto pubblico locale – una prospettiva per l'Italia*, Bologna: Il Mulino.

Christiansen, P. and Loftsgarden, T. (2011), *Drivers Behind Urban Sprawl in Europe*, TØI (Institute of Transport Economics, Norwegian Center of Transport Research) Report 1136/2011, available at https://www.toi.no/getfile.php?mmfileid=17329.

Chunqin, Z., Zhicai, J., Weite, L. and Guangnian, X. (2016), 'Do the organizational forms affect passenger satisfaction? Evidence from Chinese public transport service', *Transportation Research Part A*, **94**, 129–48.

Currie, G. and Delbosc, A. (2010), 'Exploring public transport usage trends in an ageing population', *Transportation*, **37** (1), 151–64.

Dal Fiore, F., Mokhtarian, P.L., Salomon, I. and Singer, M.E. (2014), 'Nomads at last? A set of perspectives on how mobile technology may affect travel', *Journal of Transport Geography*, **41**, 97–106.

Dalen, D. and Gòmez-Lobo, A. (2003), 'Yardstick on the road: regulatory contracts and cost efficiency in the Norwegian bus industry', *Transportation*, **30** (4), 371–86.

Diana, M. (2012), 'Measuring the satisfaction of multimodal travellers for local transit services in different urban contexts', *Transportation Research Part A*, **46** (1), 1–11.

European Commission (2005), 'Proposal for a regulation of the European Parliament and of the Council on public passenger transport services by rail and by road', COM (2005) 319 Final, *Official Journal of the European Communities*, Brussels.

European Commission (2011), 'Concerning the application of EU public procurement law to relations between contracting authorities ("public-public cooperation")', Commission Staff Working Paper, SEC(2011) 1169 Final, Brussels.

European Commission (2013), 'Factsheet: Horizon 2020 budget', available at http://ec.europa.eu/research/horizon2020/pdf/press/fact_sheet_on_horizon2020_budget.pdf.

European Commission (2016), 'Quality of life in European cities 2015: Flash Eurobarometer 419', available at http://ec.europa.eu/regional_policy/sources/docgener/studies/pdf/urban/survey2015_en.pdf.

European Commission (2016) 'Study on economic and financial effects of the implementation of Regulation 1370/2007 on public passenger transport services', available at https://ec.europa.eu/transport/themes/pso/studies/pso_en.

Fellesson, M. and Friman, M. (2008), 'Perceived satisfaction with public transport service in nine European cities', *Journal of the Transportation Research Forum*, **47** (3), 93–103.

Filippini, M., Koller, M. and Masiero, G. (2015), 'Competitive tendering versus performance-based negotiation in Swiss public transport', idEP Economic Papers, 2015/04.

Fiorio, C.V., Florio, M. and Perucca, G. (2013), 'User satisfaction and the organization of local public transport: evidence from European cities', *Transport Policy*, **29**, 209–18.

Franquelli, G., Piacenza, M. and Abate, G. (2004), 'Regulating public transport networks: how do urban intercity diversification and speed up measures affect firms "cost performance"?', *Annals of Public and Cooperative Economics*, **75**(2), 193–225.

Gagnepain, P., Ivaldi, M. and Martimort, D. (2013), 'The cost of contract renegotiation: evidence from the local public sector', *American Economic Review*, **103** (6), 2352–83.

Glaeser, E.L. and Kohlhase, J.E. (2004), 'Cities, regions and the decline of transport costs', *Papers in Regional Science*, **83** (1), 197–228.

GUTs Project (2013), 'Master study on governance', Provincia di Ferrara, Italy, available at http://www.central2013.eu/fileadmin/user_upload/Downloads/out putlib/GUTS_3.4.3_MasterStudy_Governance_FINAL.pdf.

Hamari, J., Sjöklint, M. and Ukkonen, A. (2015), 'The sharing economy: why people participate in collaborative consumption', *Journal of the Association for Information Science and Technology*, **67** (9), 2047–59.

Hensher, D.A. (2003), 'Contract areas and service quality issues in public transit provision: some thoughts on the European and Australian context', *Journal of Public Transportation*, **6**(3), 15–42.

Hensher, D.A. and Houghton, E. (2004), 'Performance-based quality contracts for the bus sector: delivering social and commercial value for money', *Transportation Research Part B*, **38**(2), 123–46.

Hensher, D.A. and Stanley, J. (2008), 'Transacting under a performance-based contract: the role of negotiation and competitive tendering', *Transportation Research Part A*, **42** (9), 1143–51.

Hensher, D.A., Yvrande-Billon, A., Macário, R., Preston, J., White, P., Tyson, B., Van de Velde, D.M., van Wee, B., Guilherme de Aragão, J.J., Medeiros dos Santos, E., Orrico Filho, R.D. and Hensher, D. (2007), 'Delivering value for money to government through efficient and effective public transit service continuity: some thoughts', *Transport Reviews*, **27** (4), 410–48.

Holmgren, J. (2013), 'An analysis of the determinants of local public transport demand focusing on the effects on income changes', *European Transport Research Review*, **5** (2), 101–7.

Karlaftis, M.G. and Tsamboulas, D. (2012), 'Efficiency measurement in public transport: are findings specification sensitive?', *Transportation Research Part A*, **46**(2), 392–402.

Keseru, I., Bulckaen, J. and Macharis, C. (2015), 'Enhancing stakeholder participation in urban mobility planning: the NISTO evaluation framework', in M. Schrenk, V. Popovich, P. Zeile, P. Elisei and C. Beyer (eds), *Proceedings of REAL CORP Tagungsband*, Ghent, 5–7 May, 271–80.

Kostal, T. (2015), 'Wiener Linien: governance and provisions of services of Local Public Transport in Vienna', in L. Bernier (ed.), *Public Enterprises Today: Missions, Performance and Governance – Learning from Fifteen Cases*, CIRIEC, New York: Peter Lang, 1–40.

Litman, T. (2016), 'Evaluating public transit benefits and costs', in *Best Practices Guidebook*, Victoria Transport Policy Institute, available at http://www.vtpi.org/tranben.pdf.

Marcucci, E. and Gatta, V. (2007), 'Quality and public transport service contracts', EP-EMS, Working Papers Series in Economics, Mathematics and Statistics, Università degli Studi di Urbino Carlo Bo.

Metz, D.H. (2000), 'Mobility of older people and their quality of life', *Transport Policy*, **7** (2), 149–52.

Miranda, R. and Lerner, A. (1995), 'Bureaucracy, organizational redundancy, and the privatization of public services', *Public Administration Review*, **55** (2), 193–200.

Moudon, A.V., Lee, C., Cheadle, A.D., Collier, C.W., Johnson, D., Schmid,T.L. and Weather, R.D. (2005), 'Cycling and the built environment, a US perspective', *Transportation Research Part D*, **10** (3), 245–61.

Mouwen, A. and Rietveld, P. (2013), 'Does competitive tendering improve customer satisfaction with public transport? A case study for the Netherlands', *Transportation Research Part A*, **51**, 29–45.

Mouwen, A. and Van Ommeren, J. (2016), 'The effect of contract renewal and competitive tendering on public transport costs, subsidies and ridership', *Transportation Research Part A*, **87**, 78–89.

Neirotti, P., De Marco, A., Cagliano, A.C., Mangano, G. and Scorrano, F. (2014), 'Current trends in Smart City initiatives: some stylised facts', *Cities*, **38**, 25–36.

Ottoz, E., Fornengo, G. and Di Giacomo, M. (2009), 'The impact of ownership on the cost of bus service provision: an example from Italy', *Applied Economics*, **41** (3), 337–49.

Oueslati, W., Alvanides, S. and Garrod, G. (2015), 'Determinants of urban sprawl in European cities', *Urban Studies*, **52** (9), 1591–614.

Pedro, M.J.G. and Macário, R. (2016), 'A review of general practice in contracting public transport services and transfer to BRT systems', *Research in Transportation Economics*, **59**, 94–105.

Pesaresi, N., Sinnaeve, A., Guigue-Koeppen, V., Wiemann, J. and Radulescu, M. (2012), 'The new state aid rules for Services of General Economic Interest (SGEI): the Commission Decision and Framework of 20 December 2011', *Competition Policy Newsletter*, 2012/1, available at http://www.ec.europa.eu/competition/publications/cpn/2012_1_11_en.pdf.

Polat, C. (2012), 'The determinants for urban public transport services: a review of the literature', *Journal of Applied Sciences*, **12** (12), 1211–31.

Roy, W. and Yvrande-Billon, A. (2007), 'Ownership, contractual practices and technical efficiency: the case of urban public transport in France', *Journal of Transport Economics and Policy*, **41** (2), 257–82.

Schaaffkamp, C. (2014), 'How can customer focus be strengthened in competitive tendering?', *Research in Transportation Economics*, **48**, 305–14.

Shaheen, S., Chan, N., Bansal, A. and Cohen, A. (2015), 'Shared mobility: definitions, industry development and early understanding', White Paper, Transportation Sustainability Research Center, University of California at Berkeley and Caltrans, California Department of Transportation, available at http://innovativemobility.org/wp-content/uploads/2015/11/SharedMobility_WhitePaper_FINAL.pdf.

Valeri, E., Stathopoulos, A., Marcucci, E., Gatta, V. and Blomberg Stathopoulos, A.I. (2011), 'Local Public Transport: service quality and tendering contracts', in E. Venezia (ed.), *Urban Sustainable Transit*, Milano: Franco Angeli, 1–14.

Van de Velde, D.M. (1999), 'Organisational forms and entrepreneurship in public transport: classifying organisational forms', *Transport Policy*, **6** (3), 147–57.

Van de Velde, D.M. (2008), 'A new regulation for the European public transport', *Research in Transportation Economics*, **22**, 78–84.

Veeneman, W. and Van de Velde, D.M. (2016), 'Developments in public transport governance in the Netherlands: a brief history and recent developments', *Research in Transportation Economics*, **59**, 116–22.

Warner, M. and Bel, G. (2008), 'Competition or monopoly? Comparing privatization of local public services in the US and Spain', *Public Administration*, **86** (3), 723–35.

Yin, J., Qian, L. and Singhapakdi, A. (2016), 'Sharing sustainability: how values and ethics matter in consumers' adoption of public bicycle-sharing scheme', *Journal of Business Ethics*, **2**, 1–20.

Yvrande-Billon, A. (2006), 'The attribution process of delegation contracts in the French urban public transport sector: why competitive tendering is a myth', *Annals of Public and Cooperative Economics*, **77** (4), 453–78.

Zatti, A. (2012), 'New organizational models in European local public transport: from myth to reality', *Annals of Public and Cooperative Economics*, **83** (4), 533–59.

11. The European gas sector: political-economy implications of the transition from state-owned to mixed-owned enterprises

Roberto Cardinale*

11.1 INTRODUCTION

In recent decades, the European gas markets have undergone major changes brought about by the extension of the European Single Market policy to the energy sector. This policy was based on the logic of market liberalization, which held that consumers' interests could be best served by forbidding national governments to protect state-owned enterprises (SOEs) from competitive market pressures. It has had the effect of unbundling transmission networks from production (or import) and distribution phases, whilst at the same time fragmenting supply chains and encouraging cross-border mergers within the European Union (EU) (Florio, 2013). In this context, privatization of former SOEs was expected to create the conditions for a more equal competition among old operators and new entries[1] (Parker, 1999). More generally, privatization was deemed necessary in the light of the European economies' recent transition to an advanced stage of economic development, which entailed the need to reshape direct state intervention in the economy (Cardinale, 2013).

However, in key European countries, market opening has not been accompanied by full privatization. In fact, privatization has only been partial, and has generated hybrid arrangements in the ownership of former SOEs, bringing to the rise of mixed-owned enterprises (MOEs).[2] The coexistence of public and private shareholders within energy companies raises important questions, especially on how their respective interests can be reconciled within the company's strategy.

This issue has not been addressed extensively in the literature, probably because privatization and the rise of MOEs in Europe are still relatively recent. In fact, the literature on SOEs and MOEs has been dominated by the themes of performance and profitability, especially before and during the process of privatization (De Alessi, 1980; Millward, 1982; Boardman and Vining, 1989; Shirley and Nellis, 1991; Laffont and Tirole, 1993; Domberger and Piggott, 1986; Newbery, 1999; Dewenter and Malatesta, 2001; Meggison and Netter, 2001; Bortolotti and Siniscalco, 2004; Florio, 2004). Fewer contributions focus on the relevance of SOEs for economic policy (Toninelli, 2000; Florio, 2004; Chang, 2007; Victor et al., 2012; Christiansen, 2013; Florio, 2013) and even less so in the context of MOEs (Brophy Haney and Pollitt, 2013; Florio, 2013; Pollitt, 2015).

The aim of this chapter is to shed light on MOEs' role as a tool of economic policy. This is done by investigating the extent to which MOEs' ownership structure, characterized by private management and the presence of private shareholders along with the public share, makes it possible for European governments to pursue objectives of public policy. More specifically, this analysis sheds light on the extent to which the state is able to pursue economic objectives for improving the competitiveness of the national economic system, objectives of a social nature that concern consumers' welfare, and political objectives of strategic and commercial relevance.

The analysis builds on the assumption that private shareholders are profit-seekers whilst the state is mainly oriented by objectives of public policy. On the basis of this assumption, I argue that despite the different levels of state influence in MOEs, which usually depend on the nature of shares held and the statutory regulation, the presence of private shareholders will most likely orient the management to prioritize profitability over public policy goals, or at best to pursue both. Alternatively, if public policy goals are pursued at the expense of profitability, private shareholders would lose the incentive to hold their shares. Therefore, mixed ownership implies that public policy objectives are pursuable only if reconciled with profitability.[3]

Based on these assumptions, this chapter shows that the governance of MOEs makes it possible for European states to pursue only some of the traditional objectives of public policy they used to pursue previously in the context of full public ownership (namely, through SOEs). However, European states are still able to pursue some other objectives thanks to the major shares held in MOEs. For instance, they are still able to positively influence energy deals for energy procurement through diplomatic action, as well as guarantee energy security by vetoing divestment from import infrastructure. The chapter argues that the major economic, social and political implications of the gas sector ultimately explain why privatization of former incumbents occurred only partially.

This chapter suggests that privatization of SOEs has caused effects beyond the microeconomic level. In fact, intervention in key governance aspects of former SOEs, which accounted for the whole national production and distribution of gas, has induced structural changes in the whole gas sector. Even more so, given the strategic nature of the gas sector, the chapter shows that privatization of SOEs has had systemic implications of an economic, social and political nature. The sectoral and systemic implications of privatization reinforce the idea that privatization has represented a Policy Framework Reform (PFR) rather than a mere 'policy signal' (see Florio, this volume). In fact, whereas changes in policy signals might affect the governance of the energy sector only indirectly, for instance, by influencing prices or quantities produced, PFRs imply changes at the legislative and regulatory level that directly affect key governance factors of sectoral relevance, in this case the control and management of energy companies accounting for a remarkable share of the national gas market.

The chapter is structured as follows. Section 11.2 reconstructs the traditional objectives of public policy pursued through full public ownership of SOEs before privatization. Section 11.3 investigates the extent to which European governments can pursue the traditional objectives of public policy in the new framework of MOEs. Section 11.4 brings the chapter to a close, reflecting on the need to consider innovative ways to pursue traditional objectives of an economic and social nature when these are not pursuable in the framework of contemporary MOEs.

11.2   THE ECONOMIC, SOCIAL AND POLITICAL OBJECTIVES OF SOEs

SOEs have proven to be able to address a wide range of public policy objectives, most notably ensuring adequate levels of economic development, and pursuing objectives of a social nature such as consumers' price affordability and geographical access (Chang, 1994; Florio, 2004; Millward, 2005; Christiansen, 2013). SOEs have also been used as a tool of foreign policy by states with the aim to achieve objectives of strategic and commercial relevance (Victor et al., 2012), for instance, by ensuring energy security or strengthening economic and political cooperation with foreign countries. These objectives, which had an economic, social and political nature, were effectively pursued by European SOEs involved in the gas sector, because of the increasingly strategic role played by gas in the European economies since the second half of the twentieth century.

With respect to the objectives related to the economic sphere, SOEs' role has been pivotal in post-WWII for solving market failures connected with stagnation and underdevelopment of the gas industry (Cronshaw et al., 2008), which in turn hampered economic growth, which was a priority objective in early stages of development. Stagnation and under-development derived primarily from the risk aversion of private energy firms, which made them reluctant to engage in long-term investments for technological upgrade, but also from the lack of adequately developed financial markets able to support the nature and size of the investment needed.[4] However, the rationale for the creation of SOEs lay mostly in the systemic importance of gas: since gas is a key input for both industrial and household consumers, the gas sector is highly interdependent with other sectors, and has major implications for production costs and technological upgrade.

The creation of SOEs in the gas sector, and particularly the financial and political backing provided by the state, was essential to take advantage of the strategic nature of gas (Victor et al., 2006), especially in a context of technological backwardness and political-economic weakness. The public investments for the adaptation and development of new technolo-gies aimed to create adequate industrial capabilities for the production and import of gas, which would make it possible not to rely on foreign import-ers. This has greatly contributed to the reduction of production costs and the spread of technological spillovers in the other interdependent sectors of the economy. The reduction of gas prices has improved the industrial competitiveness by means of an increase in the industrial value added; consumers' welfare has also risen.

Nevertheless, public ownership has also proven to be effective for pursu-ing public policy objectives of social relevance in a direct way, for instance, by pursuing consumers' price affordability (Florio, 2004; Brophy Haney and Pollitt, 2013) and geographical access (Chang, 2007). In terms of consumers' price affordability, the public nature of the monopoly was con-ceived to avoid a private monopolist or private oligopoly benefiting from the bargaining power towards consumers. In fact, a private monopolist, in the absence of specific regulatory measures, would tend to produce lower levels of output with respect to the socially desirable level and raise prices. A public monopoly, instead, could afford to produce higher quantities and prioritize consumers' price affordability over profitability. Geographical access represented a further objective of social relevance that justified public monopoly. The market failure in this case consisted in the fact that in remote areas, marginal cost of gas supply is higher than the price that consumers are willing or able to pay, so that gas provision in those areas would not be profitable for private energy firms.

The political role of SOEs was performed at both the internal and external spheres of state intervention. In the internal sphere, the economic objectives of growth and technological upgrade have proven to be essential for the pursuit of political and electoral purposes, for instance, because they raised employment rates and income levels. The increase in the employment rates occurred not only indirectly, namely, as a consequence of the systemic benefits of economic growth provided by SOEs, but also as the result of direct hiring from SOEs (Capobianco and Christiansen, 2011). The latter has, in some cases, occurred at the expense of profitability.

In terms of the objectives pursued in the external sphere of state intervention, as well as in view of long-term internal implications, energy security and political-economic cooperation with foreign countries were among the most relevant and interrelated objectives. Both have been pursued through synergies between SOEs and the diplomatic bodies (Giacomello and Verbeek, 2011; Davis et al., 2016). In particular, energy security has benefited from the diplomatic platforms already set in the frameworks of political-economic cooperation with producing countries, but also from ad hoc political support for specific deals of energy imports (Victor et al., 2006), or for the joint development of energy projects, that is, production of gas fields, development of transnational infrastructure and other relevant projects. In this context, SOEs have often acted as a government branch for foreign energy affairs, in charge for both the negotiations and the technical development of gas fields in joint ventures with foreign counterparts.

In some cases, SOEs have even played a key role in opening new diplomatic and economic relations with foreign countries. SOEs' effectiveness as a tool of foreign policy has made it possible for the state to pursue objectives related to both the economic and political spheres. Concerning the economic sphere, the stipulation of energy deals often provoked the mobilization of satellite activities, but also a chain reaction in other sectors, contributing positively to increase exports in a wide range of sectors. For what concerns the political sphere, energy cooperation often represented the starting point for exploring broader strategic alliances and increasing political influence on certain areas of the globe, for purposes related to national defence or energy security.

In conclusion, SOEs have proven to be suitable for the pursuit of multiple objectives of an economic, social and political nature. In particular, the objectives related to the economic sphere have greatly benefited from the internalization of political support, because of the particular constraints deriving from the stage of development, as well as the economic and political implications of the gas sector. Furthermore, political objectives, for example, energy security and political-economic cooperation with foreign countries, have also benefited from the growth of the gas industry and SOEs' ability to penetrate foreign markets. Ultimately, the economic and political synergies have certainly influenced the social sphere, not only in terms of geographical access and price affordability for gas consumers, but more broadly for the indirect systemic benefits of economic development.

11.3   THE ECONOMIC, SOCIAL AND POLITICAL OBJECTIVES OF MOEs

Starting from the 1980s and speeding up in the 1990s, European SOEs underwent an extensive process of privatization in a wide range of key sectors, including gas (Florio, 2013). However, in several cases, the privatization of SOEs was not fully accomplished: states retained a major share, creating the conditions for the rise of the hybrid model that characterizes MOEs. On the basis of the Organisation for Economic Co-operation and Development (OECD) indicators Energy, Transport and Communications Regulation (ETCR), Table 11.1 shows the extent to which privatization of the gas sector occurred in EU 15 countries (where in a range from 6 to 0, 6 indicates full public ownership whilst 0 indicates full private ownership).

Table 11.2 lists the main vertically integrated former SOEs currently operating and the public share held on them.

The rationales for privatization can be broadly identified in two main

Table 11.1   *ETCR reform indicators of gas sector privatization in the EU 15, 1975 and 2013*

	1975	2013
Austria	4.53	2.76
Belgium	5.34	2.22
Denmark	6	4.5
Finland	5.88	1.44
France	6	2.4
Germany	0	0
Greece	6	3.88
Ireland	6	5.82
Italy	6	1.8
Luxembourg	4.26	2.75
Netherlands	3.75	3.49
Portugal	–	0.48
Spain	6	0.08
Sweden	–	0
UK	6	0

Source: Author's elaboration of OECD data.

Table 11.2   State shares held in the main vertically integrated European gas companies (EU 15)

	Public share (%)	Country of origin
British Petroleum	0	UK
British Gas	0	UK
Dong Energy	50.1	Denmark
EDF	85.6	France
Engie	32.76	France
Total	0	France
Enel	23.6	Italy
Eni	30.1	Italy
Galp	7	Portugal
Gasunie	100	Netherlands
Hellenic Petroleum	35.5	Greece
OMV	31.5	Austria
Gas Natural Fenosa	0	Spain
Repsol	0	Spain

Source: Author's elaboration of Eurobarometer data.

causes. One is connected with the EU-led change of policy paradigm and the objective to create a Single Market in which European energy companies compete (Parker, 1999). In this context, the profit-oriented nature of privatized companies and decreasing levels of political interference would have best suited the competitive market structure envisaged. Competition, instead, was expected to both increase the profitability of the most efficient energy companies,[5] and lower gas prices for consumers, enhancing the overall economic welfare (Brau et al., 2010). The other reason for privatization is connected to the competitiveness of the private energy industry and its ability to provide adequate levels of investments, which reflected the transition from an early to an advanced stage of development in Europe. Nevertheless, the two causes seem to be interconnected, since it is not unlikely that the change in the EU policy paradigm would have also been influenced by the transition to an advanced stage of development and the need to create more room for private initiative.

Despite that, the rationale for the state to retain major shares in national energy companies, and more specifically Golden Shares,[6] has been justified by the major political, economic and social implications of the energy sector (Cardinale, 2015; Picot et al., 2015), and particularly gas, because of its increasing importance in the energy mix. However, the extent to which the state could pursue public policy objectives through MOEs has been limited to those that could be reconciled with profitability, an unavoidable priority in privately managed firms such as European MOEs.

Concerning the economic sphere, traditional objectives extensively pursued through SOEs, for instance, economic and technological development, seem to have lost their priority nature in the new context of MOEs, at least to some extent. In fact, the existence of private shareholders, some of which are characterized by a short-term investment perspective (e.g. private equity firms), certainly implies that short-term capital gains assume greater importance. Therefore, one might argue that the increasing emphasis on short-term profitability could penalize long-term strategies for innovation, and indirectly the economic competitiveness, given the relevance of gas as an input for the rest of the economy (see Section 11.2 for a more detailed explanation).

However, this might not be the case if contemporary MOEs balance short-term with long-term investments in a way that reconciles profit and innovation. Even more so, a more balanced mix is justified by the characteristics of the new context in which European MOEs operate, namely, an advanced stage of development. In fact, despite the systemic importance of the gas sector, which has not changed in the transition from SOEs to MOEs, the transition to an advanced stage of development has made it possible to partially shift the emphasis from long-term development to short-term profitability, due to the lower margins of development that characterize the current phase (Cardinale, 2013). In the context of early stages of development, instead, the long-term logic usually prevails over the short-term one, which explains the traditional emphasis of post-WWII SOEs on capital formation and technological upgrade at the expense of short-term profitability.

The transition to MOEs has also potential social implications, for instance, in terms of consumers' price affordability and geographical access. In these cases, the problem is directly connected with the private management characterizing MOEs. The public shareholder, in fact, would face non-negligible opposition from private shareholders if it attempted to alleviate certain critical conditions for consumers through unprofitable corporate strategies, as happened in the context of SOEs. For instance, the private shareholders of MOEs would not accept a cut of fuel price aimed at improving consumers' price affordability, or economically unviable investments in gas infrastructure to supply remote areas and improve geographical access.

For these reasons, adequate incentives must be negotiated and implemented at the regulatory level outside the frameworks of single corporate entities. In this context, state subsidies at least equal to losses might be necessary in order to prevent the opposition from MOEs' private shareholders towards unprofitable investments aimed to provide a public service.

Concerning the political objectives pursuable through MOEs, the influence on the management still allows the states to pursue energy security and other political-economic objectives, especially those related to MOEs' external sphere of action. The contribution to energy security might derive from both ad hoc measures and long-term strategies. The ad hoc measures have mostly an emergency nature, and consist of the state's possibility to exercise its veto for specific decisions taken by MOE's management. For instance, the veto power could block strategies aimed at divesting from crucial assets for national energy security (Adolff, 2002; Grundmann and Moslein, 2004), such as transnational infrastructure for energy supply. Instead, companies characterized by full private ownership would be unlikely to attempt to reconcile profitability and energy security of the country of origin, unless specific (formal or informal) agreements between the state and the management are in place.

Along with the veto power, the state-appointed non-executive managers in the board of directors might advocate the adoption of investment strategies that reconcile energy security with profitability, for instance, by investing in producing countries that are geographically closer and politically compatible to the country of origin. Therefore, the coexistence of public (e.g. energy security) and private (e.g. profitability) objectives in MOEs could ultimately induce the corporate management to adopt strategies leading to the achievement of both, which in some cases entail mutual synergies. For instance, the bargaining power provided by the state in the negotiations for long-term gas supplies, or the military protection against pirates provided throughout the commercial routes, would benefit energy security as well as private shareholders in terms of lower uncertainty over end market's (national) supplies, thus over profits. In addition, the public shareholder could also benefit from private management if the latter adopts cost-effective strategies. In this case, energy security could be achieved more efficiently, for instance, by maximizing the use of transnational pipelines for energy import, or managing energy storage more effectively.

Beside energy security, the state could orient MOEs' commercial strategies towards projects and countries that provide systemic benefits in political-economic terms, once such strategies have proven to be profitable. In fact, as the state is able to monitor and even influence the strategies for energy security, the same mechanism might be applied to other objectives related to the external action which were extensively carried out by SOEs before the partial privatization. These are related mainly to the maintenance and penetration of strategic markets for the control of energy resources and transport routes, to create the basis for new political alliance with foreign counterparts or to strengthen the existing ones, and to launch or strengthen new initiatives of multi-sectoral trade. MOEs still have the potential to pursue these objectives despite the changes in the national and international contexts. In fact, as in the epoch of SOEs' monopoly, they still own and operate a remarkable amount of assets for gas production and transportation overseas, whilst having accumulated a great amount of knowledge and trusted relations with the producing countries. Therefore, it is not surprising that many European states still benefit from their influence on MOEs to serve national interests.

However, after the European Commission declared the potential illegality of some uses of Golden Shares,[7] many states have decided to change their legal position in the MOEs by keeping only a 'Golden Power' (Bassan, 2014). The latter entails the possibility for the state to only veto corporate actions that represent an evident threat to energy security. However, the decreasing state influence over MOEs could make it difficult to pursue some of the long-term strategies for energy security, as well as the pursuit of the aforementioned political-economic objectives through MOEs. The European Member States' ability to pursue these objectives will probably decrease further in the light of the forthcoming EU provisions for the oil and gas sector (European Commission, 2016), which envisage the EU Commission's supervision and approval of each Intergovernmental Agreement stipulated by Member States with non-EU countries.

11.4   CONCLUSIONS

The transition from SOEs to MOEs in Europe's gas sector was the result of extensive privatizations carried out over the last decades. The introduction of private management and private shareholders in former SOEs reflected the need to rethink suitable governance arrangements for the new competitive market structure brought about by the European Single Market policy. It also reflected the need to reshape state intervention in the economy after the European economies' transition to more advanced stages of development.

The introduction of private management and private shareholders in MOEs has implied the emergence of profitability as the primary objective for the corporate management. Nevertheless, the European states' major shares held in the MOEs are a legacy of former European SOEs in their traditional function of economic policy tools. This legacy is justified by the strategic relevance of former SOEs, and the economic, social and political implications deriving from them.

In this chapter, I have shown that the ownership structure of MOEs makes it possible to pursue some of the traditional objectives of public policy, especially those related to the external sphere of action, whilst several others are in principle not pursuable because they would occur at the expense of profitability. For instance, energy security and political-economic cooperation with foreign countries are still pursuable through MOEs because this may be achieved along with profitability. In this case, public and private objectives could potentially benefit from mutual synergies.

Nevertheless, the state would not be able to pursue economic and social objectives directly related to the internal sphere of action, that is, at the national level, for instance, to undertake large-scale investments for industrial upgrade, as well as to ensure consumers' price affordability and geographical access.

Large-scale investments were strategic to improve economic competitiveness in earlier stages of development, whilst they became relatively less necessary in the current stage due to the lower margins of technical improvement and the lower levels of socially desirable investment required. Nonetheless, the gas sector has maintained its systemic relevance, still being an important input for all the sectors of the economy. This, in turn, implies that too much emphasis on short-term profitability might hamper the long-term competitiveness of the whole economy.

Objectives of a social nature also seem to be difficult to pursue through MOEs. In fact, consumers' price affordability and geographical access usually occur at the expense of energy firms' profitability, and are therefore unlikely to be pursued in the context of profit-oriented MOEs.

In conclusion, the transition to MOEs in the gas sector can be explained by the attempt of some European states to adapt the governance of key energy players to a renovated context of market competition, whilst keeping a certain degree of control over them because of their strategic role in relevant political-economic areas. Nevertheless, the introduction of private management and the competitive context in which MOEs operate make it difficult to pursue sensitive objectives of an economic and social nature that were pursued before SOEs' privatization. This suggests the need to consider how to pursue such objectives not through MOEs, but by devising innovative governance mechanisms that take into account the new energy market context whilst balancing the interests of the main stakeholders, namely, states, energy firms and consumers.

NOTES

* I would like to express my gratitude to Massimo Florio and an anonymous reviewer for providing insightful comments on an earlier draft of this chapter. I would also like

to thank Umberto De Lorenzo, Maria Manolova, Ivan Miroshnychenco and Paula Podolska for their contribution to the preliminary discussion that inspired this chapter.

1. The creation of the European Single Market was conceived in the aftermath of World War II (WWII), and it was based on the idea that increasing levels of economic interdependence among European states would have decreased the probability of future wars. Only in subsequent phases, once the threat of an intra-European war vanished, the emphasis shifted to objectives related to the economic sphere, such as allocative efficiency and market competition.

2. For the purpose of this chapter, it is useful to refer to MOEs as companies in which the state holds a minority share that is nonetheless significant enough to have an influence on management strategy. This ownership structure is by far the most common in EU 15, as Table 11.1 shows. The governance of other companies will be left for future research. This chapter refers to SOEs as the former, fully state-owned companies that were prevalent before the privatization. Therefore, this chapter's definition of SOEs is not the same as the current OECD definition (Christiansen, 2011), which includes all the ownership structures in which the state holds more than 50 per cent of the shares. This is necessary for the purpose of this research, because it makes it possible to analyse the effects of the transition from fully owned to MOEs.

3. This assumption is widely accepted. However, the nature of private and public objectives is usually more complex than the simplified one assumed in this chapter. As Florio (2004) notes, one could further disaggregate objectives pursued by the state because these often reflect the interests of different institutional apparatuses. The same logic might be applied to the multiple nature of the interests representing the private shareholders.

4. In addition to the gas sector, SOEs have prevailed in other key sectors of the economy, as well as in other energy industries, most notably nuclear, oil and electricity (Millward, 2005). Although the main reason for the creation of SOEs in key sectors was to stimulate economic growth, public ownership also aimed to overcome critical conditions determined by external events such as economic crises (e.g. the oil crisis of the 1970s).

5. The idea that market competition would represent the only, or at least the main, determinant for energy firms' success or failure has not so far proved correct, at least in some areas. For instance, it is not yet clear if renewable energy can compete with traditional energy sources without large-scale public incentives (see Alberici et al., 2014).

6. The Golden Share is a set of 'special rights that have been attached to a [public] share' (Adolff, 2002, para. 8; see also Grundmann and Moslein, 2004). This, in many cases, has granted the control of the company, even if the latter is usually not contemplated in the context of minority shares such as those held by European states in contemporary MOEs. However, even in the absence of the Golden Share, a minority public share ranging between 20 per cent to 50 per cent, which occurs in most contemporary European MOEs, also grants a significant degree of influence on the management, especially when this is considerably greater compared to the shares held by the other shareholders.

7. According to the European Commission, the Golden Share makes it possible for the state to veto major external investments in the company for reasons other than the explicit threats to vital interests such as energy security; for instance, to maintain the leadership in strategic markets. This behaviour would breach the provisions of the EU Treaty on the free movement of capitals (Grundmann and Moslein, 2004; European Commission, 2012).

REFERENCES

Adolff, J. (2002). 'Turn of the Tide? The Golden Share: Judgements of the European Court of Justice and the Liberalization of the European Capital Markets', *German Law Journal* **3** (8), paras 1–36.

Alberici, S., S. Boeve, P. van Breevoort, Y. Deng, S. Förster, A. Gardiner, V. van Gastel, K. Grave, H. Groenenberg, D. de Jager, E. Klaasen, W. Pouwels, M. Smith, E. de Visser, T. Winkel and K. Wouters (2014). *Subsidies and Costs of EU Energy*, Report prepared for the European Commission, Directorate-General for Energy, 11 November.

Bassan, F. (2014). 'From Golden Share to Golden Power: The European Shift of Paradigm for State Intervention in the Economy', in *Studi Sull'integrazione Europea*. Bari: Cacucci Editore, pp. 57–80.

Boardman, A.E. and A.R. Vining (1989). 'Ownership and Performance in Competitive Environments: A Comparison of the Performance of Private, Mixed, and State-owned Enterprises', *Journal of Law & Economics* **32** (1), 1–33.

Bortolotti, B. and D. Siniscalco (2004). *The Challenges of Privatisation: An International Analysis*. Oxford and New York: Oxford University Press.

Brau, R., R. Doronzo, C. Fiorio and M. Florio (2010). 'EU Gas Industry Reforms and Consumers' Prices', *The Energy Journal* **31** (4), 167–82.

Brophy Haney, A. and M. Pollitt (2013). 'New Models of Public Ownership in Energy', *International Journal of Applied Economics* **27** (2), 174–92.

Capobianco, A. and H. Christiansen (2011). 'Competitive Neutrality and State-owned Enterprises: Challenges and Policy Options', 1. OECD Corporate Governance Working Papers, Paris.

Cardinale, R. (2013). 'Theory and Practice of State Intervention: Italy, South Korea and Stages of Economic Development', Mimeo, Catholic University of Milan and Sungkyunkwan University.

Cardinale, R. (2015). 'The Profitability of Transnational Energy Infrastructure: A Comparative Analysis of the Greenstream and Galsi Gas Pipelines', Mimeo, University College London.

Chang, H.J. (1994). *The Political Economy of Industrial Policy*. Basingstoke and New York: Macmillan and St Martin's Press.

Chang, H.J. (2007). *State-owned Enterprise Reform*. New York: United Nations, Department for Economic and Social Affairs.

Christiansen, H. (2011). 'The Size and Composition of the SOE Sector in OECD Countries', 5. OECD Corporate Governance Working Papers, Paris.

Christiansen, H. (2013). 'Balancing Commercial and Non-commercial Priorities of State-owned Enterprises', 6. OECD Corporate Governance Working Papers, Paris.

Cronshaw, I., J. Marstrand, M. Pirovska, D. Simmons and J. Wempe (2008). 'Development of Competitive Gas Trading in Continental Europe: How to Achieve Workable Competition in European Gas Markets?', IEA Information Paper, Paris, May.

Davis, C., A. Fuchs and K. Johnson (2016). 'State Control and the Effects of Foreign Relations on Bilateral Trade', MPRA Paper 74597, Munich.

De Alessi, L. (1980). 'The Economics of Property Rights: A Review of the Evidence', *Research in Law and Economics* **2** (1), 27–8.

Dewenter, K. and P. Malatesta (2001). 'State-owned and Privately Owned Firms: An Empirical Analysis of Profitability, Leverage and Labor Intensity', *American Economic Review* **91** (1), 320–34.

Domberger, S. and J. Piggott (1986). 'Privatisation Policies and Public Enterprise: A Survey', *Economic Record* **62** (2), 145–62.

European Commission (2012). 'Commission Requests Greece to Comply with EU

Rules on Free Movement of Capital and the Right of Establishment', European Commission Press Release, Brussels, 26 April.

European Commission (2016). 'Commission Welcomes Agreement to Ensure Compliance of Intergovernmental Agreements in the Field of Energy with EU Law', European Commission Press Release, Brussels, 7 December.

Florio, M. (2004). *The Great Divestiture: Evaluating the Welfare Impact of the British Privatizations, 1979–1997.* Cambridge, MA and London: MIT Press.

Florio, M. (2013). *Network Industries and Social Welfare: The Experiment that Reshuffled European Utilities.* Oxford: Oxford University Press.

Giacomello, G. and B. Verbeek (eds) (2011). *Italy's Foreign Policy in the Twenty-first Century: The New Assertiveness of an Aspiring Middle Power.* Lanham, MD: Lexington Books.

Grundmann, S. and F. Moslein (2004). 'Golden Shares – State Control in Privatized Companies: Comparative Law, European Law and Policy Aspects', *European Banking & Financial Law Journal (EUREDIA)* 2001–2002, 623 ff.

Laffont, J.-J. and J. Tirole (1993). *A Theory of Incentives in Procurement and Regulation.* Cambridge, MA: MIT Press.

Megginson, W.L. and J.M. Netter (2001). 'From State to Market: A Survey of Empirical Studies on Privatization', *Journal of Economic Literature* **39** (2), 321–89.

Millward, R. (1982). 'The Comparative Performance of Public and Private Ownership', in Lord Roll of Ipsden (ed.), *The Mixed Economy.* London: Palgrave Macmillan, pp. 58–93.

Millward, R. (2005). *Private and Public Enterprise in Europe: Energy, Telecommunication and Transport, 1830–1990.* Cambridge and New York: Cambridge University Press.

Newbery, D. (1999). *Privatization, Restructuring and Regulation of Network Utilities.* Cambridge, MA: MIT Press.

Parker, D. (1999). 'Privatization in the European Union: A Critical Assessment of Its Development, Rationale and Consequences', *Economic and Industrial Democracy* **20** (1), 9–38.

Picot, A., M. Florio, N. Grove and J. Kranz (eds) (2015). *The Economics of Infrastructure Provisioning: The Changing Role of the State.* Cambridge, MA: MIT Press.

Pollitt, M. (2015). 'New Models of Public Ownership in Energy', in A. Picot, M. Florio, N. Grove and J. Kranz (eds), *The Economics of Infrastructure Provisioning: The Changing Role of the State.* Cambridge, MA: MIT Press, pp. 386–405.

Shirley, M. and J. Nellis (1991). 'Public Enterprise Reform: The Lesson of Experience', World Bank, Economic Development Institute, Washington, DC.

Toninelli, P.M. (ed.) (2000). *The Rise and Fall of State-owned Enterprise in the Western World.* Cambridge and New York: Cambridge University Press.

Victor, D.G., A. Jaffe and M.H. Hayes (eds) (2006). *Natural Gas and Geopolitics: From 1970 to 2040.* Cambridge: Cambridge University Press.

Victor, D.G., D.R. Hults and M.C. Thurber (eds) (2012). *Oil and Governance: State-owned Enterprises and the World Energy Supply.* Cambridge and New York: Cambridge University Press.

Index

Switzerland
  local public transport (LPT) services
    203, 211
  telecommunications industry 99,
    100, 103, 105, 106
System Average Interruption Duration
  Index (SAIDI) 144–5
System Average Interruption
  Frequency Index (SAIFI) 144–5

taxation reform 3
technical harmonisation, railways 74–5
Technical Specifications for
  Interoperability (TSIs) 75
technological changes 22, 158–9, 198
telecommunications industry 157–8,
  166
  accessibility 166
  consumers, impact of reform 164–6
  developments in 158–9
  EU policy reforms 160–61, 172
  price and quality drivers 159–60
  prices, and policy reforms 164–5
  quality, and policy reforms 165
  reform patterns across Europe
    162–4, 172
  restructuring 34
telecommunications industry,
  ownership and firm performance
    99–102, 112–14
  data 105–9
  empirical analysis 109–12
  major state-invested enterprises
    (SIEs) in Europe 102–4
Thatcher, Margaret 29, 30
theory of reform, development of 3–4
Total 226
Trans-European Networks (TENs)
  174–5
Trans-European Rail Freight Network
  (TERFN) 74
transparency, and railways reform 72, 73
transport, local *see* local public
  transport (LPT) services
Transport for London (TfL) 201
Transports Metropolitans de Barcelona
  (TMB) 205
transposition of legislation 76–7
Trenitalia 179, 182
Tsutsui, M. 59

unbundling 8–9, 220
  effects of 34
  electricity industry 44, 45, 47, 48–9,
    49–50, 59, 141, 146, 147, 153
  railways 72–3, 175, 177
  as variable 15
United Kingdom (UK)
  electricity industry 45, 46, 48, 49,
    52–3, 54, 55, 56–7, 58, 60, 62,
    146, 147, 148, 149, 150, 151,
    152, 153–4
  gas industry 225, 226
  local public transport (LPT) services
    201, 204
  postal services 121, 123, 124, 125,
    131, 132
  railways 68, 80, 81, 82, 83, 86, 87, 88,
    89, 90, 91, 178, 188
  telecommunications industry 99,
    100, 105, 106, 163–4
United States (US), electricity industry
  141–2
urban sprawl 198

Van Ommeren, J. 211
variables, methodological issues 10,
  14–15
Vattenfall 57, 61, 147
vertical integration 171, 172
  electricity industry 34, 47, 48, 49–50,
    139
  gas industry 226
  railways 34, 68, 173–4, 185, 186
  telecommunications industry 160
Vertical Integration Index (OECD)
  49–50
Volume Development Index (postal
  services) 122

wages, and privatisation 32
welfare economics perspective 3–4,
  6–7
welfare effects, defining and measuring
  18–21
welfare weights 19
Wiener Linien 203
WIK-consult 117, 122, 123–4, 126, 131
Willner, J. 33

Yu, M. 101